Davidson
1981

CORPUS
SACRAE SCRIPTURAE
NEERLANDICAE
MEDII AEVI

MISCELLANEA

VOLUMEN I

CORPUS SACRAE SCRIPTURAE NEERLANDICAE
MEDII AEVI

MISCELLANEA

VOLUMEN I

TEXTUS ET IMAGINES
IN
CODICIBUS SACRAE SCRIPTURAE
NEERLANDICIS SAEC. XV
IMAGINIBUS ORNATIS

AUCTORE

SANDRA HINDMAN

LEIDEN
E. J. BRILL
1977

VERZAMELING VAN MIDDELNEDERLANDSE
BIJBELTEKSTEN
MISCELLANEA
DEEL 1

TEXT AND IMAGE
IN
FIFTEENTH-CENTURY
ILLUSTRATED DUTCH BIBLES

BY

SANDRA HINDMAN

LEIDEN
E. J. BRILL
1977

Dit boek is gedrukt met financiële hulp van de Nederlandse Organisatie
voor Zuiver Wetenschappelijk Onderzoek (Z.W.O.)

ISBN 90 04 04901 0

Copyright 1977 by E. J. Brill, Leiden, The Netherlands

PRINTED IN THE NETHERLANDS

CONTENTS

PREFACE

A number of codices of the 'First History-Bible' that were copied in the Northern Netherlands in the fifteenth century have a special place among Middle Dutch translations of the Bible because of the miniatures they contain. These splendid manuscripts have already attracted the attention of art-historians, who have indeed studied the miniatures with considerable thoroughness but have so far paid little attention to the relationship between text and illuminations. The miniatures, intended to stimulate the interest of the reader in the Bible story, are an integral part of the text. Professor Sandra Hindman has in the present work shown the unity of text and illustration. The results of her researches are therefore very much in their place in the Corpus Sacrae Scripturae Neerlandicae Medii Aevi and we are pleased that she has agreed to their being published in this series.

May, 1977
Leiden

C. C. DE BRUIN

ACKNOWLEDGEMENTS

Numerous friends and colleagues assisted me in various ways during the completion of this study: Professor R. G. Calkins, Dr. Jan Deschamps, Professor Robert Deshman, Professor James D. Farquhar, Dr. David Freedberg, Professor Sir Ernst Gombrich, Dr. J. P. Gumbert, Dr. Ulli Jenni, Professor J. J. John, Professor Herbert Kessler, Professor James Marrow, Professor Peter Parshall, Professor Lawrence Silver, and Dr. Eleanor Spencer. To Professor C. C. de Bruin, who oversaw publication of this study in the *Corpus*, I owe a special debt of gratitude.

Research in Europe on this topic was made possible through generous grants from the Samuel K. Kress Foundation from 1970 to 1973, and without this opportunity this study would not have been possible. For her continuing interest and encouragement, I wish to thank Miss Mary Davis, Executive Vice-President of the Kress Foundation. I am particularly grateful to members of the staff of the Warburg Institute in London who extended their help during my three years as Samuel H. Kress Fellow there. I would also like to thank the ZWO (Nederlandse Organisatie voor Zuiver-Wetenschappelijk Onderzoek) for a generous grant subsidizing publication of the final study.

I would like to thank the staffs of the following European libraries who gave freely of their time to meet my requests for manuscripts: Brussels, Bibliothèque royale; The Hague, Koninklijke Bibliotheek and Museum Meermanno-Westreenianum; Leiden, Universiteitsbibliotheek; London, The British Library; Oxford, the Bodleian Library; Paris, Bibliothèque nationale; Utrecht, Universiteitsbibliotheek; and Vienna, Oesterreichische Nationalbibliothek. Photo credits are extended to the following institutions: Antwerp, Museum Plantin-Moretus; Cambridge, Fitzwilliam Museum; Cambridge (Mass.), Harvard University Library; the Hague, Koninklijke Bibliotheek and Museum Meermanno-Westreenianum; London, British Library; Munich, Staatsbibliothek; Nuremberg, Stadtbibliothek; Paris, Bibliothèque nationale; and Vienna, Oesterreichische Nationalbibliothek.

The late Professor L. M. J. Delaissé contributed more than anyone else to my initial interest in Dutch manuscripts and to the final formulation of some of the problems. For this, and for his *humanitas* as both friend and scholar, I thank him.

November, 1975   SANDRA HINDMAN
Baltimore

LIST OF FIGURES*

* All reproductions are courtesy of their respective libraries.

LIST OF MANUSCRIPT ABBREVIATIONS

Brussels Bible	Brussels Bibliothèque royale, Mss. 9018-23
The Hague Bible	The Hague, Koninklijke Bibliotheek, Ms. 78 D 38
London Bible	London, British Library, Add. Ms. 10043
Lochorst Bible	London, British Library, Add. Ms. 38122
Munich Bible	Staatsbibliothek, Cod. germ. 1102
Nuremberg Bible	Stadtbibliothek, Ms. Solger 80
Vienna Bible	Österreichische Nationalbibliothek, Mss. 2771-72

INTRODUCTION

In the fifteenth century, the First History Bible, or *Eerste Historiebijbel*, was one of the most popular books in the North Netherlands. Its text consisted basically of a juxtaposition of the Bible with Petrus Comestor's twelfth century *Historia Scholastica*, executed so that each passage from the Bible immediately preceded the relevant commentary on that passage from the *Historia Scholastica*. Thirty-six manuscripts (see Appendix I) of this text are extant,[1] and at least twelve other manuscripts are known to have existed, for the text has been identified on twelve single-folio fragments.[2] Of these thirty-six manuscripts, fourteen received illustrations; the remainder are simply written copies of the text. Contemporary colophons reveal the approximate period of production of the illustrated exemplars: the earliest manuscript (Brussels, Bibliothèque royale, Ms. 9018-23) is dated 1431; and the latest (London, British Library, Add. Ms. 16951) is dated 1473-74. Thus, their production spans the middle two quarters of the century. Although their original provenance is not so easily established by internal evidence, three of the illustrated codices (London, British Museum, Add. Mss. 10043 and 38122, and Vienna, Oesterreichische Nationalbibliothek, Mss. 2771-72) display arms of well-known ecclesiastics in Utrecht.[3]

---

[1] The most complete published list of manuscripts is in Jan Deschamps, *Middelnederlandse Handschriften uit Europese en Amerikaanse Bibliotheken*, Brussels, 1970 (catalogue of an exhibition at the Bibliothèque royale), no. 50, pp. 152-156. However, the following four manuscripts are omitted in Deschamps' list: British Library, Add. Ms. 38122; The Hague, Koninklijke Bibliotheek, Ms. 129 C 3, The Hague, Koninklijke Bibliotheek, Ms. K. A. XXXII; and Utrecht, Bibliotheek der Rijksuniversiteit, Ms. 2 B 13. Deschamps' number for Utrecht, Bibliotheek der Rijksuniversiteit, Ms. 6 E 5 should read Ms. 5 E 6.

[2] Brussels, Bibliothèque royale, Mss. IV. 636, IV. 650. The first contains two fragments and the second contains ten, each folio of which clearly belonged to a different codex.

[3] Arms of the Lochorst family occur in British Library, Add. Ms. 10043 and Add. Ms. 38122 (see Appendix I). Herman van Lochorst was deacon of the Cathedral from 1400 to 1428. The arms of Evart van Soudenbalch, canon of Utrecht Cathedral from 1445 to 1503, are found on fol. 10r of the Vienna Bible (Österreichische Nationalbibliothek, Ms. 2771-2772). In the Lochorst Bible, the arms of the Lochorst family occur on numerous folios with those of the city of Utrecht and those of other families. This raises the question of whether the heraldry alludes to a political program perhaps referring to the schism in which the Lochorsts were actively involved. It also suggests the possibility of alternate ownership, which closer examination of the placement of the heraldry might elucidate.

Previous Scholarship and the Problems

Scholarship on the First History Bible has been sharply divided between two separate disciplines — philology and art history. In the
eighteenth century, LeLong[4] was the first scholar to distinguish the text
of the First History Bible from other vernacular renditions. Following his
work, van Druten[5] and Ebbinge Wubben[6] collated the various manuscripts of this text, noting differences between them and placing them
within the general tradition of Bible translations. Most recently, de Bruin's
work[7] has been concerned with the original fourteenth century translation from which the extant fifteenth century manuscripts derive. The first
art historian to discuss the first vernacular Bibles as an artistic group was
Vogelsang[8] who devoted a chapter to them in his monograph on Dutch
illumination published in the late nineteenth century. Their most extensive art historical treatment, however, has been in a series of books
and articles by Byvanck,[9] whose contributions were supplemented by
Hoogewerff[10] and de Wit.[11] New observations on the First History Bibles
and their relation to larger problems have appeared in Delaissé's monograph on Dutch illumination[12] and Gumbert's study on Carthusian book
production in Utrecht.[13]

---

[4] Isaac Le Long, *Boek-zaal der Nederduytsche Bybels*, Amsterdam, 1732.

[5] H. van Druten, *Geschiedenis der Nederlandsche Bijbelvertaling*, Eerste Deel: *Geschiedenis
der Nederlandsche Bijbelvertaling tot het jaar 1522*, Leiden, 1895.

[6] C. H. Ebbinge Wubben, *Over Middelnederlandsche vertalingen van het Oude Testament*,
The Hague, 1903.

[7] C. C. de Bruin, "Bespiegelingen over de 'Bijbelvertaler van 1360,' Zijn milieu, werk,
en persoon," *Nederlandsch Archief voor Kerkgeschiedenis* 48 (1968), pp. 39-59, 49 (1969), pp.
135-154, 50 (1969), pp. 11-27, 51 (1970), pp. 16-41.

[8] W. Vogelsang, *Holländische Miniaturen des Späteren Mittelalters*, Strassburg, 1899
(Studien zur Deutschen Kunstgeschichte, XVIII).

[9] A. W. Byvanck, "Aanteekeningen over handschriften met miniaturen. VII: Het
atelier der Utrechtsche Miniaturen," *Oudheidkundig Jaarboek* 9 (1929), pp. 136-145; *De
Middeleeuwsche Boekillustratie in de noordelijke Nederlanden*, Antwerp, 1943; *La miniature dans
les Pays-bas septentrionaux*, Paris, 1937; "Noordnederlandsche Miniaturen der XVe eeuw
in handschriften van den Bijbel," *Bulletin van den Nederlandschen Oudheidkundigen Bond*, 2e
serie, 10 (1917), pp. 260-275; "Utrechtsche miniaturen," *Het Gildeboek* 6 (1923-1924), pp.
1-11, 63-80, 106-117, 179-195.

[10] A. W. Byvanck and G. J. Hoogewerff, *La miniature hillandaise et les manuscrits illustrés
du XIVe au XVIe siècle aux Pays-Bas septentrionaux*, The Hague, 1922-1926, and G. J. Hoogewerff, *De Noord-Nederlandsche Schilderkunst*, Vols. 1-2, The Hague, 1936-1947.

[11] C. de Wit, "Het Atelier der Utrechtsche Miniaturen en een Kapittel uit de Geschiedenis van het Karthuizerklooster Nieuw-Licht," *Oudheidkundig Jaarboek* 7 (1929), pp. 264-271.

[12] L.M.J.Delaissé, *A Century of Dutch Manuscript Illumination*, Berkeley/Los Angeles, 1968.

[13] J. P. Gumbert, *Die Utrechter Kartäuser und ihre Bücher im frühen fünfzehnten Jahrhundert*,
Leiden, 1974.

Philologists have been almost exclusively concerned with the text of the First History Bible. Few even mention its illustrations. Van Druten and Ebbinge Wubben[14] have treated the linguistic peculiarities of the various manuscripts and the deviations in the contents of the First History Bible from other vernacular renditions. However, the historical and religious circumstances surrounding the production of the fifteenth century First History Bible remain obscure. This is primarily because philologists' principal aim has been reconstructing the fourteenth century text which served as a model for the fifteenth century copies. de Bruin[15] treated the historical circumstances which must have motivated the translation of the Bible in the fourteenth century; but even his concern lies more with a reconstruction of the original text.[16] Thus, a clear picture of the fifteenth century First History Bibles as written and illustrated books has not emerged from philological scholarship.

Nor have art historians been concerned with the First History Bibles as both written and illustrated books. Art historical scholarship has concentrated on two problems — the separation and identification of miniaturists' hands and the localization of the manuscripts. The most significant contribution to the study of hands was Byvanck's, whose conclusions appeared in a series of four articles in *Het Gildeboek*.[17] By identifying the collaborating miniaturists, Byvanck established two basic groups of miniaturists working on the Bible illustrations. Illuminators from the first group worked on eight of the illustrated *Eerste Historiebijbels* which date from the second quarter of the fifteenth century: London, British Library, Add. Ms. 15410; Amsterdam, Oudheidkundig Genootschap, Ms. 61; Brussels, Bibliothèque royale, Ms. 9018-23; The Hague, Koninklijke Bibliotheek, Ms. 78 D 38; The Hague, Museum Meermanno-Westreenianum, Ms. 10 A 18-19; Middelburg, Zeeuws Genootschap voor Wetenschappen; Munich, Staatsbibliothek, Cod. germ 1102; and Nuremberg, Stadtbibliothek, Ms. Solger 8°. In the third quarter of the fifteenth century, one of the miniaturists of the Vienna Bible (Oesterreichische Nationalbibliothek, Ms. 2771-72) also did the illustrations for

---

14 van Druten, *Geschiedenis* and Ebbinge Wubben, *Middelnederlandsche vertalingen*.

15 de Bruin, *NAK*, 49, pp. 135-154, 51, pp. 16-41.

16 The first published edition of the text of the *Eerste Historiebijbel* will appear in de Bruin (ed.), *Corpus Sacrae Scripturae Neerlandicae Medii Aevi. Series Maior*, Leiden (1977 and 1978).

17 Byvanck, *Het Gildeboek*, pp. 1-11, 63-80, 106-117, 179-195.

a two-volume Bible preserved in Ghent (Universiteitsbibliotheek, Ms. 430) and The Hague (Koninklijke Bibliotheek, Ms. 78 D 39).

Not only did Byvanck establish that the Dutch vernacular Bibles form a coherent group probably emanating from a single milieu, he also set out to prove that their place of execution was the Carthusian monastery of the Nieuwlicht in Utrecht.[18] This suggestion was originally made by S. Müller, the chief Utrecht archivist of the nineteenth century whose notes Byvanck followed.[19] Byvanck's own conclusions, as well as his argumentation, were never completely accepted by his contemporary scholars; de Wit[20] and Hoogewerff,[21] for example, were both dissenters. However, some modern scholarship terms these Bibles, the "Carthusian Bibles."[22] In the light of recent, more definitive scholarship categorically rejecting the Bibles as Carthusian products,[23] it is worth reviewing the controversy here.

The identification of the Bible atelier as the Carthusian monastery of the Nieuwlicht rests on Byvanck's assumption that two other manuscripts emanate from this production center.[24] These two manuscripts are a four-volume copy of the Vulgate in Brussels (Bibliothèque royale, Mss. 106-107, 204-205) and a copy of Nicolas of Lyra's *Postilla in prophetas minores et maiores* (Utrecht, Universiteits Bibliotheek, Ms. 252).[25] The latter manuscript possesses one miniature by the anonymous Master of Otto van Mordrecht,[26] so called after the donor of the book; and the former contains a single historiated initial depicting the Death of Alex-

---

[18] *Ibid.*, pp. 1-11.

[19] Gumbert, *Die Utrechter Kartäuser*, p. 184, note 75.

[20] de Wit, *Oudheidkundig Jaarboek*, pp. 264-271, consists of a rebuttal of the theses in Byvanck's *Het Gildeboek* articles.

[21] In Byvanck and Hoogewerff, *La miniature hollandaise*, pp. xxi-xxiii, Hoogewerff simply summarizes Byvanck's conclusions. However, in *Noord-Nederlandsche Schilderkunst*, I, pp. 376, 387, II, pp. 309-310, Hoogewerff presents a case against Byvanck's hypothesis.

[22] Two most recent assertions that the First History Bibles are products of Nieuwlicht occur in *De Gouden Eeuw der Boekverluchting in de Noordelijke Nederlanden*, Brussels, 1971 (catalogue of an exhibition at the Bibliothèque royale), p. 19, and in D. J. A. Ross, *Illustrated Medieval Alexander Books in Germany and The Netherlands*, Cambridge, 1971, pp. 160 and 178. Other recent examples of this appellation are cited by Gumbert, *Die Utrechter Kartäuser*, p. 80, note 7.

[23] Gumbert, *Die Utrechter Kartäuser*, pp. 181-185.

[24] Byvanck, *Het Gildeboek*, pp. 1-11.

[25] Further details on these manuscripts may be found in Byvanck and Hoogewerff, *La miniature hollandaise*, nos. 9, 24, pp. 5-5, 10.

[26] *Ibid.*, pl. 5.

ander.[27] Both manuscripts have contemporary *ex libris'* of the monastery of Nieuwlicht.[28] The fact that both books were known to belong to the monastery and that both contain miniatures is accepted as evidence by Byvanck that Nieuwlicht was an active scriptorium producing both written and illustrated books.

Byvanck further supports his theory of Carthusian activity in book production by eliminating Oude Gracht, the monastery of the Augustinian canons regular in Utrecht, as a contender. First, he cites the existence of a "steady trickle" of manuscripts produced in Utrecht from 1400 to 1470, some with a Carthusian provenance and some with an Augustinian canons regular provenance.[29] Secondly, historical factors are presented to prove the incapacity of the Augustinian monastery during part of this period.[30] Between 1428 and 1432 the canons vacated their monastery, some moving to Westfalia and some to Doetinchem as a result of the Utrecht Schism. When they returned in 1432, the cloister was penniless and would not have had sufficient funds for the production of luxury manuscripts. And in 1439, still another disaster befell the monastery; only the prior and a few canons were spared from the plague of that year. Since some of the extensively illustrated First Bibles are known to date from these years of Augustinian trouble, Byvanck assumes that they were

---

[27] *Ibid.*, Pl. 201.

[28] The Vulgate (Brussels, Bibliothèque royale, Mss. 106-107, 204-205) has three inscriptions, the first of which (Ms. 106, fol. 238v) reads: "Anno Domini millesimo quadringentesimo secundo decima septima mensis Januarii hoc volumen finitum est per manus Henrici de Aernhem. Orate pro eo." The second (Ms. 204, fol. 222v) is similar: "Anno Domini millesimo quadringentesimo tercio feria quarta in die cinerum hec Biblia est finita in quatuor voluminibus Deo dante gracia per manus Henrici de Aernhem. Orate pro eo." The inside covers of the bindings of Mss. 106-107, 204 bear the annotation: "Pertinet ad Carthusienses prope Traiectum." The inscriptions in Nicolas of Lyra's *Postilla in prophetas* (Utrecht, Universiteitsbibliotheek, Ms. 252, fol. 246v and inside cover) read: "Pertinet ad Carthusienses prope Traiectum, quem scribi fecit Magister Otto, dudum canonicus Sancti Martini Traiectensis, postea monachus ac prior huius domus" and "Iste liber est fratrum Carthusiensium prope Traiectum quem scribi fecit Dominus Otto tempore noviciatus sui, completus post eius professionem." It is clear from the inscriptions that both manuscripts belonged to the monastery; but neither colophon testifies to their having been written at Nieuwlicht.

[29] Byvanck, *Het Gildeboek*, p. 11. Most of the fifteenth century manuscripts belonging either to Nieuwlicht or the Oude Gracht are preserved today in the Bibliotheek der Rijksuniversiteit in Utrecht, where they have been catalogued by J. D. Hintzen, "De geïllumineerde handschriften der Utrechtsche Universiteitsbibliotheek," *Het Boek* 10 (1921), pp. 1-13, 263-264, and J. F. van Someren, *De Utrechtsche Universiteitsbibliotheek*, Utrecht, 1909.

[30] Byvanck, *Het Gildeboek*, p. 11.

produced in a Carthusian monastery, like the illustrated Vulgate and the Nicolas of Lyra text mentioned above.[31]

Byvanck's misinterpretation of the evidence has been discussed by Gumbert in his study entitled *Die Utrechter Kartäuser und ihre Bücher*.[32] According to Gumbert, neither the illustrated Vulgate nor the Nicolas of Lyra manuscript was produced in the Carthusian monastery. The Brussels copy of the Vulgate was probably commissioned by the Carthusians, but its colophon states that it was written "per manus Henrici de Aernhem" who was a scribe enrolled in the lay gild in Utrecht.[33] The inscription in the Nicolas of Lyra text states that the book was a gift to the monastery from the Carthusian prior, Otto van Mordrecht, at the termination of his novitiate. However, its execution in the monastery cannot be assumed from the inscription, and indeed its features of production do not correspond with those employed in documented Carthusian products.[34] Moreover, Gumbert pointed out that the Rules of the Carthusian order specifically discouraged the use of *curiositas* or "illustrations" in manuscripts of that order.[35] That such a regulation was adhered to at Nieuwlicht is supported by the absence of *any* manuscripts produced by the cloister in which illustrations occur.[36] Only three manuscripts from the Utrecht Carthusian's library contain illuminations, and each of these was written elsewhere.[37]

Alternative theories to an exclusive Carthusian production of the Utrecht Bibles have been proposed. De Wit[38] argued that lay artists were

---

[31] *Ibid.*

[32] Gumbert, *Die Utrechter Kartäuser*, pp. 181-185. The relevant chapter is entitled "Bildlicher Schmuck."

[33] *Ibid.*, p. 184, note 71.

[34] *Ibid.*, p. 184-185.

[35] *Ibid.*, pp. 10, note 14; 182; 316.

[36] *Ibid.*, p. 181. However, at least one contemporary charterhouse did produce some illuminated manuscripts, the Charterhouse of St. Barbara in Cologne discussed in Richard Marks, *The Medieval Manuscript Library of the Charterhouse of St. Barbara in Cologne* (Analecta Cartusiana, XXI-XXII), 2 vols, Salzburg, 1974.

[37] St. Bernard's Commentary on the Song of Songs (Utrecht, Universiteits Bibliotheek, Ms. 155) has a single historiated initial containing a portrait of a seated abbot (fol. 1r). The Brussels Vulgate contains the previously mentioned miniature of the Death of Alexander (Ms. 205, fol. 1r); and the Lyra manuscript contains the portrait of Lyra (fol. 44r) and another miniature depicting a seraphim (fol. 43v). The Bernard manuscript was a gift to the cloister from Wilhelmus van Rhenen from the eastern Netherlands; the Brussels Vulgate was probably commissioned by the cloister and produced in Utrecht; and the Lyra manuscript was a gift from Otto van Moordrecht, perhaps also produced in Utrecht, according to Gumbert, *Die Utrechter Karthäuser*, pp. 57, 68, 77-79.

employed by the Carthusians. This solution compensated for the insufficient number of monks at Nieuwlicht necessary to undertake the production of such a large number of illustrated manuscripts. However, it hardly remains a viable alternative, given the fact that no illustrated books can be shown to derive from the Utrecht Carthusian workshop. Hoogewerff's suggestions[39] were similar to de Wit's. The former postulated a joint scriptorium, shared by the Carthusians and the Augustinians in Utrecht and participated in by lay artists from the same city. However, none of the extensively illustrated manuscripts are known to have been produced by the Augustinians. Nor is Delaissé's suggestion of an Augustinian Bible workshop tenable.[40] It rests on the reasoning that the Brussels Vulgate could not have been written by the Carthusians because it was finished in 1403, only eleven years after the founding of Nieuwlicht. On this basis, Delaissé assumes that "the Bible was written by the Regular Canons of the same town,"[41] for the Carthusian community was still too young. However, Gumbert has proven that Henricus de Aernhem, the copyist of this Bible, was in fact a lay scribe who it seems free-lanced both for the Carthusian monastery and Utrecht Cathedral.[42]

Scholarship on the First History Bibles has suffered considerably from focusing almost exclusively on the problem of localization. With the exception of Gumbert's study, scholarly accounts suggest that only two solutions are possible. Either the Bibles must have been produced by the Carthusian monastery or the Augustinian cloister. Why monastic production of illuminated Bibles should be essential in The Netherlands when lay production of illuminated manuscripts at this time was more common elsewhere[43] has never been properly clarified. Evidence revealing

---

[38] de Wit, *Oudheidkundig Jaarboek*, p. 265.

[39] Hoogewerff, *Noordnederlandsche Schilderkunst*, I, pp. 376-385.

[40] Delaissé, *Dutch Manuscript Illumination*, p. 16.

[41] *Ibid.*

[42] Gumbert, *Die Utrechter Kartäuser*, pp. 184, note 71.

[43] For example, in the South Netherlands Burgundian production is characterized by publishing houses which were run by a "director" and employed on a regular basis both scribes and illuminators. The most detailed study of Burgundian methods of production remains L. M. J. Delaissé, *Le siècle d'or de la miniature flamande, le mécenat de Philippe le Bon*, Brussels, 1959 (catalogue of an exhibition at the Bibliothèque royale). In fourteenth and fifteenth century Paris a slightly different situation existed. Miniaturists and scribes resided in a single quarter of the city, and when a patron wanted to commission a book, a "manager" would select the required artists and scribes. Thus, any given product from this center is likely to vary in some degree from any other. Nevertheless, in both centers, the majority of the production was essentially in lay hands.

Devotio Moderna activity in book production[44] is not sufficient reason for the localization of all Dutch manuscripts in monastic circles. Utrecht alone had a large number of lay artists and scribes registered in its gild,[45] of which Henricus de Aernhem was only one.

The preoccupation with the question of localization has virtually obscured any internal evidence presented by the Bible manuscripts themselves. Their texts, miniature cycles, and the relationship of text to picture have never been thoroughly investigated. Only Vogelsang[46] considered these questions, but his summary conclusions were overlooked by later scholars. In his examination of the texts of the unillustrated *Eerste Historiebijbel*, he noted evidences of monastic provenance.[47] Furthermore, he conjectured that the production of vernacular biblical texts may have served the aims of the *Devotio Moderna* in their instruction of the laity.[48] And, in his stylistic analysis of the manuscripts Vogelsang was partly concerned with the contents of the miniatures. These, he observed ,were executed with the primary aim of faithfully illustrating the text: "Ueber das Inhaltliche sei hier nur noch nachgetragen, dass der Zweck stets ist, eine knappe Illustration des Textes zu geben."[49]

Following the directions implicit in Vogelsang's inquiry, this study will investigate the Bibles as an artistic and historical phenomenon. Their texts, miniatures, and the relationship of one to the other will be considered in turn. First, an examination of the contents of the texts should suggest the purpose for which the First History Bibles were conceived — the audience to whom they were directed and the use these readers were instructed to make of the texts. Secondly, an analysis of the system of illustration in the miniature cycles in relation to other illuminated Bibles is likely to reveal the characteristic features of the Dutch cycles. Two factors can be shown to govern the choice and treatment of subjects in the miniature cycles: an interest in narrative illustration and an interest in

---

[44] The copying and illuminating of books by the Brothers of the Common Life is discussed by R. R. Post, *The Modern Devotion. Confrontation with Reformation and Humanism*, Leiden, 1968, pp. 349, 367; A. Hyma, *The Christian Renaissance*, Hamden (Conn.), 1965 (reprint), pp. 115-116; and W. Oeser, "Die Brüder des gemeinsamen Lebens in Münster als Bücherschreiber," *Archiv für Geschichte des Buchwesens* 5 (1964), pp. 198-398.

[45] Extracts from the gild are published by G. van Klaveren, "Utrechtsche schrijvers en verlichters van miniaturen," *Maandblad van 'Oud-Utrecht'*, 10 (1935), pp. 35-37.

[46] Vogelsang, *Holländische Miniaturen*.

[47] *Ibid.*, p. 37.

[48] *Ibid.*, p. 39.

[49] *Ibid.*, p. 44.

pictorial realism. Each of these interests will be investigated, noting the relationship of the contents in both narrative and realistic miniatures to the contents of the accompanying text. In addition, analysis of the actual physical relationship between text and pictures may clarify the extent to which the First History Bibles were conceived as integrated written and illustrated books.

Once a clear picture of the Bibles as a textual and pictorial group has been constructed, the historical and religious circumstances motivating their production will be considered. Any factual evidence contained within both the illustrated and unillustrated manuscripts will be presented; many possess colophons and scribal notations. Then, the reasons for such a widespread interest in this particular vernacular text can be examined, and the motivation behind the interest in narrative illustration and pictorial realism can be assessed. Since the concerns of the *Devotio Moderna* closely parallel the interests apparent in both text and pictures in the First History Bibles, the role that this religious movement may have played in their production will be discussed. The attitudes of certain writers of the *Devotio Moderna* towards vernacular texts and Bible reading will be closely examined. In addition, other evidence suggesting an interest in vernacular Bible texts in circles of the *Devotio Moderna* will be presented.

It is necessary to impose certain limitations on this study. The interesting and varied styles evident in the miniatures are beyond the scope of an investigation of the relationship between text and illustration. Likewise, the separation and identification of hands, extensively treated by Byvanck, will not be considered. The identity and number of the workshops responsible for the production of the Bibles will be treated only peripherally in the discussion of the historical and religious background. An investigation of one group of manuscripts, related to each other by text as are the Dutch Bibles, does not provide sufficient evidence for a definitive solution to such a problem. Rather the problem of localization requires a different approach, one dependent on a complete codicological study, and subsequent comparison, of all the diverse manuscripts which are associated with Utrecht. An analysis of the style and the number of hands in the miniatures would constitute one aspect of a codicological investigation.

Nor will this study treat in the same detail all the illustrated exemplars of the First History Bible. On the basis of their number of illustrations and their placement in the text, the illustrated First History Bibles divide into two groups. The first group consists of manuscripts illustrated only by one introductory miniature prefacing each book of the Bible; their cycles of illustration are thus relatively short. This group is composed of the following manuscripts: Amsterdam, Oudheidkundig Genootschap, Ms. 61; Middelburg, Zeeuws Genootschap voor Wetenschappen;[50] The Hague, Museum Meermanno-Westreenianum, Ms. 10 A 18-19; The Hague, Koninklijke Bibliotheek, Ms. 78 D 39; Ghent, Universiteits Bibliotheek, Ms. 430; and London, British Museum, Add. Ms. 15410. Since the Amsterdam and Middelburg Bibles, like the ones in The Hague (Ms. 78 D 39) and Ghent, originally were one manuscript, four First History Bibles belong to the first group. On the other hand, manuscripts from the second group contain extensive numbers of miniatures inserted within the text of the Bible at short intervals. The remaining manuscripts make up the second group: Brussels, Bibliothèque royale, Mss. 9018-23; The Hague, Koninklijke Bibliotheek, Ms. 78 D 38; London, British Library, Add. Mss. 10043, 16951, 38122; Munich, Staatsbibliothek, Cod. germ. 1102; Nuremberg, Stadtbibliothek, Ms. Solger 8°; and Vienna, Oesterreichische Nationalbibliothek, Mss. 2771-72.[51]

For an investigation of the relationship between text and illustration, the second group is of more crucial importance. And, indeed, the themes of the prefatory miniatures in the first group do not depart significantly from well-established medieval traditions of biblical illustration.[52] Thus, the second group will form the focus of this study, although the textual contents of the first group will be considered with that of the second. In addition, internal evidence presented by manuscripts in both groups, as well as by the unillustrated examples, will be dealt with to elucidate the historical and religious milieu which produced the First History Bible in the fifteenth century.

---

[50] This manuscript was apparently destroyed in a fire in Middelburg in 1945, according to correspondence with the librarian, Drs. A. W. M. van Kraay. Published photographs of it exist in Byvanck, *Het Gildeboek*, Pls. 33, 37, 38, and Byvanck and Hoogewerff, *La miniature hollandaise*, Pls. 113-114, fig. 59.

[51] Hereafter, the manuscripts will be referred to by their abbreviated references on p. XI.

[52] M. R. James, "The Pictorial Illustration of the Old Testament from the Fourth to the Sixteenth Centuries," in *A Book of Old Testament Illustrations of the Middle of the 13th Century*, London, 1927, pp. 1-55.

CHAPTER ONE

THE PLACE OF THE FIRST HISTORY BIBLE'S TEXT IN DUTCH BIBLICAL TRADITION

The texts of the Dutch vernacular Bibles have received much attention in scholarship. As early as the eighteenth century, a Dutch scholar, Isaac Le Long, described each version of the vernacular Bible in the chronological order of their appearance, publishing at the same time the prologues from each text.[1] Le Long pioneering work was resumed in the late nineteenth and early twentieth centuries by the philologists, van Druten[2] and Ebbinge Wubben.[3] These two scholars attempted to provide an outline of the development of the textual tradition of the vernacular Bibles in Holland, pointing out philological and historical interrelationships between the various versions. Most recently, de Bruin's research on the first Dutch vernacular Bible deserves mention. It was he who has attempted an identification of the translator of this text, the milieu in which he worked, and his literary output.[4] And, de Bruin's forthcoming edition of the first Dutch vernacular Bible[5] should provide a firm basis for further research on this text. However, none of the research has been aimed at establishing the place of the *Eerste Historiebijbel* in the development of the vernacular Bible tradition in Holland with regard to the purpose of its translation.

The first Dutch version of the vernacular Bible, the *Eerste Historiebijbel*, was translated around 1360 from the Latin by an anonymous monk working in the Benedictine abbey of Affligem in Brabant in the southern Netherlands.[6] Since the nineteenth century, it has been termed the *Tweede Historiebijbel* in scholarly literature owing to a scribal error which resulted in the mistaken dating of another version of the Dutch vernacular Bible. A contemporary colophon dated one manuscript of this second

---

[1] Le Long, *Boekzaal*.

[2] van Druten, *Geschiedenis*.

[3] Ebbinge Wubben, *Middelnederlandsche vertalingen*.

[4] de Bruin, *NAK*.

[5] For his forthcoming edition is *CSSN*, de Bruin is using a British Library exemplar of the *Eerste Historiebijbel* (Add. Ms. 15310-15311).

[6] de Bruin, *NAK*, 51, pp. 16-41.

version in 1358, that is two years before the execution of the Brabant version. Only recently Deschamps elucidated this error, pointing out that the 1358 manuscript was actually completed in 1458 by Johannes Scutken, a member of the Windesheim Congregation.[7] As a result, the nomenclature has been revised, and the *Tweede Historiebijbel* has assumed its rightful place in fifteenth century tradition of biblical translation, while the *Eerste Historiebijbel* now refers to the edition executed in Brabant.

In its strictest sense, the term *Eerste Historiebijbel* signifies only the translation of the historical books of the Old and New Testaments, with their commentaries, executed between 1359 and 1361.[8] These included the Pentateuch, Joshua, Judges, Ruth, the four books of Kings, Tobit, Judith, and Esther, translated from the Vulgate and accompanied by the relevant translations from the *Historia Scholastica*. In addition, the Old Testament part of this version contained Cyrus, Alexander, Maccabees, and the Destruction of Jerusalem in a translation reworked from Petrus Comestor's *Historia Scholastica* and from Jacob van Maerlant's *Rijmbijbel*, *Spiegel Historiael*, and *Wrake van Iherusalem*. From the New Testament a Gospel Harmony, derived from a thirteenth century vernacular *Leven van Ihesus*,[9] and the Acts of the Apostles, both with commentaries from the *Historia Scholastica*, completed this translation.

Somewhat later, the same anonymous translator worked on other books of the Bible but without corresponding texts from the *Historia Scholastica*.[10] In 1384, he translated the major prophets, Isaiah and Jeremiah, and in the 1390's he translated the poetic books of the Old Testament which included Proverbs, Ecclesiastes, Song of Songs, the Book of Wisdom, and Ecclesiasticus. During the same period, the Psalter was also translated by him into Dutch. Many manuscripts of the *Eerste Historiebijbel* contain other sections of the Bible which were not the work of our translator, amongst which are the Apocalypse, the Epistles, and

---

[7] Deschamps, *Middelnederlandse Handschriften*, p. 157.

[8] de Bruin's and Deschamps' nomenclature and dating of the *Eerste Hiatoriebijbel* are followed here, as set forth in de Bruin, *NAK*, 50, pp. 14-15, and Deschamps, *Middelnederlandse Handschriften*, pp. 152-156. The description of the contents of the original translation derives from de Bruin, *NAK*, pp. 14-15. Unfortunately, the extent to which the fifteenth century manuscripts follow an original fourteenth century exemplar is as yet unclear, as a manuscript *stemma* has not been published. This should be remedied in de Bruin's forthcoming philological edition of the text in *CSSN* (1977).

[9] An edition of this thirteenth century text has been published by J. Bergsma, *De Levens van Jezus in het Middelnederlandsch*, Leiden, 1898.

[10] de Bruin, *NAK*, 50, pp. 14-15.

readings from the minor prophets.[11] In all probability these were copied and modified from still earlier translations of such books, such as the thirteenth century translation of the Apocalypse and the numerous vernacular lectionaries and epistolaries which contained readings from the Epistles and Prophets.[12]

A considerable number of manuscripts of the *Eerste Historiebijbel* are extant.[13] However, of the thirty or so surviving texts, none contain the complete translation by the "translator of 1360" which would have consisted of the historical and poetic books of the Old and New Testaments, the Psalter, and the major prophets. Closest in text to the original is an unillustrated codex in the British Library (British Library, Add. Ms. 15310-11).[14] This manuscript omits only the Psalter and the major prophets and includes none of the supplementary books such as the Apocalypse and the Epistles. Most of the remaining manuscripts are pastiches of the original, some containing only the historical books of the Old Testament, like the three other British Library Bibles (British Library, Add. Mss. 10043, 15410, 38122), and some containing most of the complete work of the "translator of 1360" with the Apocalypse and Epistles, as in The Hague Bible.[15] The fact that all the extant manuscripts date from the fifteenth century rather than the fourteenth, the earliest from about 1425, may in part explain the wide discrepancy between their textual contents and that of the 1360 exemplar. Moreover, only a few of the manuscripts were executed in the southern Netherlands and none in Brabant. the place of origin of the translation.[16] The vast majority come

---

[11] *Ibid.*, p. 15.

[12] This suggestion is made by S. Axters. *Geschiedenis van de Vroomheid in de Nederlanden*, II, *De Eeuw van Ruusbroec*, Antwerp, 1953, p. 382.

[13] The list of manuscripts appears in Deschamps, *Middelnederlandse Handschriften*, no. 50, pp. 154-5.

[14] *Ibid.*, no. 50, p. 152-156.

[15] Because the Hague Bible bears a colophon stating that it was completed in 1360, it was once thought to be the original manuscript of the translator. However, scholars now recognize that it was completed in the fifteenth century and that the colophon copies that of its model.

[16] An article by James Marrow, "Dutch Illumination, and the 'Devotio Moderna'," *Medium Aevum* 42 (1973), pp. 251-258, questions the localization of fifteenth century vernacular Bible production in the North Netherlands. He states that several manuscripts of the *Eerste Historiebijbel* have linguistic features characteristic of the South Netherlands and adds that there was a tradition of vernacular translation in the South, to which Jacob van Maerlant belonged. The South Netherlandish Bible manuscripts are cited by J. Deschamps, "Middelnederlandse Bijbelhandschriften uit het klooster Sint Catharinadal te Hasselt," *Liber amicorum aangeboden aan Magister Jan Gruyters*, Hasselt, 1957, pp.

from the North Netherlands, many probably from Utrecht,[17] another factor which may have contributed to their departure from the model by the "translator of 1360."

The religious climate in Brabant where the translator of the *Eerste Historiebijbel* worked was particularly favorable to renditions of theological texts.[18] The "translator of 1360" alone translated no less than fourteen texts, amongst which were lives of the saints and the church Fathers, Gregory's Homilies on the Gospels, a mystical text on spiritual love, and Jacobus de Voragine's *Golden Legend*, in addition to his biblical translations.[19] Another center in Brabant was also prolific in vernacular translations; Ruysbroec's abbey of Rooklooster near Groenendaal was a veritable "translatorium" which produced large quantities of saints' lives and mystical texts, many by Ruysbroec himself.[20] The translation movement in Brabant did not begin with these two abbeys in the fourteenth century. Seeds for its development existed in the thirteenth when the Beguines and Beghards, popular religious foundations, turned out vernacular texts.[21] Two of the earliest Netherlandish translators of biblical texts, Lambert le Bègue of Liège and Jacob van Maerlant, worked in this milieu, producing respectively a Flemish *Acts of the Apostles* and the *Rijmbijbel*, the latter a direct precursor to the *Eerste Historiebijbel* in its translations of the *Historia Scholastica*.[22]

By the fifteenth century, the North Netherlands acquired preeminence over its southern neighbors as a center of vernacular theological translations. In fact, the South Netherlands virtually ceased to contribute to this endeavor, although vernacular translations of literary and historical

193-233. However, de Bruin, *NAK*, 48, p. 50, clearly states that most of the fifteenth century manuscripts were produced and used in the North: ". . . opmerkenswaardige feit dat het gros van deze teksten in de noordelijke Nederlanden afgeschreven en daar ook in gebruik geweest was." See below, p. 15 for the diffusion of interest in vernacular translations from the South to the North.

[17] pp. 1, 101.

[18] The most recent survey of vernacular translation activity in the Netherlands appears as the general introduction to *CSSN*, Series Minor, Vol. I: *Het Luikse Diatessaron*, pp. xv-xxx, by de Bruin. See also, S. Axters, *Vroomheid*, I, pp. 377-464.

[19] A list of the anonymous translator's works is given by de Bruin, *NAK*, 50, pp. 14-15.

[20] On the library at Groenendaal see P. Vermeeren, "Op zoek naar de librije van Rooklooster," *Het Boek*, 35 (1962), pp. 142-155.

[21] On these important religious groups see Ernest W. McDonnell, *The Beguines and Beghards in Medieval Culture with special emphasis on the Belgian scene*, New Brunswick (New Jersey), 1954.

[22] See S. Axters, *Vroomheid*, I, p. 380. On Jacob van Maerlant, see J. te Winkel, *Maerlant's werken beschouwd als spiegel van de dertiende eeuw*, Leiden, 1877.

texts were plentiful there. This fact may be due, in part, to the patronage of the Dukes of Burgundy who inspired the cultivation of courtly, Parisian tastes. In the mid-fifteenth century Brussels, formerly an active center in the heart of Flemish mystical traditions, became the "Paris of the North" under the influence of the Duke Philip the Good's court. But this was not before spiritual leaders from the North had absorbed some of the essential features of Brabantian mysticism. The diffusion of southern traditions to the North occurred partially through the work of one man, Geert Groote, the founder of the *Devotio Moderna*. His southern heritage has long been noted, and his lengthy sojourn in the Augustinian monastery of Rooklooster during Ruysbroec's life was a factor contributing to his absorption of the mystical ideals.[23] Here, too, he must have read Ruysbroec's translations and indeed many others which formed part of the extensive library in that cloister. Shortly thereafter, on his return to his northern homeland, Groote translated the Psalter and then the Book of Hours. And his translation of the latter, of which more manuscripts survive than of any other single text in the North, was adopted in the fifteenth century as the standard form for all Books of Hours produced by houses and monasteries affiliated with the Windesheim Congregation.[24]

In the northern Netherlands, fifteenth century leaders of the *Devotio Moderna* followed Groote's interest in biblical texts. Scutken's retranslation of the Bible and *Historia Scholastica*, the *Tweede Historiebijbel*, in 1458 has already been mentioned, although the motivation behind this translation is as yet unclear.[25] At the same time, the Windesheim Congregation worked on a corrected translation of the Latin Vulgate which, on completion, was standardized as the Windesheim version of the Bible, like the Book of Hours had been earlier.[26] But the fact which evidences the most extensive interest in vernacular biblical translations is the

---

[23] Two recent monographs contain the best biographical studies on Geert Groote: G. Épiney-Burgard, *Gérard Grote (1340-1384) et les débuts de la Devotion Moderne*, Wiesbaden, 1970, and T. van Zijl, *Gerard Groote, Ascetic and Reformer (1340-1384)*, Washington, 1963 (The Catholic University of America Studies in Medieval History, New Series, 18). Épiney-Burgard, pp. 86-136, treats Groote's relation to mysticism.

[24] Groote's version of the Book of Hours is discussed and edited in N. van Wijk (ed.), *Het Getijdenboek van Geert Groote naar het Haagse handschrift 133 E 21*, Leiden, 1940.

[25] On the *Tweede Historiebijbel* see the catalogue entry by Deschamps, *Middelnederlandse Handschriften*, no. 51, pp. 156-158, and van Druten, *Geschiedenis*, pp. 75-79.

[26] The Windesheim revision is discussed by Post, *Modern Devotion*, pp. 304-308, and in greater detail in N. Greiteman, *De Windesheimse Vulgaatrevisie in de vijftiende eeuw*, Hilversum, 1937.

printing in 1477 in Delft of a revised version of the *Eerste Historiebijbel* by Mauricius Yemantszoon van Middelborch and Jacob Jacobszoon van der Meer. It was this edition which served as the model for the famous Cologne Bible published around 1480 and insuring dispersion of the text across northern Europe.[27] It would be difficult to deny that essays at biblical translations beginning in Brabant in the thirteenth century and continuing in the fourteenth and fifteenth centuries in South and North, alike, paved the way for the great Erasmian and Lutherian attempts at Bible translation in the sixteenth century.

Bible production was a by-product of certain common characteristics which unified these three religious movements: Brabantian mysticism of the Beguines and Beghards, southern mystical movements of the canonical orders, and northern *Devotio Moderna*. All three were popular religious movements which, in their reaction against features of the traditional church, sought to reach a wider audience. This audience was the laity, considered as yet untainted by the faults of members of the more conventional religious orders. The chief gripes of the reformers were both practical and ideological. On a practical level, they saw in the growing exclusiveness within the church a resultant deterioration, whereby failings and even deviations were more often than not overlooked. Simony, for example, was rampant, and Groote himself became one of its most outspoken adversaries.[28] One of the ideological permutations of this exclusiveness was scholasticism and its application to theological writings. This resulted in the teachings of the church reaching only an elite, often university educated, minority, and then only in the form of dogma removed many times from the original sources on which it relied. Therefore, to combat this exclusiveness in its practical and ideological guises, religious leaders, still *within the confines* of the church, translated simple texts such as the Bible for the ordinary people in an attempt to return to the purity of the early church.

The composition of the laity towards whom these texts were directed changed during the three centuries when vernacular translations were common. Particularly in the thirteenth century, but also in the fourteenth, it was primarily the nobility and to a certain extent the emerging bourge-

---

[27] On the revised *Eerste Historiebijbel* see van Druten, *Geschiedenis*, pp. 121-138. An account of its printing is given in M. Campbell, *Annales de la typographie néerlandaise au XVe siècle*, The Hague, 1874, no. 290, pp. 76-77.

[28] Groote's views on simony were set forth in his essay *De simonia ad beguttas* edited by W. de Vreese, *De simonia ad beguttas; de Middelnederlandse tekst*, The Hague, 1940.

oisie who were able to afford to purchase and subsequently to utilize hand-written manuscripts. While Maerlant's *Rijmbijbel* still has a stylized courtly tenor which may indicate the reading public's desires, we know that Jan Tay, a burger from Brussels, commissioned the translation of the *Eerste Historiebijbel* from our anonymous monk in the fourteenth century.[29] The existence of numerous fifteenth century non-luxury manuscripts of the *Eerste Historiebijbel* testifies to a more extensive reading public. Written on paper instead of parchment, in a cursive script, and often accompanied by hasty pendrawn illustrations, these were the medieval "paperback" illustrations for the less wealthy sectors of the population.[30] A corresponding change in literary style follows this change in audience. Gradually, the high aesthetic standards noticeable in the earlier translations such as the *Rijmbijbel* gave way to a simplification of language most apparent in the *Tweede Historiebijbel*.

Nevertheless, the main purpose of each of the biblical translations was didactic, despite changes in the audience and a resultant development in the style of the texts. The place of the *Eerste Historiebijbel* in the development of biblical textual tradition and its didactic aims may best be elucidated by a comparison of its text with those of its predecessors and its immediate successors. For this purpose, the *Rijmbijbel*, translated in 1280 by Jacob van Maerlant, the *Eerste Historiebijbel* and its revised printed edition, the *Tweede Historiebijbel*, the Windesheim Congregation's experiments with the Vulgate, and Erasmus' translations will be considered in chronological order.

Jacob van Maerlant's Rijmbijbel

Jacob van Maerlant's *Rijmbijbel* was a loose translation and reworking in poetry of Petrus Comestor's prose text, the *Historia Scholastica*, originally written between 1169 and 1176.[31] The Dutch translation of Comestor's text into the vernacular was not unique in European textual history. In

---

[29] de Bruin, *NAK*, 48, p. 45.

[30] Amongst the illustrated manuscripts the following are on paper: Ghent, Universiteitsbibliotheek, Ms. 430; The Hague, Koninklijke Bibliotheek, Ms. 78 D 39; and Munich, Staatsbibliotheek, Ms. germ. 1102. However, many of the unillustrated exemplars were also written on paper, as for example: The Hague, Koninklijke Bibliotheek, Mss. 75 E 7, 129 C 3, 128 C 2, 133 D 31; Leiden, Universiteitsbibliotheek, Mss. Ltk. 1128, 234, 232.

[31] An edition of Jacob van Maerlant's text has been published by J. David, *Rijmbijbel van Jacob van Maerlant*, 3 vols., Brussels, 1858-1859.

fact, vernacular renditions of this text sprang up all over northern Europe in the thirteenth century, the most popular of which was Guyart Desmoulin's *Bible historiale*.[32] This text was a straightforward prose translation of the Latin *Historia Scholastica*. But Jacob van Maerlant's version differed from that of Guyart Desmoulins in two fundamental respects. In contents, he omitted the third part of Comestor's text in favor of a translation of Flavius Josephus' *Bellum Judaicum*, and in style, his poetry allowed him to take considerable liberties with Comestor's text, so that the end product bears the unmistakable stamp of Maerlant. Amongst the stylistic peculiarities of the *Rijmbijbel*, we find a highly personal and a markedly courtly style. Continual interjections such as *verstaen wi* or "we understand" and *nu merct ghi* or "now we observe" heighten the readability of the *Rijmbijbel* by Maerlant's direct appeals to his readers. At the same time, the use of a courtly iconography, as for example in the characterization of Cain as a robber baron, give the work an artificial stylization.[33]

In his introduction to the *Rijmbijbel*, Maerlant specified the aims of his work as being both didactic and personal.[34] First, he tells his audience that they will read what it is "necessary to know" or *wat nutschap hier an sal wesen* in the text. He furthermore states that his text contains no fables or falsehoods; it only consists of "true rhyme and true words," *vraye rime ende ware word*. Secondly, Maerlant makes a plea to his readers to pray for his sins. Such a plea was a relatively common occurrence amongst me-

---

[32] The *Bible historiale* is discussed in S. Berger, *La bible française au moyen age. Étude sur les plus anciennes versions de la bible écrites en prose de langue d'oil*, Paris, 1884 (reprint, 1967). On this and other vernacular renditions of the *Historia Scholastica* see G. Lampe (ed.), *The Cambridge History of the Bible*, Vol. 2: *The West from the Fathers to the Reformation*, Cambridge, 1969, pp. 380-385, 430-435, and 448-450. Unfortunately, there is neither a critical edition nor a detailed scholarly study of Petrus Comestor's text. However, a brief account of the *Historia Scholastica* appears in the following works: Beryl Smalley, *The Study of the Bible in the Middle Ages*, Oxford, 1952, pp. 178-180; M. Manitius, *Geschichte der lateinischen Literatur des Mittelalters*, Vol. 3, Munich, 1931, pp. 156-159; N. Jung, "Pierre Comestor," *Dictionnaire de théologie catholique*, Vol. 12 (2), Paris, 1935, cols. 1918-22; F. Stegmüller, *Repertorium Biblicum Medii Aevi*, Vol. 4: *Commentaria, Auctores N-Q*, Madrid, 1954, pp. 280-300, nos. 6543-6592; A. Landgraf, "Recherches sur les écrits de Pierre le Mangeur," *Recherches de théologie ancienne et médiévale* 3 (1931), pp. 292-306, 341-372; and R. N. Martin, "Notes sur l'oeuvre littéraire de Pierre le Mangeur," *Recherches de théologie ancienne et médiévale*, 3 (1931), pp. 54-66. The Latin manuscripts of the *Historia Scholastica* are listed in Stegmüller, *Repertorium Biblicum Medii Aevi*, Vol. 4, pp. 288-290.

[33] Courtly iconography in the Rijmbijbel is discussed briefly by K. F. Proost, *De Bijbel in de Nederlandsche Letterkunde als spiegel der cultuur*, Deel 1: *De Middeleeuwen*, Assen, 1932, p. 63.

[34] Maerlant's introduction is published by Le Long, *Boek-zaal*, pp. 160-161.

dieval scribes and authors who consistently terminated their texts with the request that their sins might be exonerated in repayment for their holy labor. But Maerlant's request was far more specific as he stated that amongst his sins were the many books which he naively wrote in his youth and for which he now begged forgiveness. Perhaps Maerlant was thinking of such works as his *Der Kerken Claghe*, a biting poetic satire in which the evils of the church were soundly denounced.[35] Nevertheless, the request that readers pray in his favor was secondary to his primary intent of informing his audience of the essential elements of the Scripture. It was this goal which he specified even earlier in the introduction to his *Spiegel Historiael*, a translation in 1256 of Vincent of Beauvais' *Speculum Historiale*.[36] Here, he stated that he hoped to "enlighten the laity on the holy mysteries of the Bible," or *dat hi leeken weten dede uter Bibelen die heimelichede*.

Maerlant's almost exclusive use of one text, the *Historia Scholastica*, for his translation suggests the possibility of a similar intent in the two texts, the commentary and the *Rijmbijbel*. The *Historia* was composed in 1169 as a compendium of earlier biblical commentaries, drawing on such writers as Augustine, Jerome, Gregory, Josephus, Pliny, and Methodius. Its purpose was primarily a didactic one, as is evident from its use. In the twelfth century, it was incorporated into the university curriculum where it was used to provide the foundation in biblical history considered essential for the program of scholastic learning set forth in Hugh of St. Victor's *Didascalicon*.[37] Comestor's prologue[38] clarifies some of the aims of the *Historia Scholastica*. In particular, he states that his work is one to which readers may recur to obtain "the historical [or literal] truth [of Holy Scripture]." The "sea of mysteries," i.e. the figurative truths or

---

[35] *Der Kerken Claghe* is published by A. C. Bouman, *Middelnederlandse Bloemlezing met Grammatica*, Zutphen, 1948, pp. 138-153.

[36] An edition of this translation appears in M. de Vries and E. Verwijs, *Jacob van Maerlant's Spiegel historiael*, 3 vols., Leiden, 1863.

[37] On the use of the *Historia Scholastica* in medieval universities see H. Rashdall, *The Universities of Europe in the Middle Ages*, Vol. 3, Oxford, 1936 (2nd edition), pp. 158, 246. In the thirteenth century, Comestor's text was considered a complement to Petrus Lombard's *Sentences* and, although it did not retain its status as a textbook, it remained popular in the universities until the end of the Middle Ages.

[38] J. P. Migne, *PL*, Vol. 198, cols. 1053-1054: Causa suscepti laboris fuit instans petitio sociorum. Qui cum historiam sacrae Scripturae in serie, et glossis diffusam lectitarent, brevem nimis et inexpositam, opus aggredi me compulerunt: ad quod pro veritate historiae consequenda recurrerent ... Porro a cosmographia Moysi inchoans, rivulum historicum deduxi, usque ad ascensionem salvatoris, pelagus mysteriorum peritioribus relinquens, ...

meanings of Scripture, he leaves to the more skilled to deal with. Although he did not always observe these limits, Comestor clearly wanted to present the basic historical biblical narrative rather than its allegorical or tropological meanings.

In many places, Maerlant's text demonstrates an emphasis on the biblical narrative similar to that indicated in Comestor's prologue. First, he supplemented the narrative by answering questions implicitly posed in the Bible. For example, the reason for God's rest on the seventh day of creation in the book of Genesis must have seemed unclear. Maerlant interpreted this not as the completion of creation, but as a rest interlude before the resumption of creation on the eighth day.[39] Even when the narrative was self-explanatory, Maerlant expanded the story in various ways. The origin of Eve's name was naively explained as deriving from the first sounds uttered by infants, "e" by girls and "a" by boys.[40] Locations were provided for various biblical events, as for example those surrounding Noah which we learn took place in Persia and India.[41] The names of events or persons contemporaneous with those mentioned in the Bible are supplied in the *Rijmbijbel*: Jacob lived in Prometheus' time and Moses during the reign of King Abderas; the biblical period of the book of Judges was identical with that of the famous events at Troy.[42] Such details were probably provided in part to instill a certain familiarity with biblical persons and events, although we may wonder at their complete success when Prometheus was perhaps less well-known to the average reader than Jacob.

The didactic intent in the *Rijmbijbel* was not limited to an imparting of factual information for the edification of its readers. Their spiritual enlightenment was further advanced by Maerlant's suggestions of the tropological significance of certain passages whereby their literal meanings acquired another dimension in moral lesson. Such meanings were also drawn from the *Historia Scholastica*. For example, in the *Rijmbijbel* and in the *Historia Scholastica*, Lamech's "unfortunate" life was related to his bigamy, the implicit message being that in order to reap the rewards of a good life an individual must remain monogamous.[43] Most frequently, however, these moral lessons were directed towards the clergy. Maerlant

---

[39] Proost, *Bijbel in de Nederlandsche Letterkunde*, p. 64.
[40] *Ibid.*, pp. 63-64.
[41] *Ibid.*, p. 63.
[42] *Ibid.*
[43] *Ibid.*, p. 70.

related Aaron's entrance into the tabernacle to pray at the altar, contrasting Aaron's abstinence from wine with the rampant drunkenness of contemporary priests.[44] Tobias was praised for sharing his material wealth with the entire family during his visit to Sara, while the deceitful accumulation of goods by the clergy who nevertheless "cry poor" was deplored.[45] Simony in all its guises was likewise attacked in the *Rijmbijbel*, in the story of Simon from Acts, in the incident of the money changers in the temple, and in the story of Gehazi and Nanam.[46] Maerlant's continual barbs leveled at the practices of official members of the church were, therefore, couched in the moral meanings of Old Testament stories.

Clarification of the literal and tropological meanings of the narrative was not the only feature which characterizes the *Historia Scholastica*, and likewise the *Rijmbijbel*, as didactic. The *Historia* also frequently pointed out the typological meaning of the narrative of the Old Testament in relation to the New. These were the sections of its text which Maerlant most often adapted in his translation, adding other typological relationships not found in the commentary. Maerlant's exposition of the story of Jacob's Dream is a case in point, as Proost has noted:[47] the ladder signifies the mother of God; the door of heaven is the open wound in Christ's body; Jacob's staff is the cross; and God is the church. Such typological relationships occur in abundance throughout the *Rijmbijbel* where, for example, types prefiguring both Mary and Christ abound. Sara, the fall of manna, and Aaron's staff all signify Mary for various reasons explained by the poet, while Abel, Melchizedek, Isaac, and Joseph each prefigure Christ.[48] Jewish Old Testament figures are also consistently presented as prefiguring those responsible for Christ's suffering in his Passion: Esau was rough and red because his hands were soiled with Christ's blood; Cain was a Jew and as a result was dirty, impure and false like the Jews in the New Testament.[49] Maerlant's emphasis on typology over narrative is not surprising, particularly if we recall his translation of Vincent of Beauvais' *Speculum Historiale* some twenty years earlier which held that everything in the New Testament was to be found in the Old Testament either by implication or through symbols.[50]

---

[44] van Druten, *Geschiedenis*, p. 73.
[45] *Ibid.*, pp. 73-74.
[46] Proost, *Bijbel in de Nederlandsche Letterdunke*, p. 66.
[47] *Ibid.*, p. 68.
[48] *Ibid.*
[49] van Druten, *Geschiedenis*, p. 72.
[50] Lampe (ed.), *Cambridge History of the Bible*, II, p. 291.

The Eerste Historiebijbel

Like the *Rijmbijbel*, the *Eerste Historiebijbel* contains a translation of the *Historia Scholastica*, but the presence of a translation of the Vulgate distinguishes it from its precedessor. In the first Dutch vernacular Bible, it is the biblical text which acquires preeminence, whereas the *Rijmbijbel's* dependence on the commentary alone assigned a special importance to that work. In fact, the anonymous monk implies an intention in his prologue to closely follow his biblical model. He states that he will translate carefully letter by letter, word by word, and sentence by sentence,[51] a statement which recalls Maerlant's expressed intent to provide *vraye rime en ware word*. However, Maerlant's statement applies to the general character of his translation, not to the specific methods employed in the translating procedure and alluded to by the "translator of 1360." This emphasis on the text of the Bible itself is further suggested by the justification provided by the translator for his inclusion of the *Historia Scholastica*. Only because the Bible is *soe doncker van verstandenissen* or "so difficult to understand" is the *Historia Scholastica* appended to its text.[52] And then the translator tells us it is to be set off from the text of the Bible by the red lettering of its introductory glosses, thus insuring the independence of each text and minimizing confusion between them.[53] The functions of the glosses from the commentary are further specified by the translator in the prologue; they will be used both to the *profijt*, or "advantage," and *orbere*, or "necessity," of the meaning of the biblical passages,[54] but the preeminence of the biblical passages themselves remains clear.

The difference between the *Eerste Historiebijbel* and the *Rijmbijbel* is due partly to differing interpretations of the roles of the translator. Whereas Maerlant's role is creator as much as translator of his model, the "translator of 1360" remains a middle man, closely conveying the original's content and form to the reader. As such, the "translator of 1360" stands at the beginning of a tradition of textual translation in the Netherlands which utilized one of the first tenets of philological methodology, the integrity of the textual models, in this case the Bible and the *Historia Scholastica*.

---

[51] The prologue to the *Eerste Historiebijbel* is published in Le Long, *Boekzaal*, pp. 235-240, and in Ebbinge Wubben, *Middelnederlandsche vertalingen*, pp. 66-76.

[52] *Ibid.*, p. 239.

[53] *Ibid.*

[54] *Ibid.*

This return to the text of the Bible as an independent unit resulted, almost inevitably, in a closer examination of its literal contents. The translator was certainly aware of the various levels of meaning which a given text could contain, for in his prologue he distinguished between the many weighty books written in the past which attempted to unfold the Scripture through *allegorie* and *tropologie* and his own translation wherein the *historie* of the Bible could be found.[55] This division of scriptural writings into three types — *historie*, *allegorie* and *tropologie* — ultimately derived from Gregory's tripartite division of scriptural interpretation into its literal or historical, allegorical or typological, and moral or tropological meanings.[56] But it may well have been from Petrus Comestor himself that the anonymous translator's use of these categories derives. An illustration of the translator's division is the metaphor in which each of the three types represents a different structural part in a building. *Historie* is equated with the building's foundation, while *allegorie* and *tropologie* are equated with its walls and roof respectively.[57] As such, *historie* has the greatest structural importance, for it is the support on which the others depend and without which they cannot exist. When the translator compared his text to books which unfolded the Scripture through *allegorie* and *tropologie*, he added that "for this reason" *historie* was the foundation, thereby alluding to its place in the metaphor.[58] In Comestor's prologue, the same three categories are mentioned, as is the identical metaphor relating each to a structural part of a building.[59]

In the First History Bible the importance of *historie* was stressed by a further metaphor which related it to water. Like the water which never ran dry in Abraham's well, the bounty of the *historie* was so great that it may be drawn upon unendingly without ever being depleted.[60] The benefits for the reader who referred to this bounty of the *historie* were described as personal enlightenment and the correction of his spiritual state.[61] Maerlant's translation was seen as fulfilling a similar function by

---

[55] "Op deze twee leste partien [allegorie and tropologie] hebben die heilighen vele pinen gehadt om die Scriftuer te ontbinden, ende hebben ons daer of ghelaten menighe scone boeken. Hierom, als wi voorseit hebben, so is die historie dat fondament." *Ibid.*, p. 237.

[56] On the history of the various senses of scriptural meaning, see H. de Lubac, *Exégèse médiévale; les quatres sens de l'Écriture*, 4 vols,. Paris, 1959-1964.

[57] Le Long, *Boekzaal*, pp. 235-236.

[58] *Ibid.*, p. 237.

[59] Migne, *PL*, vol. 198, cols. 1053-54.

[60] Le Long, *Boekzaal*, p. 237.

providing an individual with "what it was necessary to know" presumably also with reference to his spiritual state. But for Maerlant the literal meanings in the Bible had to be supplemented with allegorical and tropological analogies which, in fact, were more prevalent. However, in the work of the "translator of 1360," as in Comestor's work, the *historie* alone was considered more than self-sufficient, supplanting almost entirely the use of allegory and typology.

The contents of the extant manuscripts of the *Eerste Historiebijbel* witness this emphasis on the *historie* of the text. Certain sections of the Bible with its commentary seem to have been transcribed with more frequency than others, a frequency perhaps attributable to their narrative contents. As mentioned earlier, only the British Library exemplar among the unillustrated codices and the illustrated Hague Bible (Koninklijke Bibliotheek, Ms. 78 D 38) reflect the completeness of the fourteenth century model. The majority of the remaining twelve illustrated manuscripts contain portions of the Old Testament alone,[62] in which the exposition of biblical history was in the form of a continuous readable narrative. Only four of these contain the New Testament sections of the Bible,[63] which in addition to the narrative of the life of Christ devoted considerable space to religious teachings. That such a phenomenon is not an accident of preservation seems probable when we consider that the New Testament appears in only three of the twenty-odd extant unilluminated codices of this text.[64] And, when the Gospels accompany the Old Testament translation, their format is a Gospel harmony, in which the story could be easily followed in one book rather than reconstructed piecemeal from four.

---

[61] "Ende men machse wel beduden bi den water. Want si is wel ghelijc Abrahams putte, dien si heten Bersabee, dats overvlodicheit; want, wat menre wtsciep, si bleef altoes even vol. Also ist bi der historien, daer mach elc na sinen staet gheestelic wtnemen dat hem betaemt, nochtant bliven si even vol." *Ibid.*, p. 237.

[62] London, British Library, Add. Mss. 10043, 38122, 1540; Amsterdam, Oudheidkundig Genootschap, Ms. 9; Middelburg, Zeeuws Genootschap; The Hague, Museum Meermanno-Westreenianum, Mss. 10 A 18-19; Munich, Staatsbibliothek, Ms. germ. 1102; Nuremberg, Stadtbibliothek, Ms. Solger, 8°.

[63] Brussels, Bibliothèque royale, Mss. 9018-9023; The Hague, Koninklijke Bibliotheek, Ms. 78 D 38; Ghent, Universiteits Bibliotheek, Ms. 430; and Vienna, Oesterreichische Nationalbibliothek, Mss. 2771-2772. Although Ms. 78 D 39 in the Koninklijke Bibliotheek in The Hague contains only the Old Testament, it is the first volume of the illustrated Ghent Bible which does contain the New Testament. Therefore, it cannot be counted with the Old Testament exemplars.

[64] The Hague, Koninklijke Bibliotheek, Mss. 128 C 2, and London, Dutch Church, Austin Friars, Ms. 9; Utrecht, Bibliotheek der Rijksuniversiteit Ms. 2 B 13.

It seems that the fifteenth century transcribers for the most part eliminated the non-expository books of the Bible as unessential to the narrative. The inclusion in many manuscripts of narrative apocryphal texts, such as the Legend of Alexander[65] and the Destruction of Jerusalem, to the exclusion of New Testament books provides further evidence for such a selective process. Moreover, the translator gives concrete proof that his exclusion of certain books was a conscious choice. At the end of the text of Maccabees he states: "the books of the prophets should here follow, but because they are so difficult for the laity to understand, I have left them out."[66] And in the illustrated codices, where the narrative of the text was to be visually complemented by miniatures, it is perhaps significant that half the extant examples contain only the historical books of the Old Testament, Genesis through Job.[67] The poetic books which are highly allegorical, rather than expository, and therefore difficult to illustrate, are omitted, as interestingly enough, they were by Comestor in his *Historia Scholastica*.

The particular use of the *Historia Scholastica* in relation to the Bible in the *Eerste Historiebijbel* demonstrates the emphasis on the *historie* or the narrative of the Bible text. For, in fact, excerpts from the commentary that were most frequently translated were those which enhanced the literal meaning of biblical passages. Three methods were used to enhance the narrative in the well-known story from Genesis (Genesis 37-50) of the sale of Joseph to the Ishmaelites, his sojourn in Egypt, and his reunion with Jacob, to cite one example. First, a non-narrative framework is provided to justify Joseph's brothers' successive trips to Egypt to buy grain. The famine, mentioned in the Bible (Genesis 45:6), is crucial to

[65] The Legend of Alexander is included in five of the illustrated First History Bibles: The Hague, Koninklijke Bibliotheek, Mss. 78 D 38, 78 D 39; Brussels, Bibliothèque royale, Mss. 9018-9023; Middelburg, Zeeuws Genootschap; and Vienna, Oesterreichische Nationalbibliothek, Mss. 2771-2772. Its absence in the remaining manuscripts does not mean that it had an optional use, for its normal position in the text was between the poetic books and Maccabees. The text in all the remaining manuscripts stops short of the poetic books, with the exception of the Nuremberg Bible which terminates just at the point where the Legend of Alexander would have begun. On the use and models of this apocryphal text in the First History Bibles, see Ross, *Medieval Alexander Books*, p. 168ff.

[66] de Bruin, *NAK*, 50, p. 19.

[67] Five illustrated manuscripts contain only the historical books: The Hague, Museum Meermanno-Westreenianum, Ms. 10 A 18-19; London, British Library, Add. Mss. 10043, 16951, 31822; and Munich, Staatsbibliothek, Ms. germ. 1102. With the exception of The Hague Bible, all of these belong to the second group of the First History Bibles, the group containing extensive cycles of miniatures inserted within the text.

the story for it is the direct cause of these "shopping sprees." So the *Historia Scholastica* relates the climatic conditions and geographic lay-out in Egypt which would account for the abundance of staples there and the dearth in neighboring lands.[68] The reader learns that although Egypt, like the surrounding area, had little rainfall, the irrigational benefits of the Nile permitted the flourishing of vegetation there.

The second method used in the commentary to enhance the narrative is illustrated in passages which augment the actual narrative sequence. This is achieved either by relating an incident absent in the progression of episodes in the Bible or by the addition of auxiliary details to an already described incident. Following Joseph's sale to the Ishmaelites, the Bible states that Reuben returned to the pit, and failing to find Joseph, went to his father (Genesis 37:29). In the *Historia Scholastica* Reuben's initial re-actions on seeing the empty pit are described, as is the change in his re-action after seeing his brothers:

> Reuben thought that when he did not find Joseph he had been killed while he was away. But, when he found out that he was still alive, he was outraged.[69]

Later in the Joseph cycle, the Bible relates Potiphar's temptation of Joseph (Genesis 39:7-15), but the means by which she contrives to im-plement her plot are omitted in the Bible and subsequently elaborated in the *Historia Scholastica*:

> Josephus says that on a certain feast day all the women were required to attend in good spirits. And when this wife [Potiphar's] saw that she could not win Joseph with cunning words, she thought how she could get him alone so as to persuade him to lay with her. On this feast day she pretended to her husband that she was sick so that she could remain in the house alone.[70]

Thus, the occurrence of the festival and Potiphar's wife's malingering are

---

[68] London Bible, fol. 35v. When possible, the text of this manuscript will be used for textual references.

[69] Ruben dochte, doe hi Josep niet en vant, dat si en gedoot hadden binnen dien dat hi wech was. Mer doe hi wiste dat hij levede, so sweech hij. *Ibid.*, fol. 31r.

[70] Josephus seit datmen op ene tijt feest had, dair alle die vrouwen schuldich waren behagel te wesen. Ende doe dit wijf sach dat si an Joseph niet en const gewinnen mit woirden, so peynsede si hoe si en alleen gecrigen mochte dat si en dwingen soude bi hair te leggen. Ende te deser feesten maecte si hair sieck voir horen man, om dat si thuus bliven soude. *Ibid.*, fol. 32v.

recounted, additional features in the narrative preparatory to her attempted seduction of Joseph.

An example of the addition of auxiliary details occurs following the biblical account of Joseph's feast with his brothers in Egypt. The Bible states that Benjamin had five times as much to eat at the feast as his brothers (Genesis 43:34), a perfectly clear remark. However, the *Historia Scholastica* elaborates on this in an amusing fashion:

> Josephus says that Benjamin had twice as many courses, so since they had five courses and he had each two times, he had five courses more than the others.[71]

Neither the "fact" from the Bible that Benjamin had five times as much food as his brothers nor Josephus' statement that Benjamin had double courses are presented as self-explanatory. The commentary performs the mental arithmetic necessary for the reader to determine that Benjamin, thus, had five additional courses.

A third group of passages accompanying the Joseph story clarifies written details in the biblical narrative, by furnishing more lucid restatements of certain verses, by providing definitions for little known or ambiguous words, or by explaining the etymology and significance of place-names. During the feast of Joseph and his brothers, the Bible states that the Egyptians dined with them, but because of religious convention the three groups were not permitted to eat at the same table (Genesis 43:32). The *Historia Scholastica* appends to this verse the simple statement: "Thus there were three tables."[72] When the pit into which Joseph was thrown is first mentioned in the Bible (Genesis 37:22), the Dutch translation from the Latin for "pit" is transcribed as *cysterne*. In order that the reader will have a clear understanding of the word's definition, an explanatory gloss from the commentary succeeds the word: "A cistern is a dry well without water."[73] And, finally, when Jacob journeys to the land of Goshen to be reunited with his son (Genesis 46:28-29), the commentary catalogues several past and present names for the country, interwoven with an explanation of its religious significance.[74] Presumably,

[71] Josephus seit dat Benyamen had dubbelde gerechten op datsi vijf gerechten hadden, ende hij elc dubbelt had, so had hi vijf gerechten meer dan die ander hadden. *Ibid.*, fol. 35r.
[72] Dus warenre drie tafelen, *Ibid.*, fol. 35r.
[73] Cysterne is een verdroecht put sonder water. *Ibid.*, fol. 30r.
[74] *Ibid.*, fol. 76v.

one intent of the gloss is to instill familiarity with an otherwise foreign location. If the reader did not know the name of the country as it existed in the Bible, perhaps he would recognize one of its cognates in the commentary. If not, the lengthy passage might encourage familiarity through prolonged exposure or its explanation of a comprehensible meaning.

Underlying all the accompanying glosses is a pervasive concern with the biblical narrative, expressed in an artless, straightforward style and with encyclopedic scope. Not only is the narrative expanded or clarified by the commentary, but a background is provided for its occurrence and questionable points in the descriptive text are elucidated. In short, it seems that the contents of the commentary set out to provide the answers to any possible questions directly related to the story itself which the reader might pose. Comestor's selective use of his sources verifies his interest in the narrative of the Bible. That statements from Augustine, Jerome, and Gregory are included certainly demonstrates his familiarity with the early church Fathers. Yet, quotations from these authorities are often restricted to narrative points extracted from their original context in complex theological proofs. Comestor's far more extensive and direct borrowings from Josephus, the historian of Jewish antiquities, is not surprising considering the preference of both writers for biblical narrative over speculative theology.

Indeed, the attempt to reconstruct a lucid historical past, evidenced in the interest in historical events and their circumstances, in toponymy and philology, in the first Dutch vernacular Bible demonstrates its closer affinity to the genre of historiography than to exegesis. This interest in the circumstances surrounding historical events was also noted in the text of Maerlant's *Rijmbijbel*, where it likewise derived in large part from the *Historia Scholastica*. However, in Maerlant's text an emphasis on historical events was subordinated to an interest in allegory and tropology, which as we have seen could also be found in the *Historia Scholastica*. We may wonder whether this interest in allegory and tropology was completely absent in the fourteeth century Bible, despite the assertion of the "translator of 1360" that these two levels of scriptural meaning were less important than the *historie* of the Scripture. His reliance on the *Historia Scholastica*, suggests the fruitfulness of a search for allegorical and tropological emphases in the *Eerste Historiebijbel* as well.

As in the *Rijmbijbel*, moral interpretations may be found in the *Eerste Historiebijbel*, although their frequency has diminished and their moral tenor is less polemic. Incidents of simony were noted in the first Dutch

vernacular Bible, as in Maerlant's text, and the punishment for such
moral wrongs was specified as in the story of Gehazi and Naman. Here,
we learn first that Gehazi had many leprous children and the reason for
this was that he engaged in simoniacal actions, divinely punished by the
taint of leprosy on the offspring.[75] The commentary proceeds to give the
distinction between *simonie* and *ghiesite* derived from the stories of Simon
and Gehazi and signifying the sale and purchase of spiritual goods respectively. Two differences between this and the *Rijmbijbel's* treatment of
moral meanings are notable. First, the factual objective approach, content with providing definitions of terms, in the *Eerste Historiebijbel* is in
marked contrast to Maerlant's approach where the allegory of the Old
Testament provided a springboard for a vitriolic attack on contemporary
practices. Secondly, the ostensible reason for the presence of this passage
from the commentary is an explanation of the narrative, of the fact that
Gehazi bore leprous children. The moral lesson is secondary, almost a
by-product of the explication of the story itself, whereas in Maerlant's
text it was of primary importance.

This inclusion of tropology employed in service to the narrative is
apparent also in the story of Lamech in the *Eerste Historiebijbel*.[76] Both the
first Dutch vernacular Bible and the *Rijmbijbel* record the immorality of
Lamech's two marriages, which they cite as a reason for Lamech's unfortunate life. But the moral lesson in the *Eerste Historiebijbel* is virtually
lost in the subsequent lengthy passage where the particular skills of
Lamech's sons, born to each wife, were set down. This was followed in
turn in the commentary by the story of the death of Cain, insufficiently
explained in the text of the Bible; and the commentary concludes with a
further reference to Lamech's two wives who are said to have mistreated
Lamech as a result of his sins. Nevertheless, the purpose of the entire
passage was primarily narrative in its explanation of Lamech's lineage
and Lamech's murder of Cain. Tropological references to the immorality
of Lamech's two marriages, while present, appear as mere token inclu-
sions in an otherwise narrative exposition.

Allegorical indications occur more frequently in the *Eerste Historiebijbel*
than tropological interpretations. When places and persons in the Old
Testament prefigure those in the New this is briefly stated in the commentary. For example, the miraculous incidents surrounding births in the

---

[75] Nuremberg Bible, fol. 88v.
[76] London Bible, fol. 10r.

Old Testament, in which the names of the children were foretold before their births, namely the cases of Ishmael, Samuel, and Samson, are recorded as prefigurations of the case of John the Baptist.[77] The location both of Rachel and Jacob's burial is given as Bethlehem prefiguring, of course, Christ's birth.[78] We learn that the three Annas in the Old Testament, namely Samuel's mother, Tobit's wife, and Raquel's wife,[79] prefigure Anna, Mary's mother, and Anna, the prophetess in the temple in the New Testament. The common types of Old Testament events are also mentioned: for example, Melchizedek as a type for the Last Supper and Moses' brazen serpent as a type for the Crucifixion.[80] Without exception though, such references occupy only a minimal space in the text of the commentary which is devoted primarily to the narrative.

The proliferation of types for each element in one story, as it occurs in the *Rijmbijbel*, no longer exists in the *Eerste Historiebijbel*. In Maerlant's account of Jacob's dream each element acquired a different symbolic importance, an interpretation which was significantly altered and simplified in the later text. This text states that Jacob foretells the law of the temple and Christ's Passion.[81] Thus, the door of heaven and heaven itself reached by the ladder symbolized Christ's Passion and his law respectively, for through the Passion Christ's law became accessible to mankind. Even the style of the prose text implies a conscious simplification resulting from a desire to present a straightforward typology. The translator's phrase introducing the typological interpretation reads: "here is nothing other than God's house...".[82] This emphasis on the symbols in the Old Testament which prefigure Christ's Passion is another feature which distinguishes the use of typology in the first vernacular Bible from the *Rijmbijbel*. Only the Passion receives repeated reference in typological symbols in the *Eerste Historiebijbel*, a fact which may not be unrelated to the widespread production of Dutch Passion texts in the late fourteenth and fifteenth centuries.

---

[77] *Ibid.*, fol. 17v.

[78] *Ibid.*, fol. 30r.

[79] *Ibid.*, fol. 170r.

[80] *Ibid.*, fols. 16v and 89r.

[81] *Ibid.*, fol. 26r.

[82] "Hier en is anders niet dan gods huys, dat beduut den tempel, dat hi daer staen soude." *Ibid.*

The Tweede Historiebijbel

The contents of the *Tweede Historiebijbel* suggests that it, like the *Eerste Historiebijbel*, was designed to emphasize the narrative of the Bible.[83] Its text omitted all the poetic books of the Old Testament and the entire New Testament, including for the most part only the historical books of the Old Testament. Only the Pentateuch, Joshua, Judges, Ruth, and Kings were translated from the Vulgate; two additional sections of its text depend for their translation on the *Historia Scholastica* and the *Rijmbijbel* respectively. The integrity of the text of the Bible, a feature noted in the *Eerste Historiebijbel*, is even more apparent in the second version of the vernacular Bible where the commentary accompanying the historical books was omitted altogether. Although the *Historia Scholastica* is present as a model for the entire translation of Tobit, Daniel, Judith, Esdras, and Esther, the Bible is absent in this section. This exclusive use of separate textual models — the Bible, the *Historia Scholastica*, and the *Rijmbijbel* — for each major section of the translation was perhaps motivated by a respect for the integrity of the separate texts. The pre-eminence of the biblical narrative is obvious in the first section of this exemplar which includes only the Bible text, but an emphasis on narrative is also apparent in the remaining sections of the text. For example, the inclusion of the Legend of Alexander and the historical events surrounding the Maccabees, directly following the book of Esther, to the exclusion of the poetic books of the Old Testament and the New Testament, can only have been implemented to enhance the historical continuity in the narrative of the Bible.

However, several features of the *Tweede Historiebijbel* characterize it as *retardataire*, particularly compared to the translation almost a century earlier of the first Dutch vernacular Bible. Its dependence on the thirteenth century *Rijmbijbel* was so extensive that it originally led scholars to attribute this text to Jacob van Maerlant as well.[84] The translator's use

---

[83] A brief survey of the *Tweede Historiebijbel* appears in van Druten, *Geschiedenis*, pp. 64-74.

[84] J. van Harderwijk, *Verslag van een handschrift, bevattende Jacob van Maerlants Nederduitsche prozaische bijbelvertaling, met aanteekeningen en bijlagen*, The Hague, 1831, and P. Leendertz, "De prozabijbel aan Jacob van Maerlant toegeschreven," *De Navorscher* 11 (1861), pp. 337-346, attribute the *Tweede Historiebijbel* to Jacob van Maerlant. In van Druten, *Geschiedenis*, pp. 68-74, there is a refutation of this theory through a detailed comparison of the two texts.

of earlier models is further emphasized by the analogies between his
prologue in the *Tweede Historiebijbel* and a fourteenth century text of
personal piety, *Der Sielen Troost*.[85] Once again, this resemblance misled
late nineteenth century scholars who attributed the second Dutch vernacular Bible to an anonymous fourteenth century author, an attribution
apparently corroborated by the mistaken dating of the text in 1358.[86] But
two factors suggest that this fifteenth century vernacular Bible was something of an anomaly in the textual tradition of Dutch Bibles, lacking the
widespread popularity of its predecessor. It exists in only seven extant
manuscripts and a few fragmentary copies,[87] compared with the thirty
manuscripts of the *Eerste Historiebijbel*. And, when a text was sought in
Holland to provide a model for the printing of the vernacular Bible, it
was the earlier *Eerste Historiebijbel* which was used, not the near-contemporary *Tweede Historiebijbel*.

The Printed Delft Bible

The very fact of the printing in 1477 of the Delft Bible suggests that it
was intended to reach a wide, probably lay, audience. This is further
supported by its inclusion of the prologue from the earlier *Eerste Historiebijbel* where it stated that the translation was intended for those *die
ongheleert is van clergien*, or those who were "unlearned of clerical matters."[88]
Thus, like its predecessors, the purpose of the Delft Bible was primarily a
didactic one. Although this Bible was essentially an adaptation and revision of the text of the *Eerste Historiebijbel*, the alterations in it illustrate the
changes in the use of the Bible and its commentaries for didactic purposes. Only the Bible text was included; all the accompanying commentaries placed with the text in the *Eerste Historiebijbel* were omitted.[89]

---

[85] On the resemblances between the Second History Bible and the *Sielen Troost* see M.
Anderson-Schmitt, "Über die Verwandtschaft der Alexandersagen im Seelentrost und
in der ersten niederländischen Historienbibel," *Münstersche Beiträge zur Niederdeutschen
Philologie* 1960, pp. 78-104 (*Niederdeutsche Studien* 6).

[86] van Druten, *Geschiedenis*, p. 70.

[87] The Hague, Koninklijke Bibliotheek, Ms. 133 M 32; Copenhagen, Kongelige
Bibliotek, Ms. Thott 124, fol.; Leiden, Bibliotheek der Rijksuniversiteit, Ms. Ltk, 231,
337, and B.P.L. 1800; Paris, Bibliothèque Nationale, fonds néerl. 2; and Utrecht, Universiteitsbibliotheek, Ms. 4 E 3, according to Deschamps, *Middelnederlandse Handschriften*,
no. 51, pp. 156-159.

[88] The prologue of the Delft Bible is published by Le Long, *Boekzaal*, pp. 367-370.

[89] For the contents of this Bible see van Druten, *Geschiedenis*, pp. 121-138.

Moreover, the text of the Bible included only the Old Testament books —
historical, poetic, and prophetic — omitting the New Testament and the
Psalter. From its contents, we may deduce that it was the narrative, the
historie, of the Bible which was considered most important for didactic exposition, as it was in the *Eerste Historiebijbel*. But, unlike the first vernacular
Bible, in the printed version this narrative must have been considered
self-sufficient and no longer dependent on explanatory glosses for an
understanding of its meaning.

This increased integrity of the biblical text led naturally to a greater
concern with the correctness of its contents and composition, a concern
perhaps further stimulated by the more exacting requirements of the
printing process compared with the hand copying of manuscripts. The
translator of the Delft Bible makes it clear that accuracy was one of his
aims when he states that he has carefully "corrected and respelled" his
model.[90] Such an expressed concern is reminiscent of those of Jacob van
Maerlant and the "translator of 1360" who each stated an intention to
translate their texts carefully, in "true words" and "letter by letter, word
by word, and sentence by sentence." However, in the Delft Bible the
specific mention of corrections and spellings suggests an incipient interest
in a critical philological methodology, rather than the simple desire to
convey the correct sense of the passages implied by the earlier statements.

An interest in the methods of philology is further suggested by the
composition of the Delft Bible. Not only are the commentaries absent,
but all apocryphal texts, such as the frequently transcribed Legend of
Alexander, were omitted. The original Bible text thus remained intact,
devoid of foreign elements. In Dutch vernacular Bible tradition the composition of this Bible text was itself new. For the first time, the Delft Bible
made available in one edition a virtually complete Old Testament with
historical, poetic, and prophetic books following each other in their
correct sequence. Both in the critical concern with individual words and
the interest in the composition of the entire text, the Delft Bible represented the first concrete statement, in a vernacular form, of the search for
the purity of the Bible in Holland.

The Windesheim Revision of the Vulgate

The textual tradition of the Vulgate in Holland demonstrates a similar

---

[90] Le Long, *Boek-zaal*, p. 369.

concern with the search for a pure Bible text. At the monastery of Windesheim the brothers undertook the task of creating a standard Latin Bible: "they attempted to reduce all the 'original' books of the Old and New Testaments to the text as translated by St. Jerome from Hebrew into Latin, using the best models obtainable."[91] The purpose of this was to establish uniformity in choir services and Bible readings amongst the houses belonging to the chapter.[92] For their project, they gathered together and compared as many Latin Bibles as possible, one of which belonged to the Knights of St. John. This text possessed a colophon stating that it had been compiled from the library of St. Jerome, a notation mistaken by the brethren to signify that it had actually been copied from the Bible of St. Jerome. While we may smile at their naiveté in using primarily this text simply because of its colophon, it is nevertheless revealing of the spirit, if not the results, of their labor. Like the translator of the Delft Bible after them and apparently already in the *Eerste Historiebijbel* before, they sought to apply a critical phililogical methodology to the texts. And this meant a return to the original Latin Bible of Jerome, rather than a straightforward standardization of the Latin Bibles currently in use.

Erasmus and Dutch Bible Tradition

It was Erasmus who developed more fully the philological methodology of the Windesheim group in his translation of the New Testament from the original Greek.[93] In his treatise, the *Ratio seu methodus compendio perveniendi ad veram theologiam*,[94] which in an abbreviated form was originally the preface to the New Testament, Erasmus elucidates the importance of philology for spiritual learning. His basic premise was that the Bible was the foundation of all theology and as a result only through study of this text in its original form could spiritual understanding be attained. As corollaries to this premise, Erasmus recommended that

---

[91] Johannes Busch, *Chronicon Windeshemense* edited by K. Grube in *Geschichtsquellen der Sachsen*, 19 (1880), quoted from Post, *The Modern Devotion*, p. 305. For a complete study of the Windesheim Vulgate see Greiteman, De *Windesheimse Vulgaatrevisie*.

[92] This suggestion is made in Post, *Modern Devotion*, p. 307.

[93] Erasmus' relation to medieval biblical tradition is discussed in Lampe (ed.), *Cambridge History of the Bible*, II, pp. 492-505. For a good overall view of Erasmus' relation to humanism see H. A. Enno van Gelder, *The Two Reformations of the 16th Century. A study of the religious aspects and consequences of Renaissance and humanism*, The Hague, 1961.

[94] The treatise is discussed in Lampe (ed.), *Cambridge History of the Bible*, II, pp. 492-503.

biblical quotations never be taken out of their immediate or extended context within the Bible as a whole.[95] Commentaries were thus to be used only with caution, necessitating a simultaneous study of the Bible. Erasmus' view of the relative unimportance of commentaries is perhaps clearest from his suggestion that the most useful book for Bible study was a concordance.[96] In this way, it would be possible to trace not only words but ideas through the Bible, thereby understanding them through their original context, rather than through a reading of the commentaries.

Conclusions

Certainly, Erasmus introduced many new features to theological thought and to Bible study, influenced largely by humanism, but his work also shares some of the main concerns of vernacular translators from the two preceeding centuries. The integrity of the text of the Bible was now an explicit goal and the methods for executing critical editions, in order to best maintain its integrity, were improved. As we have seen, vernacular translations demonstrated a gradual development towards this same end. At the beginning of the development stands the *Rijmbijbel* where commentary and Bible text were indistinguishably mixed with little regard for the integrity of either text. With the *Eerste Historiebijbel*, the commentaries and biblical passages were clearly separated, and the translator's concern with the literal meaning of the latter led to a closer attention to the Bible text. The *Tweede Historiebijbel* and the revised *Eerste Historiebijbel*, or the Delft Bible, assigned an even greater prominence to the text of the Bible itself, excluding its accompanying commentaries. And the translator of the Delft Bible extended his interest in the integrity of the text to a concern with its accuracy, explicitly referred to in his statement mentioning "corrections and respellings." Still earlier in the century, the application of a philological methodology to the Windesheim revision of the Vulgate betrays concerns with the Bible text similar to those which were eventually to occupy vernacular translators.

This development of a philological methodology for textual editions of the Bible may be viewed partially as a direct result of the persistent regard for the didactic character of the Bible. Maerlant's *Rjmbijbel* remained fully rooted in medieval tradition in its interest in the figurative

---

[95] *Ibid.*, p. 504.
[96] *Ibid.*

meanings of the Bible over its literal sense. But with the *Eerste Historie-bijbel* the importance of the literal meaning of the text re-emerged, through a use of the *Historia Scholastica* designed to stress the historical truth of the Scripture and through a clear physical separation of Bible and commentary. Finally, in the last two vernacular editions considered, the absence of the commentaries certainly implies the significance of literal readings alone. Once the literal meaning acquired chief import-ance, accuracy in the text was therefore essential. Erasmus' emphasis on philological correctness in the Bible leads us to expect that it was the literal meaning for him as well which was most crucial. However, this is not the case, as is evident from his lengthy discourse on the literal and figurative senses of the Bible in *Ratio . . . perveniendi ad veram theologiam.* Here, he distinguishes between the many layers of scriptural meaning, all of which can be found in the Bible itself, and he further states that in some places only the figurative sense is the correct reading.[97] Neverthe-less, Erasmus' distinction between the various meanings owes little to a medieval heritage and has been seen rather as anticipating modern theological speculation.[98] And to be sure, he owes to his immediate pre-decessors, such as Petrus Comestor and the "translator of 1360," an abandonment of the wholesale application of allegory and tropology in favor of a close perusal of the *historie* of the text.

What was the reason for such an interest in the didactic character of the Bible, and the resultant philological methods for presenting its text? The *Devotio Moderna* with its single-minded emphasis on a return to the original writings of the church — the Bible and the early church Fathers — imme-diately comes to mind as a motivating factor behind vernacular Bible translations. Bible production could have been an instrument for extend-ing the influence of religion beyond the confines of exclusive monastic communities to the entire lay population. The Windesheim revision of the Vulgate was certainly the product of a group associated with the *Devotio Moderna*, as the translation of the *Tweede Historiebijbel* seems to have been the work of one of its members. Indeed, Erasmus' early train-ing in a monastery of the *Devotio Moderna* and his all-consuming interest in the Bible are perhaps more than coincidental.[99] However, the precise

---

[97] *Ibid.*

[98] *Ibid.*

[99] Between 1487 and 1493, Erasmus resided in the Augustinian monastery of Steyn near Gouda, a member of the Chapter of Sion which had close connections with the Congregation of Windesheim. Erasmus' connections with the *Devotio Moderna* may be

effect of this movement on vernacular Bible production has remained elusive in scholarship, some suggesting a causal relationship and some denying it.[100] It is to this question which we will later return in a consideration of both text and picture cycles in the first vernacular Bible.

---

dated even earlier, for he was educated in two schools run by the Brothers of the Common Life. In 1483, he studied at Deventer and in 1484 at 's-Hertogenbosch.

[100] Post, *Modern Devotion*, while admitting a connection between the Vulgate and the *Devotio Moderna*, believes that the movement had nothing to do with the production of vernacular Bibles. On the other hand, de Bruin, *NAK*, 48, sees the *Devotio Moderna* as the motivating force behind vernacular Bible translation.

CHAPTER TWO

NARRATIVE ILLUSTRATION IN THE MINIATURE CYCLES

Medieval Narrative Illustration

With the introduction and spread of Christianity, a tradition of narrative biblical illustration developed, adopting well-established methods of narrative representation commonly employed for other types of texts. As Weitzmann has demonstrated,[1] the Early Christian period produced extensive cycles of miniatures for individual books of the Bible. Some three hundred illustrations existed in the now-fragmentary Cotton Genesis (British Library, Cott. Ms. Otho B. VI),[2] and similarly lengthy cycles can be reconstructed for other sections of the Bible such as the Pentateuch, the Books of Kings, Job, and the Acts of the Apostles.[3] In each of these cycles certain features characteristic of narrative illustrations appear: a multiplication of individual episodes each represented in separate illustrations, an economy of detail, an emphasis on the expressive gestures of the participants, and often a close physical relationship between the elements of text and illustration.

It was not until the Carolingian period that complete illustrated Bibles were produced, such as the Vivian Bible (Paris, Bibliothèque Nationale, fonds. lat. 1) and the Grandval Bible (British Library, Add. Ms. 10546), both products of the school of Tours. These Turonian Bibles apparently adapted cycles of single biblical books for their miniatures, and like their Early Christian models their mode of illustration was fundamentally narrative.[4] But the early practise of extensively illustrating biblical books did not continue on the same scale. By the Carolingian period, the creation of liturgical books called for a different system of illustration, in which biblical events were represented according to their place in the

---

[1] K. Weitzmann, *Illustrations in Roll and Codex. A study of the origin and method of text illustration*, Princeton, 1947 (Studies in Manuscript Illumination, 2).

[2] *Ibid.*, p. 259.

[3] *Ibid.*, p. 132.

[4] H. Kessler, "'Hic Homo Formatur': the Genesis Frontispieces of the Carolingian Bibles," *Art Bulletin* 53 (1971), pp. 143-160.

liturgy, rather than their narrative context in the Bible itself. This meant that some episodes, primarily New Testament ones, were illustrated with more frequency, in sacramentaries and lectionaries, for example, while others were virtually dropped from the *repertoire* as unnecessary to liturgical illustration. And, in order to meet the requirements of this type of book, the characteristics of narrative illustration were supplanted either by a more hieratic, formal scheme of representation or by a markedly abbreviated one, both less reliant, on the narrative of the Bible.[5]

The illustrations for devotional manuscripts, common in the Romanesque and particularly the Gothic eras, present a similar phenomenon. Here, too, the miniatures developed away from the biblical texts which they originally depicted, often becoming symbolic of the event rather than representative of it. However, Old Testament events borrowed directly from Bibles continued to appear as illustrations to devotional manuscripts. For example, the illustrations of the story of David from the much-discussed Paris Psalter (Bibliothèque nationale, fonds gr. 20) were probably taken over from a Byzantine Book of Kings.[6] And the miniature of David and Bathsheba for the Seven Penitential Psalms in a fifteenth century Book of Hours originally occurred in a thirteenth century *Bible moralisee.*[7]

Evidence presented by two manuscripts attests to the fact that Old Testament narrative illustration, based ultimately on an Early Christian tradition, never actually ceased in the Middle Ages. In the late twelfth century, a cycle of narrative illustrations was produced to accompany a Middle High German vernacular Bible known as the Millstatt Genesis (Klagenfurt, Mus. Rudolfinum, Ms. VI. 19).[8] According to Weitzmann, these miniatures probably derive from an Early Christian biblical recension like the Cotton Genesis.[9] The thirteenth century Morgan Picture

---

[5] K. Weitzmann, "The Narrative and Liturgical Gospel Illustrations" in *New Testament Manuscript Studies*, edited by M. Parvis and A. P. Wickgren, Chicago, 1950, pp. 151-174.

[6] Weitzmann, *Roll and Codex*, p. 107.

[7] L. M. J. Delaissé, "The Importance of Books of Hours for the History of the Medieval Book," *Gatherings in Honor of Dorothy Miner* (edited by Ursula E. McCracken, Lilian M. C. Randall, Richard H. Randall, Jr.), Baltimore, 1974, p. 210.

[8] Illustrations of the Millstatt Genesis may be found in H. Voss, *Studien zur illustrierten Millstätter Genesis*, Munich, 1962 (Münchener Texte und Untersuchungen zur Deutschen Literatur des Mittelalters, 4).

[9] Weitzmann, *Roll and Codex*, p. 140.

Bible (New York, Pierpont Morgan Ms. M. 638)[10] contains an extensive narrative cycle for the books of the Bible from Genesis through Samuel which, as Buchthal has pointed out, may derive from an illustrated Byzantine Octateuch.[11]

In the Gothic era, the vast programs of speculative theology displayed on cathedral facades certainly speak for the prevalence of non-narrative representation in the visual arts. Where narrative biblical scenes occur in sculptural programs, they were employed primarily to elucidate allegorical or typological relationships between the events of the Old and New Testaments.[12] However, the same period also witnessed the production of numerous literary texts, often extolling the knightly ideals of chivalry, such as the *Roman de la Rose* and *Lancelot*. Frequently produced as luxury illuminated manuscripts for the nobility, these texts required the creation, or at least the adaptation, of cycles of narrative illustration, and some were taken over from the Bible itself.[13] The same dualism of theological and narrative representation, noticeable in sculpture and literary texts, also existed in Bible production during the Gothic period. On the one hand, the *Bible moralisée* produced for Saint Louis[14] is the manuscript equivalent of facade programs. In this text, eight medallions are grouped in pairs on each folio, each medallion being accompanied by a short explanatory text. Four of the medallions are juxtaposed on one page in such a way as to convey the typological relationships between two Old Testament episodes and two New Testament events, while four others suggests the moral significance of biblical situations to contemporary life. On the other hand, the *Bible historiale completée* was also a product of the thirteenth century.[15] This work provided a text of the Bible and the *Historia Scholastica* in which the biblical narrative proceeded

---

[10] A facsmile of this manuscript has been published by Sydney C. Cockerell and John Plummer, *Old Testament Miniatures, A Medieval Picture Book with 283 Paintings from the Creation to the Story of David*, London, 1969.

[11] H. Buchthal, *Miniature Painting in the Latin Kingdom of Jerusalem*, Oxford, 1957.

[12] See E. Mâle, *L'Art religieux du XIIIe siècle en France*, Paris, 1902, pp. 160-201.

[13] M. A. Stones, *The Illustration of the French Prose Lancelot in Belgium, Flanders, and Paris 1250-1340*, London, 1971 (Unpublished doctoral dissertation).

[14] A. De Laborde, *La bible moralisée illustrée*, Paris, 1911-1927.

[15] *Bible historiale completée* is the term used by Berger, *La bible française*, p. 157, to designate the French translation of the Bible and the *Historia Scholastica*, whereas the *Bible historiale* refers simply to the French translation of the *Historia Scholastica*. However, following later scholars, the term *bible historiale* will be used hereafter to signify the *bible historiale completée*.

in its proper chronological sequence. Thus, however abbreviated its cycle of illustration originally ways, it called for a chronological visual narrative to accompany the text.

General Characteristics of Narrative Illustration in the First History Bibles

The Dutch versions of the *Bible historiale complétée*, the *Eerste Historiebijbel*, possess lengthy cycles of illustration, the number of which certainly suggests an interest in narrative illustration. In the Hague Bible 491 miniatures accompany a translation of the entire Bible, which contains in addition numerous historiated initials, many also with narrative scenes. Even the manuscripts containing a shortened Bible text possess extensive cycles of illustration. For example, in the London Bible which contains only the text of the Octateuch plus Tobit, 243 miniatures illustrate the text, the same number used in the Brussels Bible to illustrate Maccabees and the New Testament. The Lochorst Bible, the Munich Bible, and the Nuremburg Bible each with between one and two hundred illustrations present shorter, though far from brief, cycles. Not only are the cycles of illustration extensive in these Bibles, their miniatures are placed within the individual chapters of the text, another feature characteristic of narrative illustration. Both from the number of illustrations and their general format the Dutch vernacular Bibles suggest that their underlying motivation was the desire to create a continuous written and illustrated story.

In the northern Netherlands, such extensive cycles of biblical illustration were unprecedented. Copies of Jacob van Maerlant's *Rijmbijbel* rarely possessed more than one hundred miniatures,[16] and one of the only extant illustrated Vulgates (Cambridge, Fitzwilliam Museum Ms. 289) predating the copies of the *Eerste Historiebijbel* was decorated with just 56 miniatures. Some of the *Bibles historiales* produced in France[17] were also decorated with lengthy cycles, such as the fourteenth century Bible of Jean de Vaudetar (The Hague, Museum Meermanno Westreenianum, Ms. 10 B 23)[18] containing 263 illustrations and the Arsenal Bible (Paris,

---

[16] One of the most extensively illustrated manuscripts in The Hague (Museum Meermanno-Westreenianum, Ms. 10 B 21) possesses 73 miniatures.

[17] A catalogue of the illustrated and unillustrated French manuscripts of this text appears in Berger, *La bible française*, pp. 321-435.

[18] *Ibid.*, pp. 429-430.

Bibliothèque de l'Arsenal, Ms. 5212)[19] with its 338 illustrations from the same period. But on closer examination, the majority of the miniatures in the Bible of Jean de Vaudetar are grouped in fours preceding each book of the Bible. The full-scale miniatures in the Arsenal Bible also precede each book, while the remaining scenes are contained in historiated initials, many of non-narrative subjects, dispersed throughout the text. Neither Bible, therefore, provides a parallel with the illustrations of the *Eerste Historiebijbel*, either in its number of illustrations or their placement within the text.

One French *Bible historiale* (Paris, Bibliothèque Nationale, fonds. fr. 152)[20] does contain a cycle of 344 illustrations approaching the number in the Dutch cycles, and the majority of these are arranged within the text. However, this Bible is something of an anomaly in the tradition of French *Bibles historiales*. Not only are the number and placement of its illustrations different from its French relatives, its text betrays many linguistic peculiarities which led Berger to suggest its execution in Picardy in North France.[21] Most of the illustrated *Bibles historiales* were produced not in the North but in and around Paris under the courtly patronage of King Charles V and his ducal brothers, particularly the Duke of Berry.[22] For the most part, there is nothing exceptional in the style of illustrations in this *Bible historiale*, which throughout the book are representative of fourteenth century provincial French illumination. But, as Berger noticed,[23] the miniatures accompanying the Psalter have been repainted in a completely different style which, to my knowledge, appears only in a group of manuscripts associated with the court in the northern Netherlands at the beginning of the fifteenth century.[24] Given the

---

[19] *Ibid.*, p. 368.

[20] *Ibid.*, pp. 329-330.

[21] *Ibid.*, p. 329.

[22] For the group of Bibles belonging to the Duke of Berry see *Ibid.*, p. 216-218.

[23] *Ibid.*, p. 329.

[24] The manuscripts belonging to this group include: three copies of Dirc van Delft's *Tafel van den Kersten Ghelove* (British Library, Add. Ms. 22288; Walters Art Gallery, Ms. W. 171; and Pierpont Morgan Ms. M. 691), a *Biblia Pauperum* (British Library, Kings Ms. 5), a *Rijmbijbel* (Koninklijke Nederlandse Akademie van Wetenschappen, on deposit in The Hague, Koninklijke Bibliotheek, Ms. K.A. XVIII), two Vulgate Bibles (Cambridge, Fitzwilliam Museum Ms. 289 and Brussels, Bibliothèque royale, Mss. 205-206), the *Saksenspiegel* (Berlin, Staatsbibliothek der Stiftung Preussischer Kulturbesitz, Ms. germ. fol. 820), a Breviary (Darmstadt, Hessische Landesbibliothek, Ms. 975), a text of Dominican Sermons (Copenhagen, Royal Library, Ms. Thott 70) and two Books of Hours (New York, Kraus Collection, and Lisbon, Gulbenkian Foundation). Many of

similar length of cycles in this manuscript and the Dutch vernacular
Bibles and their relationship to the text, we might speculate whether
the French exemplar actually found its way to the Netherlands in the
fifteenth century. Whether or not this was the case, the Paris manuscript
does present one near-contemporary precedent for the Dutch *Eerste
Historiebijbels*.

From an examination of several miniatures in the Dutch vernacular
Bibles, the nature of their narrative illustration may be characterized.
In the London Bible the miniature representing *Elijah Causing Fire from
Heaven to Consume the Burnt Offering* (Fig. 1) depicts Elijah in the center
kneeling before an altar on the right, with four men standing behind him
on the left. Flames descend from the sky on the right towards the burning
wood on top of the altar. A trench filled with water surrounds the altar,
and liquid droplets appear on the side of the altar table between the
wood and the trench. The event takes place in a landscape setting.

This episode is related in the first book of Kings, and the exact moment
depicted in the miniature corresponds with the verse:

> Then the fire of the Lord fell, and consumed the burnt sacrifice, and the
> wood, and the stones, and the dust, and licked up the water that was in the
> trench. (I Kings 18 : 38)

This verse, then, explains the presence of the descending flames, the
burning wood on the altar, the water in the trench, and the liquid
droplets on the side of the altar. But other features of the illustration owe
their inclusion to preceding and following verses. Elijah kneels in prayer
before the altar in illustration of the verse directly preceding:

> Hear me, O Lord, hear me, that the people may know that thou art the
> Lord God, and that thou hast turned their heart back again. (I Kings 18 :37)

The presence of the group of people behind Elijah, as well as their
astonished expressions, must have been suggested by a following verse,
where the peoples' reactions to the miracle are recorded. (I Kings 18:39).
And the individualization of one of these participants, setting him off
from the others, suggests that he was conceived as Ahab, whose presence
is mentioned in another verse (I Kings 18:41). Even the use of a land-

---

these manuscripts have been treated in an important article by M. Rickert, "The
Illuminated Manuscripts of Meester Dirc van Delft's 'Tafel van den Kersten Ghelove',"
Journal of the Walters Art Gallery 12 (1949), pp. 79-108.

scape setting was undoubtedly due to a reading of the biblical chapter, for the gathering of stones to build an altar (I Kings 18:31-32) and the digging of a trench surrounding the altar (I Kings 18:32) connoted an outdoor rather than an indoor environment.

Each element in the miniature is therefore mentioned in the biblical text: the participants, the setting, and the props. Likewise, the positions and responses of the participants — Elijah's kneeling pose and Ahab's surprise — have been suggested by a close reading of the accompanying text. Moreover, there is an economical use of detail in the illustration; additional narrative features have been included to illustrate the appropriate verse, but the gratuitous accumulation of extraneous detail has been avoided. In the process of illustrating the biblical episode, previous and successive verses have been referred to, suggesting a careful perusal of the text for the purpose of providing a succinct, visual narrative statement.

The illustration of the *Shame of Noah* (Fig. 2) in the Munich Bible (Staatsbibliothek, cod. germ. 1102) demonstrates a similar close connection between text and miniatures. In a domestic chamber, Noah lies on a bed on the right, while two men stand over him on the left. One man in the foreground holds a garment over Noah, while the other averts his face with his hand. Farther on the left, stands Ham whose face and posture betray a smug satisfaction. The miniature is, thus, an illustration of the biblical text:

> And Shem and Japheth took a garment and laid it upon both their shoulders, and went backward, and covered the nakedness of their father and their faces were backward and they saw not their father's nakedness.
>
> (Genesis 9 : 23)

The two men represent Shem and Japheth, one of whose faces is turned "backward" as the text specifies.

As in the illustration of *Elijah Causing Fire from Heaven to Consume the Burnt Offering*, additional details were provided by a reading of the adjacent verses. Ham's manifest unabashed behavior in leading his brothers into the tent to view Noah is alluded to in the verses which describe Noah's reaction:

> And Ham, the father of Canaan, saw the nakedness of his father, and took his brethren without. . . . And Noah awoke from his wine and knew what his younger son had done to him. And he said Cursed be Canaan, a servant of servants shall he be unto his brethren. (Genesis 9: 22, 24-25)

The interior domestic setting in which the action occurs is rare in depictions of the *Shame of Noah*, but perhaps it has its source in the Bible text which states that Noah was "uncovered within his tent" (Genesis 9:21). Thus, this miniature, as well, conforms to the nature of narrative illustration which was noted in the preceding illustration: its pictorial elements were drawn from the biblical text; there is an economy of detail; and adjacent biblical verses were consulted in accumulating the essential detail.

It seems improbable that a generalized knowledge of the main incidents in the Bible resulted in such a precise rendering of entire episodes as those portrayed in the preceding miniatures. The narrative character of the illustrations in the vernacular Bibles is even more striking when they are compared with miniatures of the same subjects from a Dutch *Biblia Pauperum* (British Library, King 5)[25] illuminated less than thirty years earlier. *Elijah Causing Fire from Heaven to Consume the Burnt Offering* (Fig. 3) is represented in this manuscript simply by the inclusion of a ram standing on the ground touched by fire descending from above, while Elijah stands on the left and three other individuals stand on the right. The essential elements of the story are present — the offering, the fire, Elijah, and the people — but the dramatic rendering of the event in a narrative context is absent. The offering does not burn on the altar which Elijah had just constructed, nor do the flames dry up the water on the wood or in the trench, for they are not depicted. There is no allusion made to Elijah's prayer to God, and while an outdoor setting is implied by the rocky terrain beneath the ram, it is negated by the abstract gold background of the miniature.

The *Shame of Noah* (Fig. 4) from the same *Biblia Pauperum* presents a similarly abbreviated version of this event. Beneath a grape arbor lies Noah "uncovered", while Ham points out Noah's nakedness to his brothers, Shem and Japheth, on the right. In this miniature, Noah's reclining position, Ham's behavior, and the brothers' covering their faces all derive from the biblical text. But the garment used to cover Noah and the interior setting are both absent. This divergence in illustrations of the

---

[25] This important manuscript has never been sufficiently studied. It was described by G. F. Warner and J. P. Gilson, *British Museum Catalogue of Western Manuscripts in the Old Royal and Kings Collections*, London, 1921, Vol. III, pp. 2-3, and by E. Maunde Thompson, "Bibliographica on a manuscript of the Biblia Pauperum," *Bibliographica*, III, pp. 385-406. It is also discussed briefly in Rickert, *Journal of the Walters Art Gallery*, p. 81 and L. M. J. Delaissé, *Dutch Manuscript Illumination*, p. 18.

Biblia Pauperum is not surprising if the different orientations of the books themselves are considered. Since the *Biblia Pauperum* employed Old Testament episodes primarily as theological elucidations of events from the New Testament, only a generalized rendering of the episodes was necessary to convey its typological relationship to the viewer. Moreover, its format called for the juxtaposition of three full-page miniatures — representing one New Testament and two Old Testament events — with only a brief, accompanying explanatory passage. As a result, the miniatures were displaced from their physical context within the narrative of the Bible.

However, even when miniatures occurred within the text of the Bible in The Netherlands, as in the Dutch manuscript of the Vulgate in Cambridge, they lacked the narrative character of their counterparts in the vernacular Bibles. A comparison of the miniatures of *Moses Crossing the Red Sea* (Figs. 5 & 6) from the Cambridge Bible and a vernacular Bible in The Hague (Museum Meermanno Westreenianum, Ms. 10 A 18-19) shows clearly the difference in their methods of illustration. In the Cambridge miniature (Fig. 5), Moses and a group of the Israelites stand on a patch of land on the right, illustrating the moment after they had crossed the Red Sea to escape the Pharaoh's armies (Exodus 14:29). Moses and his Israelites are also depicted on the right in the miniature from the vernacular Bible (Fig. 6) illustrating the same verse. However, the Pharaoh in his chariot and his army appear on the left, drowning in the rising waters, a reference to the preceding verse (Exodus 14:28). The static representation of the miniature in the Cambridge Bible is in marked contrast to the narrative energy of the latter example.

In fact, the representation of *Moses Crossing the Red Sea* was always accompanied by the drowning of the Pharaoh's armies in the vernacular Bibles. The moment after the crossing of the Sea was never depicted as an isolated action in these Bibles; it was also combined with an illustration of the *Song of Moses* (Exodus 15:1-21). Pictorially, this miniature, as it appears in the Lochorst Bible (Fig. 7) and in most of the other vernacular Bibles, is closer to the Cambridge miniature (Fig. 5) than the illustration of *Moses Crossing the Red Sea*. Both represent Moses and the Israelites standing on dry land. However, in the vernacular Bibles the representation again acquires a narrative content, for the Israelites hold tamborines, lutes, and violas. They are in the process of singing their thanks and triumph in illustration of a specific biblical verse (Exodus 15:20).

The iconographic treatment of the miniatures in the Cambridge Bible rarely corresponds[26] with that in the vernacular Bibles. In the *Eerste Historiebijbel*, the story related in the apocryphal book of Tobit seems to have appealed to the Dutch artists, perhaps because of its rich narrative, for it generally received at least ten miniatures. One example from the London Bible, representing *Tobias Removing the Innards of a Fish* (Fig. 8), is characteristic of the Tobit cycle. At the bank of the river, Tobias appears busily engaged in cutting open the fish with his knife, while the angel, Raphael, stands over him (Tobit 6:3-5). The angel's arms are opened as a gesture of speech, alluding to his command to Tobias mentioned in the Bible (Tobit 6:3-4). Both the narrative character of the miniature and its close relationship to the text are obvious.

But, in the Cambridge Bible, the single miniature for the book of Tobit, illustrating *Tobit and the Angel* (Fig. 9), is not only static, but it bears little relationship to the biblical text. Presumably, the angel appears before Tobit in illustration of the beginning of the story where Tobit prays to God to intervene and help with his misfortunes (Tobit 3: 2-15). The Bible relates that an angel was sent to heal Tobit's eyes and to give Sara as a wife to Tobias (Tobit 3:17). However, at no point does the angel appear before Tobit alone; when he reveals his identity at the conclusion of the story it is to Tobit and Tobias together (Tobit 12:6-20). In the tradition of Dutch Bible illustration, picture cycles for the Vulgate provide little parallel for the rich narrative sequences in the vernacular Bibles.

Miniatures from French *Bibles historiales* approximate more closely the narrative renderings in the Dutch vernacular Bibles. In the Bible of Charles V (Paris, Bibliothèque nationale, fonds fr. 5707)[27] the scene representing the *Wisdom of Solomon* (Fig. 10) preceding the book of Wisdom depicts Solomon enthroned on the left, confronted by the two kneeling women, one of whom asks for the return of her child (I Kings 3:24-27). Behind Solomon stands one servant and on the far right is another servant who prepares to slaughter the child in order to determine the identity of its rightful mother. Both the facial expressions of the participants and their gestures combine to convey convincingly the dramatic action in what is one of the more lively illustrations from this group of manuscripts. However, in this miniature the patterned background for

---

[26] Only the illustration of Job visited by three friends (fol. 153v) in the Cambridge Bible parallels Bible miniatures in the First History Bibles.

[27] Berger, *La bible française*, pp. 348-349.

the action contradicts the liveliness of the drama by suggesting a certain timelessness. Similar diapered backgrounds were employed almost exclusively not only in this Bible but also in the Arsenal Bible and the Bible of Jean de Vaudetaur. Where this background is absent, as in the grisaille *bas-de-pages*, the gestures of the figures acquired a heightened expressiveness, and additional narrative features often accompany the illustrations. Such is the case particularly in the Bible of Jean de Cy (Paris, Bibliothèque nationale, fonds fr. 15397.[28] In the illustration of *Abraham before Abimelech* (Fig. 11) from this Bible, the former approaches the latter, his finger pointing in accusation at the King (Genesis 20:9-12). The sheep which Abimelech presented to Abraham when he restored Sara to him are also present illustrating a later verse (Genesis 20:14), and the well on the right may be an allusion to the well which appeared to Hagar in the wilderness somewhat later in Abraham's life (Genesis 21:19). It is true that *bas-de-page* illustrations traditionally employed a different and freer mode of representation. Nevertheless, no longer reliant on flat, patterned backgrounds and sharp coloristic contrasts for their aesthetic impact, these *bas-de-pages* illustrations exploit more fully the possibilities of the written narrative of the Bible.

While aesthetic considerations may have been one factor which determined the narrative content of some miniatures, the purposes of the various texts probably also played a role. Texts of the Vulgate were generally destined for a Latin-reading audience. They were undoubtedly used by the clergy to supply readings for services and by monks for private study. But more often these manuscripts, particularly the luxury editions of them such as the three-volume Cambridge Bible, must have formed part of the library of wealthy ecclesiastics.[29] As such, they were primarily show-pieces. Their illustrations fulfilled only the purposes of impressing the viewer as objects of beauty. On the other hand, the Dutch vernacular Bibles were to be read, as a unit, from cover to cover, not in extracts for the services. They were, after all, translated for this very reason, and few editions survive as luxury manuscripts. Because of the new orientation of this particular text, it is not surprising that parallels for the narrative

---

[28] *Ibid.*, pp. 357-358. This manuscript has been more completely studied by E. Panofsky, *Early Netherlandish Painting*, Cambridge (Mass.), 1953, pp. 38-39 and M. Meiss, *French Painting in the Time of Jean de Berry, the late fourteenth century and the patronage of the Duke*, New York/London, 1967, p. 20-23.

[29] The Cambridge Bible, for example, contains the arms of the Lochorst family. See Byvanck and Hoogewerff, *La miniature hollandaise*, pp. 12-13.

contents of its illustrations are not easily found in manuscripts containing the *Biblia Pauperum*, the Vulgate, or even in *Bibles historiales*. Unlike the other versions of the Bible, its illustrations were conceived to act in conjunction with the text, providing a continuous visual and written narrative.

Selection of Narrative Details from the Bible

In the process of providing a continuous visual narrative to accompany the text, there was a trend towards narrative accuracy in the illustrations. For example, close attention was paid to details of setting recorded in the Bible. In the miniature representing *Isaiah Informing Hezekiah of the Sign of the Lord* (Fig. 12) from the Nuremberg Bible the artist has included a bright sun in the upper right corner of the illustration. In this episode from the second book of Kings, Hezekiah asks that the sign of the Lord's healing power be the movement backwards by ten degrees of his shadow:

> And Isaiah said, This sign shalt thou have of the Lord, that the Lord will do the thing that he hath spoken: shall the shadow go forward ten degrees or back ten degrees? And Hezekiah answered, It is a light thing for a shadow to go down ten degrees: nay let the shadow return backward ten degrees. (II Kings 20 : 9-10)

Although the miniaturist seems to have been unable to portray the cast shadow itself, he recognized the necessity for the inclusion of the sun, absent in other miniatures in this Bible, in order to cast the shadow. Here, a detail of setting was provided as essential to conveying visually the full sense of the written narrative.

Other miniatures show a persistent attention to details of setting. In the miniature of the *Raven and the Dove* (Fig. 13) from the London Bible, Noah sends forth two birds one after another to determine the existence of dry land onto which the people and animals from the ark can alight (Genesis 8:7-11). The ark rests on a protruding peak of the mountain of Ararat, mentioned in an earlier verse of the same chapter (Genesis 8:4). Presumably, this detail of setting was included because the mountain must have suggested to Noah the possibility of the recession of the waters from the flood. But, artists went to the Bible for details of setting even when they were not particularly important for an understanding of the narrative. According to the Bible, David first saw Bathsheba "in an eventide" (II Samuel 11:2). The artist of the London Bible, thus, has represented

a golden setting sun over Bathsheda's head in the background of the minia
ture of *David and Bathsheba* (Fig. 14).

Not only was the Bible consulted for details of setting, it was also relied
on to provide numerical detail. The illumination of *Joshua Setting Up
Twelve Stones* from the Nuremberg Bible records Joshua's construction of
an altar from twelve stones near the Jordan (Joshua 4:9). Twelve rectan-
gular slabs are represented, nine already piled in a box-like construction
and three lying scattered on the ground, yet to be arranged by Joshua
who stands in the center. In a British Library Bible (British Library,
Add. Ms. 16951 fol. 173v), the twelve rods mentioned in the biblical
story (Numbers 17:8) are present witnessing the Choice of Aaron. One
of the twelve rods, depicted standing upright on the altar, blossoms as an
indication of Aaron's selection. Countless other examples of this attention
to numerical detail occur in the Bibles. For example, when the twelve
priests of Israel offer gifts at the tabernacle, precisely twelve are represented;[30] and when the hanging of Hamon's ten sons is depicted, ten
figures are illustrated suspended from the gallows.[31]

Details of kind were also selected for illustration from the biblical text.
In the book of Joshua, the procession of the ark around Jericho is narrated
(Joshua 6:13). The order of the procession is given in the Bible which
states that armed men lead the procession, followed by the priests, then
the bearers of the ark, and finally the rereward. In the miniature of the
Encircling of Jericho (Fig. 15) from the London Bible this order is repeated
almost precisely. The priests lead the procession, although they are
followed instead of preceded by the armed men; the bearers of the ark
are in the next position; and the rereward is depicted at the end of the
demi-circle. And in the miniature representing *Judah and Tamar* in the
same Bible, the three objects which Judah gave Tamar — the signet ring,
the bracelet, and the staff — are included in the scene exactly as mentioned in the biblical verse (Genesis 38:18).

Selection of Narrative Details from the Historia Scholastica

When the biblical text was considered insufficient in supplying details
necessary for a complete understanding of the literal meaning of the
text, supplementary details were borrowed from the accompanying com-

---

[30] London, British Library, Add. Ms. 10043, fol. 81r.
[31] Vienna, Oesterreichische Nationalbibliothek, Ms. 2771, fol. 271v.

mentary and incorporated into the miniatures. One of the most striking examples of this is the illustration of *Lamech Killing Cain* (Figs. 16 & 17), as it occurs in the London Bible and the Munich Bible. Cain's death after his murder of Abel is suggested although it is far from explicit in the Bible where it states simply:

> And the Lord said unto him [Lamech], therefore whosoever slayeth Cain, vengeance shall be taken on him sevenfold. And the Lord set a mark on Cain, lest any finding him should kill him . . . And Lamech said unto his wives Adah and Zil-lah, Hear my voice ye wives of Lamech, hearing unto my speech: for I have slain a man to my wounding, and a young man to my hurt. If Cain shall be avenged sevenfold, truly Lamech seventy and sevenfold. (Genesis 4 : 15, 23-24)

The implication of the biblical reading is clear. Cain was undoubtedly one of the men slain by Lamech, for which Lamech, in turn, anticipated divine retribution. However, all the details of the narrative are absent. How and where did Lamech kill Cain? And who was the second man killed by Lamech referred to in the text? The *Historia Scholastica* compensates for the enigmatic character of the narrative in the Bible by providing the answers to these questions and by supplementing the narrative even further:

> Also Josephus says that Lamech possessed divine wisdom. And since he saw that Cain was accursed he knew that he was to suffer further pain. Thus he said to his wives: because I have slain one man to my wounding and a young man to my hurt, Cain shall be avenged seventy-sevenfold. Lamech was an archer and for some time he had had poor vision, so that when he went shooting he was led by a young servant. And it gave him pleasure to shoot animals and to have the skins of the animals he had shot. Because none used the flesh of animals before the Deluge. Thus he accidentally shot Cain dead while he was lying under a thicket, for he thought he was an animal. On this matter, the youth had informed him, thereby misdirecting his aim, he was so angry with him that he struck him dead with the bow. Thus, he killed Cain by that wound and the youth by the hurt of the wound. Both of them he thus killed by their wounds. And these wounds were his damnation.[32]

---

[32] Also Josephus seit, so wiste Lameths wijsheit die godlike dingen. Ende om dat hi sach dat Cayn vermaledijt was, so wist hi oic dat hi meere pine was sculdich te hebben. Ende hi voirseide sinen wive dit aldus: Want ic heb enen man gedoot in minen woude ende enen jongelinc in minen weffel. Sevenvout sal wrake gegeven werden van Cayn, mer van Lameth sal si gegeven werden lxxvii werff. Lameth was een scutter ende van outheiden sach hi qualic. Ende doe hi ginck scieten, so had hi enen jongelinc dien leyde. Ende hi plach te scieten om sijn solaes ende om die velle dair af te hebben vanden

Both miniatures follow the story in the *Historia Scholastica*. In the British Library Bible miniature (Fig. 16), a youth on the left directs Lamech's aim of the arrow towards Cain who kneels crouched in a clump of trees on the far right. Lamech's eyes do indeed seem vacant, perhaps in an attempt to portray his poor vision. In the center, the second sequence of the action is illustrated, where Lamech in his anger raises the bow over the youth's head to strike him. In the Munich Bible (Fig. 17), Cain falls in high weeds, used to depict a thicket, as he is struck by Lamech's arrow. On the left, Lamech, eyes closed, grabs his helper by the shoulder with one hand, while he holds the bow with which he is about to strike him in the other. Although the intensity of the drama is conveyed with greater conviction and by a better artist in the Munich Bible, both miniatures do use the same details of the commentary to relate the story.

The miniature of *Deborah and Barak Smiting Sisera's People* (Fig. 18) in the London Bible demonstrates a similar reliance on the *Historia Scholastica* to clarify the obscurity of the Bible. The biblical description of the battle scene between Barak's and Sisera's armies states:

> And the Lord discomfitted Sisera, and all his chariots, and all his host with the edge of the sword before Barak, and Sisera lighted down from his chariot, and fled away on his feet. (Judges 4:15)

But how was Sisera "discomfitted" by the Lord? The *Historia* explains this:

> And the Lord humiliated Sisera and all his men by sending from heaven in their faces so great a storm of wind, hail, and lightening that their bows and swords were broken by it.[33]

Descending from the upper right in the miniature are the wind and the

---

beesten. Want men plach doe gien vleysche teten voir die diluvie. Mit ongeval so scoet hi Cayn doot dair hi onder die riseren lach, want hi waende dat hi een beest geweest had. Ende om dattie jongelinc hem gewijst had derwart te scieten, so wart hi gram opten jongelinc ende sloechen mitten boge over doot. Dus hadde hi Cayn gedoot inden woude ende den jongelinc inden weffelen der woude. Of hi hadse beiden gedoot innsinen woude. Ende sijn weffele dat was sine verdoemenisse. London, British Library, Add. Ms. 10043, fol. 9v-10r. See also Sandra Hindman, "Fifteenth-century Dutch Bible Illustration and the 'Historia Scholastica'," *Journal of the Warburg and Courtauld Institutes*, 37, 1974, pp. 131-144, Pls. 30-32.

[33] Ende die Heer vernederde Syseram ende al sijn heer ende hi seynde vanden hemel him int aensicht so groten storm van wijnde ende van hagel ende van blixem dair hair bogen ende hair slingers alle mede braken oft onnut worden. *Ibid.*, fol. 125r.

hail sent out by the Lord to arrest Sisera's success in battle. Other details also derive from the commentary. The broken swords are depicted in the right foreground and Deborah, who the Bible states accompanied Barak, stands on a hill on the left, hands clasped in prayer, according to the *Historia Scholastica's* description: "And while Barak was fighting Deborah remained on the mountain Thabor in prayer."[34]

To conclude this type of example, where the primary motive in the miniature seems to be an effort to clarify the Scripture, the illustration of *David Playing the Harp to Saul* (Fig. 19) in the Nuremberg Bible may be cited.[35] The Bible states:

> And it came to pass, when the evil spirit from God was upon Saul, that David took the Harp, and played with his hand: so Saul was refreshed and was well and the evil spirit departed from him. (I Samuel 16:23)

The presence of the devil, standing behind Saul with his hands on his shoulders while David plays his harp derives from the *Historia Scholastica*:

> When Saul was suffering from the evil spirit, David drove away this spirit with the harp. For the masters say that the sweet sound makes the happy still happier and the sad sadder. Some sages say that many devils are unable to hear that sweet sound.[36]

The devil, then, stands behind Saul as the agent who infuses Saul with the evil spirit from God, an idea derived from the reading of the commentary.

The non-biblical addition to the illustration of the *Raven and the Dove* (Fig. 13) in the London Bible is of a slightly different nature. Basically, the miniature depicts:

> ... the dove came in to him at eventide; and, lo, in her mouth an olive leaf pluckt off: so that Noah knew the waters were abated from the earth. (Genesis 8:11)

---

[34] Ende dat wijl dat Baracht striden ginc, so bleef Deborah opten berch Thabor in bedinge. *Ibid.*, fol. 125r.

[35] The subject of this miniature occurs also in The Hague Bible (Koninklijke Bibliotheek, Ms. 78 D 38, fol. 168r.)

[36] Als Saul gequelt wart mitten quaeden geest, so verjagede David den quaden geest mitter harpen. Want die meisters seggen dattet suete geluut den bliden noch blider maect ende bedroefden noch meer bedrovet. Wair saghers seggen dat voel duvelen dat soete geluut niet horen en moegen. Nuremberg, Stadtbibliothek, Ms. Solger 8⁰, fol. 39r.

However, the detail of the raven resting on a corpse in the lower right corner is unexplainable from the Bible text which simply states: "and he sent forth a raven and it went to and fro, until the waters were dried up from the earth." (Genesis 8:7). This inclusion is explainable again by the *Historia Scholastica*:

> Perhaps he [the raven] found a floating corpse in the water and rested thereon. But Josephus says that the raven, after flying all around found wetness everywhere and returned to Noah.[37]

Presumably, the miniaturist found it as unlikely as did the author of the *Historia* that the raven could fly about for seven days finding nothing on which to alight. Thus, he included the detail of the raven resting on the floating corpse in an effort to provide a more logical explanation to the story. Here, then, it was not so much the obscurity of the biblical text which inspired the additional detail, but rather the incredibility of the narrative as related in the Bible account.

Supplementary Use of the Historia Scholastica

Where the previous illustrations use details from the *Historia Scholastica* to correct the obscurity or to lend credibility to the biblical accounts, certain illustrations borrow details from the commentary even when the Bible narrative is self-explanatory. *David Slaying Goliath* is clearly described in the Bible:

> And David put his hand in his bag, and took thence a stone, and slang it, and smote the Philistine in his forehead, that the stone sunk into his forehead; and he fell upon his face to the earth. (I Samuel 17:49)

An earlier verse mentions that David carried five stones in his pouch for this purpose (I Samuel 17:40). The Bible does state, however, that David slew the giant with one stone, although it does not state the position where that stone landed. Nevertheless, in the miniature illustrating this event (Fig. 20) from the London Bible one stone lies on the ground on the right, one stone barely misses the Philistine's forehead, and the third is still in David's slingshot. The *Historia Scholastica* probably provided the

---

[37] Machschien hi vant int water enen korre vlotende ende hi bleefer op. Mer Josephus seit, om dattie raven al om ende om nat vant, so keerde hi weder tot Noe. London, British Library, Add. Ms. 10043, fol. 12v.

detail of the three stones for the illustration of this event:

> David threw three stones, one after another, at his forehead, and when the
> third struck the Philistine fell. Here the Jews say that the iron of the shield
> and of the helmet gave way to the stone which David threw, because it
> illuminated him and permitted the stone to land on the Philistine's head in
> order to kill him.[38]

In the miniature in The Hague Bible of the *Flight into Egypt* (Fig. 21),
the fallen idols on the right provide an additional detail to the traditional
medieval image of Mary and the child on an ass accompanied by Joseph
walking alongside with a pack over his shoulder. The Gospel of Matthew
in the Bible speaks quite simply of the Flight:

> And when they were departed, behold the angel of the Lord appeareth to
> Joseph in a dream, saying, Arise, and take the young child and his mother,
> and flee into Egypt, and be thou there until I bring thee word: for Herod
> will seek the young child to destroy him. When he arose, he took the young
> child and his mother by night and departed into Egypt: And was there until
> the death of Herod: that it might be fulfilled which was spoken of the Lord
> by the prophecy, saying Out of Egypt have I called my son. (Matthew
> 2:13-15)

But the *Historia Scholastica* incorporates the detail of the idols into its
description of the Flight:

> When Herod saw that the kings were not going to return to him, he won-
> dered if he had been deceived by the stars, and whether they were thus
> ashamed to return to him. And after that, he set out to search for the child.
> But then he heard what the shepherds had seen and of Simon's and Anne's
> prophecies. And he began to order all the children of Bethlehem put to
> death so that the child whom he did not know would be killed with them
> And the angel flew to Joseph commanding him to go to Egypt with Jesus
> and his mother until Herod was dead. And when our Lord Jesus entered
> Egypt all the idols of the Egyptians fell as Moses had predicted: the Lord
> shall sit on a cloud of light. That was his flesh that was born to Mary with-
> out sin. And he shall come into Egypt and the idols of the Egyptians shall be
> destroyed. Similarly, it is said that on the day when the children of Israel

---

[38] David werp hem drie stenen int voirhoeft deen naden anderen; ten derden worp so
viel die philistijn. Hier seggen die Joden dattet yser vanden halsberch ende vanden helm
wijcte den steen die David warp, want het lichte hem op ende gaf den steen stat dat hi
[op] des philistijns hoeft gaen soude om [hem] te doden. *Ibid.*, fol. 145r.

left Egypt there was no house in which there was not one dead. Thus there was no temple in which the idols had not fallen.[39]

Whereas the inclusion of the detail of the three stones in *David and Goliath* was probably executed both to enhance the narrative and to visually join the narrative of the two texts for the reader, the inclusion of the fallen idols in the *Flight into Egypt* serves another purpose as well. It is a reminder of the typological relationship between the Old and New Testament, between the prophecies and events of the Israelites and the events in the life of Christ.

Numerous other examples show a similar borrowing of narrative detail from the commentary when that in the Bible was self-explanatory. In the miniature from the Lochorst Bible representing the *Feast of Joseph and his Brothers* (Fig. 22), Joseph and his guests dine at three tables. This arrangement was probably suggested by the Bible text where the fact is stated that a meal was set for Joseph by himself, the brothers by themselves, and the Egyptians by themselves (Genesis 43:32). A gloss from the *Historia Scholastica* makes clear the actual physical layout of the tables which was then adopted in the miniature: "Thus there were three tables."[40] In the miniature of the *Slaying of Absalom* (Fig. 23), as it appears in the Nuremberg Bible, Absalom hangs by his hair from a tree in the right center of the composition, while a man on the left pierces him with a sword in illustration of a passage from Samuel. (II Samuel 18:14). However, the detail on the right where another man, sword poised, is ready to cut off Absalom's hand has no written counterpart in the biblical account. This detail again derives from the *Historia Scholastica:* "Some maintain that the

[39] Doe Herodes sach dat hem die coninghe niet weder en quamen, so waende hij dat hij bedrogen had gheweest mitter sterren, ende dat sij dair om hem scaemden weder te hem te comen. Ende hier om liet hij after tkijnt te zoekene. Mer doe hij verhoerde dattie herden gheseit hadden, ende sonderlinghe Symeons prophecien ende Annen, so wart hij gheware dat hij bespot was. Ende hij beginste raet te hebben om de kijndere van Bethleem te doeden, op dattet kijnt dat hij niet en kende, mit hem ghedoot soude werden. Ende hij om vloech Joseph mitten bevele vanden enghele mit Jhesus ende sijnre moeder in Egipten tot dat Herodes doot was. Ende doe Jhesus onse Heer binnen Egipten quam, so vielen alle die afgoede van Egipten also Moyses voirseit hadde: Die Heere sal sitten op een lichte wolken. Dat was sijn vleysch dat sonder zonde van Marien geboren was. Ende hij sal in Egipten comen ende die afgode van Egipten sullen werden beruert. Ende men seit gelijc dat optien dach doe die kijndere van Ysrael wt Egipten togen, negheen huus dair binnen en was dair en lach een dode in. Also en was nu negheen tempel in Egipten dair en waren die afgode gevallen. The Hague, Koninklijke Bibliotheek, Ms. 78 D 38, fol. 145r.
[40] London, British Library, Add. Ms. 10043, fol. 35r.

tree on which Absalom hung was a cedar and in this location his hand was cut off by a sword."[41] Several details from the commentary are depicted in the miniature of *David Preparing for Battle against the Philistines* (Fig. 24) (II Samuel 5:25) from the London Bible. David's men are gathered beneath a cluster of trees on which yellow fruit hangs, described in the *Historia Scholastica* as pear trees. And the appearance of an angel in the upper corner and falling idols on the right both owe their inclusion to their mention in the accompanying *Historia Scholastica*.[42]

Such borrowings suggest a careful reading of both texts, the Bible and the *Historia Scholastica* for the creation of the cycle of miniatures. Certainly, the close correspondence of details of setting, number, and kind in the Bible and the illustrations points to a thorough examination of the biblical text to provide the essentials of the story. And the *Historia Scholastica* was consulted to fill in gaps when the narrative of the Bible was unclear. The fact that details from the commentary were also incorporated into the illustrations when the biblical narrative was self-explanatory indicates that the commentary did not perform only a supplementary function. Rather, it was read with the same attention as the Bible. Both texts, then, supplied the pictorial details for the combined visual narrative, and it was this continuing narrative which was considered more important than the veracity of either textual version.

Some miniatures in the Dutch vernacular Bibles, which have no basis in the text of the Bible itself, owe their existence to this interest in the narrative. When a sequence in the narrative was absent altogether in the Bible, the entire episode was occasionally borrowed from the *Historia*. The story of Moses' life related in the book of Exodus commences with an account of the child's birth and his subsequent rescue from the Pharaoh's interdict. However, the following narrative skips from this to the story of Moses, as an adult, slaying the Egyptian, thereby omitting the intermediate years of his life. It is this period of Moses' life which is elaborated in the commentary and illustrated in the Bibles. For example, the *Historia Scholastica* relates and explains an incident which occurred during the youth of Moses when he was crowned by the Pharaoh, as his potential successor, threw the crown on the floor, and then placed a burning coal

---

[41] Enege wanen dat tytel dien Absolon verhief, was een segeboem dair Absolons hant in gegroveert was of gesneden. Nuremberg Bible fol. 6or.

[42] Si hadden onder den peerboem haer afgode geset. Die engelen gods maecten tgerust boven den peerboem om dat David teyken soude hebben ten stride. London Bible, fol. 156r.

in his mouth as proof that his behavior was a result of childish innocence:

> One day Termuch brought Moses to her father, the Pharaoh, for he longed to have a son. And the king was astonished at the child's beauty, so he took the crown from his head and set it on the child's head. And on the crown was engraved the image of Hamon, an Egyptian god. And the child grasped the crown and threw it at his feet on the ground so that it broke. And the priest who was sitting next to the king stood up and exclaimed that this was the child that God had revealed to him should be killed. And that he ought not to be looked after any longer. And he wanted the child killed immediately but with the king's help and a learned man's advice the child was rescued, for they said that the child acted in innocence. And in order to prove this, they presented the child with burning coals and he stuck a coal in his mouth and burned his tongue. And, thereby the Jews say that he spoke mistakenly.[43]

This incident is illustrated, exactly as described in the commentary, in the London and Lochorst Bibles (Figs. 25 & 26).[44] In the latter manuscript (Fig. 26), Moses as a young child sits on the floor placing a burning coal from the pan before him onto his tongue. The crown which he has thrown on the ground lies in front of him. On the right, the Pharaoh, accompanied by a group of standing men amongst whom are presumably both the priest and the wise man, has risen from his throne. Two women stand on the left, probably the foster mother of Moses and his nurse. In the miniature in the first Bible (Fig. 25), the first event in the sequence is depicted, while allusion is made to the following one. The Pharaoh, enthroned and again accompanied by two men on the right, crowns Moses who stands before him. The child holds the pan of coals in one hand, and Moses' foster mother and another woman stand on the left apparently interceding on Moses' behalf.

---

[43] Op enen dach daer na geviel dat Termuch Pharaoh haren vader Moisen brachte, om dat hi en oic begeren soude te hebben tot enen soen. Ende den coninc verwonderde van des kijnts scoenheit, ende nam die croen van sinen hoefde ende settese den kijnde opt hoeft. Ende an die croen was gewracht Hamons beelde, dier van Egipten god. Ende dat kijnt gegreep die croen ende werpse onder die voet optie eerde so datsi brac. Ende die priester die neven den coninc sat, stont op ende roep dat dit dat kijnt waer dat hem God vertoent had dat sijt doden souden, ende dat si hem dan niet meer en dorsten wachten. Ende hi woude doe dat kijnt doden, mer overmits des conincs hulpe ende eens vroets mans rade so wart dat kijnt verlost, want si seiden dat dit kijnt dede van onnoselheit. Ende om dit te proeven so daden si den kijnde gheven barnende colen, ende tkijnt stac een koele in sijn mont ende verbernde sijn tonge. Ende hier bi so seggen die Joden dat hi de qualiker sprac. London Bible, fol. 41r.

[44] This episode is also illustrated in the following Bibles: London, British Library, Add. Ms. 16951, fol. 87r; the Munich Bible, fol. 46r; and The Hague Bible, I, fol. 47r.

In the New Testament in The Hague Bible,[45] an event in Herod's life just preceding his death is also illustrated (Fig. 27) according to its narration in the *Historia Scholastica*. The only reference in the Bible to the death of Herod occurs in the Gospel of Matthew where it is stated: "But when Herod was dead, behold an angel of the Lord appeareth in a dream to Joseph in Egypt." (Matthew 2:19) But in the text of the *Eerste Historiebijbel* between the Gospel texts describing the Massacre of the Innocents and the Angel appearing to Joseph in Egypt, the *Historia Scholastica* elaborates in detail the events leading up to Herod's death:

> When Herod was brought back to Jericho and he heard that all the Jews looked forward to his death joyfully, he gathered all the most noble young men of Galilee and imprisoned them, and ordered his sister, Salome, to have them killed when he died so that all of Judea would weep over his death in spite of her action. And the messenger whom he had sent to Rome returned to him and brought a letter from the king which ordered that Antipater should be banned. Immediately he [Herod] pushed him [the messenger] out with a great blow and he became a little disturbed by this news. And he raised up an apple which he liked to eat, and he held a knife with which to cut it. And looking around to make certain that none would hinder him, he held out his right hand in order to stick himself with the knife. But Athiabus, his nephew, grabbed his right hand. Immediately there was a cry in the king's chamber as though he were dead. When Antipater heard this he was so glad, and he promised his attendants many goods in order to liberate them. And when Herod heard this he was more disturbed by his son's joy than he would have been by his own death. And he immediately sent his servants to have him killed, and he was buried inside Hircamon. And he hastily altered his will, designating that Archelaus should succeed him as head of the realm. It was in this manner that he should receive the crown and the realm of King Augustus.[46]

---

[45] Although Herod's suicide attempt is not illustrated in the other Bibles which contain New Testament miniatures, in its place other episodes are depicted to fill in the chronological gap between the Massacre of the Innocents and events after Christ's return. In the Vienna Bible, fol. 16r, the four brothers stand before the bishop requesting the division of Judea into four parts. And in the Brussels Bible, fol. 22r, the head of Antipater is brought to Herod. Both miniatures occur between the illustrations of the *Massacre of the Innocents* and *Christ Among the Doctors*.

[46] Als Herodes weder ghebracht was te Jericho ende hij hoerde dattie Joden sinen doot ontbeiden mit blijsscappen, so dede hij alle die edelste jongelinge wt alle Galilea vergaderen ende deedse in gevangenisse leggen, ende hij beval Salome sijnre suster also saen als hij sinen gheest gegeven hadde, dat sij se alle dede doden om dat al Judea aldus in sijnre doot weenen soude haers ondanckens. Ende die boden die hi te Romen wart geseynt hadde, quamen doe weder ende brachten een letter vanden keyser dat sij Antipater bannen soude. Ende thant so recte hij hem wt mit enen groeten vuysene ende hij bewuam

The moment when Herod's nephew, Athiabus, grabs the sword from Herod to prevent his suicide attempt is represented in the miniature (Fig. 27). Herod lies in bed, apple in one hand and sword in the other, while his sister, Salome, accompanied by another man, possibly Archelaus, stands at the foot of the bed. This episode is crucial to the Gospel narrative, for it prevents Antipater's succession, is followed by Herod's death, Archelaus' reign, and the division of Judea, thereby destroying Jesus' worst enemy and subsequently making Israel safe for his return. Thus, in the miniature as in the text, there is an attempt to create an easily understandable and continuous narrative by illustrating events derived from the *Historia Scholastica* to supplement the Gospels, which logically had to take place between the Massacre of the Innocents and Christ's return to Israel as commanded by the angel to Joseph.

A biographical interest in the lives of Old Testament figures motivated the inclusion of many episodes from the *Historia Scholastica* not related in the Bible. The illustration of *Moses and the Burning Coal* has already been mentioned, but the story of Moses' life was further supplemented in the London Bible by the illustration of a miracle which took place during Moses' young manhood, *The Driving of the Serpents from their Tents*.[47] With the inclusion of this miniature the Moses cycle was complete, providing an even distribution of scenes covering Moses' infancy, youth, early manhood, and adulthood. A similar phenomenon occurred with the Cyrus cycle in the Nuremberg Bible. Events which occurred Cyrus' reign are recorded in the book of Esdras and illustrated in the accompanying miniatures. These depict his efforts to rebuild the temple at Jerusalem and to restore to it the ecclesiastical vessels taken in the siege by Nebuchadnezzar.[48] But the events from his early life are recounted nowhere in

---

een luttel mit deser boetscap. Ende hij hiesch enen appel die hij gheern ate, ende hij haelde een mess dair hij en mede snyden soude. Ende hij sach al om [oft] yemant beletten soude ende hij haelde sijn rechter hant wt om hem selven mitten messen te stekene. Mer Athiabus, sijn neve, begreep sijn rechter hant. Ende thant wart een gheroep in des conincs sale als oft die coninc doot gheweest hadde. Doe Antipater dit hoerde, so verblide hij ende hij belovede sinen wachters vele goets, op dat sine te livereren wilden. Ende doe Herodes dit vernam, so was him zware te verdragen sijn zoens blijscap dan sijn selfs doot. Ende hij seynde thant seriante ende deden doeden, ende hij deden begraven binnen Hircamon. Ende haestelicken verwandelde hij sijn testament ende bescreef dat Archelaus na hem int rijc volgen soude, in deser manie en dat hij vanden keyser Augusto die croen ende trijc ontfangen soude. The Hague Bible, II, fol. 146r.

[47] Illustrated on fol. 41r.

[48] Nuremberg Bible, fols. 130v-132r.

the Bible; they are instead related in the commentary on the book of Daniel which precedes Esdras in the *Eerste Historiebijbel*. In illustration of the commentary, the Nuremberg Bible depicts the circumstances surrounding Cyrus' birth, the plot against his life, and his subsequent rescue as an infant.[49] Like the life of Moses, then, Cyrus' life receives a complete biographical treatment in the illustrations, the details of which derive from the Bible and commentary alike.

Not all the Old Testament characters received such an extensive biographical treatment in the cycles of illustration. The interest in Moses, as evidenced by the number of illustrations devoted to his life, was undoubtedly motivated by Moses' importance to the history of the Old Testament. He was the first type for Christ who played a major role as leader of the Israelites. But the other Old Testament heroes who appear in additional miniatures from the commentary are not amongst those who enjoyed the greatest popularity in medieval figural art — namely, David, Abraham, Saul, Solomon, or Judith. Darius and Nebuchadnezzar figure most prominently, along with Cyrus.[50] These personnages all played significant roles in the history of Jerusalem. It was Nebuchadnezzar who ravaged and destroyed the temple there, and Cyrus and Darius who lent the financial support and physical labor for its rebuilding. If we recall that the text of the *Eerste Historiebijbel*, also, highlighted the history of Jerusalem by including a translation of the Destruction of Jerusalem, the reason for these miniatures is understandable. They were motivated by a desire to present a continuous story of the events and persons surrounding Jerusalem in the Old Testament. Clearly, the narrative of either the Bible or the *Historia Scholastica* was subordinate not only to the biography of individual persons, but also to the underlying theme of the history of Jerusalem.

Entire themes, as well as details, deriving from the *Historia Scholastica* were not uncommon in Gothic art. *Lamech Kills Cain* enjoyed a long popularity in medieval art; it was, for example depicted in sculpture on the facades of Auxerre and Bourges Cathedrals.[51] The Morgan Picture Bible (Pierpont Morgan, M. 638) alone includes several illustrations with

---

[49] The Infancy of Cyrus is illustrated on fol. 130v.

[50] In the Nuremberg Bible, Darius' and Nebuchadnezzar's lives are portrayed in illustrations on fols. 106v, 114r, 114v, 115r, 115v, 118r, 119v, 132v, and 133v.

[51] Illustrated in E. Mâle, *The Gothic Image. Religious art in France of the thirteenth century*, New York, 1958, pp. 204-205, figs. 103-104.

details from the *Historia Scholastica* that were also portrayed in the vernacular Bibles — *Lamech Kills Cain*, the *Raven and the Dove*, and *David and Saul*.[52] In this Bible, Cain has just been struck by Lamech's arrow; the raven rests on a floating corpse; and the devil stands behind Saul representing the evil spirit. However, other narrative details are absent in these miniatures. Moreover, these examples are isolated borrowings from the commentary which does not occur with the Bible text. When the commentary does appear with the text, as in the French *Bibles historiales*, the illustrations are strikingly devoid of any references to it. In the extensively illustrated Paris Bible (Bibliothèque nationale, fonds fr. 152) discussed earlier the only concession to the accompanying commentary is the illustration of *Manasses' Torture of Isaiah*.[53] Neither the miniature cycle from the Picture Bible nor those from the French *Bibles historiales* demonstrate the wholesale interest in the narrative of the Bible and commentary alike, in biography and history, that the Dutch vernacular Bibles convey.

The Placement of the Illustrations in the Text

The relationship between the illustrations and the text in the Dutch vernacular Bibles demonstrates the extent to which the Dutch Bibles were constructed as integrated textual and pictorial units. Repeatedly, the break in the text for the insertion of the miniature corresponds closely with the passage which is illustrated. This is consistently the case with the early vernacular Bibles executed in the second quarter of the fifteenth century, those from London (British Library, Add. Ms. 10043 and 38122), Munich, Nuremberg, The Hague and Brussels. For example, in each of the Bibles the illustrations for the six days of creation all occur at the end of the relevant biblical passage, immediately preceding the accompanying gloss on that passage.[54] Moreover, when the miniature illustrates a passage from the *Historia Scholastica* not related in the Bible, it occurs

---

[52] Cockerell and Plummer, *Old Testament Miniatures*, Pls. fol. 2v, 2r, 26v.

[53] fol. 163v. This episode is also depicted in many of the First History Bibles: London Bible, fol. 199r; Vienna Bible, fol. 228v; Nuremberg Bible, fol. 100v; and The Hague Bible, fol. 228v.

[54] In the London Bible the Division of Light and Dark occurs between Genesis 1 (5) and the *Historia Scholastica;* the Division of the Firmament occurs between Genesis 18 and the commentary; the Fruition of the Earth occurs between Genesis 1 (13) and the commentary, and so forth.

within that text at the end of the passage which most closely describes its subject, as in Lamech Kills Cain and Herod's Suicide Attempt.[55] The departure of the Vienna Bible from this format is not surprising considering its late date of execution in the third quarter of the fifteenth century; after the original creation of a cycle, manuscripts often strayed from their model from frequent copying. Such a closeness between the elements of text and illustration suggests that the extensive cycles of miniatures were to be viewed in close conjunction with a reading of the text. As the pictorial contents of the miniatures were drawn from both the Bible and the *Historia Scholastica*, so their placement between passages of the two texts contributed to their role in providing visual synopses of the combined narrative.

This close connection between the elements of text and illustration was not particularly common in late Gothic manuscript illumination and it was most unusual in the northern Netherlands. Just the reverse was often characteristic of Dutch book production, which churned out innumerable Books of Hours, almost all containing miniatures executed on blank leaves inserted into the finished book after completion.[56] Although the devotional contents of Books of Hours did not lend themselves to an integrated program of illustration and text, this peculiar feature of Dutch manuscripts nevertheless testifies to a method of production common in centers in the North Netherlands. Other Dutch manuscripts, whose contents were more similar to the vernacular Bibles, still do not possess integrated text and illustration programs. Instead, two other systems of illustration are more frequently employed. In the spiritual treatise by Dirc van Delft, *Die Tafel van den Kersten Ghelove*, often copied in the first half of the fifteenth century, each chapter was introduced by a historiated initial.[57] And, in the Cambridge Bible, each book of the Bible was preceded by a miniature illustrating a passage from that book.

Miniatures from the *Rijmbijbel* belong to a third system of illustration, closer to that in the vernacular Bibles. Each section of the *Rijmbijbel* was

---

[55] For example, the miniature of Lamech Kills Cain in the London Bible occurs in the following place in the text: "Dus/miniature/hadde hi Cayn gedoot inden woude ende den jongelinc inden weffelen der wode."

[56] This phenomenon has been pointed out by Delaissé, *Dutch Manuscript Illumination*, p. 19.

[57] The illustrations of this manuscript have been studied by Rickert, *Journal of the Walters Art Gallery*, and the text by L. M. Daniels, *Meester Dirc van Delf, O.P., Tafel van den Kersten Ghelove*, 4 vols., Antwerp/Nijmegen/Utrecht, 1939.

introduced by a rubric briefly describing the action related in the following passages. The miniature preceding the rubric usually illustrated the contents of the rubric, and thus that of the following passage as well.[58] This was not a system of illustration unique to the *Rijmbijbel*, for it was also employed in French literary[59] and biblical manuscripts. A French *Bible historiale* containing miniatures inserted within the text, rather than preceding each book as was more common, is organized in the same way as copies of the *Rijmbijbel*. A miniature preceded a narrative passage of the Bible, the latter being introduced by a red rubric which the miniature illustrated. The *Historia Scholastica* on that passage directly followed the biblical text and was not set off by further rubrics. It thus preceded the next miniature illustrating another subject.

These manuscripts do exhibit a close relationship between text and illustration, but it is a different one from that in the Dutch vernacular Bibles. In the *Rijmbijbel* and the Paris Bible, the fact that the miniatures preceded the text which they illustrated, and in fact portrayed the text of the rubric, suggests a more distant relationship to the text than in the Dutch vernacular Bibles. Like the rubrics, they served as abbreviated indices to the following passage, allowing the reader to quickly locate a section of the Bible and the commentary appended to it. Thus, the miniatures could be, and probably were, "read" separately from the text. But the placement of the Dutch miniatures following the biblical text they illustrated and before the commentary suggests that they were to be "read" *with* the text. That the miniatures often break a single sentence in two when they occur in the midst of a passage further supports this interpretation. Instead of being abbreviated indices of the Bible alone, these miniatures represented expanded synopses of the Bible and its commentary.

This relationship between the written word and the illustrated picture in the Dutch vernacular Bibles implies a considerable degree of organization in the workshop before the manuscript could be produced. The conception of the Bible manuscripts as integrated units must have necessitated such an organization. And the existence of this preliminary organization suggests that an emerging new attitude towards the book was already present in the northern Low Countries in the first half of the fifteenth

---

[58] This system of illustration is used also in the illuminated versions of Jacob van Maerlant's *Der naturen bloeme*. See Deschamps, *Middelnederlandse Handschriften*, Pl. 34.

[59] Such as the Lancelot cycles. See Stones, *French Prose Lancelot*, pp. 8-9.

century. It was an attitude which applied specifically to the vernacular Bibles, for Books of Hours and spiritual tracts were still characterized by a more disparate relationship between text and illustration. Considering this organization, it is not surprising that the earliest dated and localized printed book in the northern Netherlands is Petrus Comestor's *Scholastica Historia super Novum Testamentum*, published in Utrecht in 1473 by Nycolas Ketelaer and Gherart de Leempt.[60] This text also formed part of the manuscripts of the *Eerste Historiebijbel*, many of which are connectable with Utrecht. And the publication four years later in Delft of the earliest printed Bible in the Netherlands used the Old Testament from the revised *Eerste Historiebijbel*.[61] Although this edition was unillustrated, its text was used for the illustrated Cologne Bible printed late in the same century.[62] The conception of the manuscripts of the Dutch vernacular Bible as integrated books, and their resultant organization, was an essential step towards the development of illustrated printed books, which also necessitated a high degree of organization before the beginning of the actual printing process.

Conclusions

In conclusion, two questions can be briefly treated. First, what was the origin of the cycle of illustrations in the Dutch vernacular Bibles? Comparisons with other cycles have shown the extent to which the artists of the Dutch Bibles departed from contemporary tradition in their creation of a narrative pictorial cycle geared to the particular text which it accompanied. Are we then to conclude that this discrepancy between the Dutch and other narrative cycles is due to the creation of a new and extensive group of miniatures for the vernacular Bibles? Secondly, what if any, was the influence of the narrative method of illustration as used in the Dutch Bibles on Netherlandish art? Because of the wholesale destruction of panel paintings during the iconoclast movement in the North,[63]

---

[60] Campbell, *Typographie néerlandaise*, no. 290, pp. 76-77.

[61] *Ibid.*, no. 1404, p. 395.

[62] The connection between the First History Bible and the Cologne Bible was stressed by Deschamps, *Middelnederlandse Handschriften*, p. 155. and in C. C. de Bruin, *Statenbijbel*. On the general relationship between the First History Bible and early printing, see Sandra Hindman, "The Transition from Manuscripts to Printed Books in the Netherlands: Illustrated Dutch Bibles," *NAK*, LVI, 1975, pp. 189-209.

[63] The effects of iconoclasm on painting have been studied in an unpublished doctoral thesis by David Freedberg, *Iconoclasm and Painting in The Netherlands (1566-1609)*, Oxford, 1972.

few panels survive from the fifteenth century. Thus, the Dutch Bibles
with their extensive cycles of miniatures provide one means of reconstructing a fifteenth century painting tradition in the northern Netherlands, one which could well have influenced later Netherlandish masters.

Other manuscripts do not provide exact counterparts for the narrative
cycles in the Dutch vernacular Bibles. Few Bible manuscripts contain
the extensive number of illustrations that the Dutch Bibles possess. Nor
do other extant manuscripts display the same reliance on the text of the
Bible to provide both the essentials and details of the action. And, the
illustrations which display details borrowed from the *Historia Scholastica*
are isolated instances; they are not from manuscripts where a continual
reading of the commentary, as well as the Bible, is evidenced. Finally, the
particular system of placing the illustrations in the text does not seem to
be borrowed from other biblical or literary manuscripts, although a
development towards this system was noted in the *Rijmbijbel* and in one
French *Bible historiale*.

In approaching the question of the origins of the picture cycle, the
earliest miniature cycle from the Bibles must be used, for it was here that
the miniaturists faced the problem either of creating or adapting a
picture cycle for a new text. For several reasons, the London Bible is
probably the earliest exemplar. Although it is undated, the style of its
miniatures seems to predate that of the so-called Claes Brouwer, active
in the third decade of the fifteenth century and chief illumination of The
Hague and Brussels Bibles.[64] On the other hand, they must postdate the
Dirc van Delft codices, dated in the first decade of the fifteenth century.[65]
And miniatures in the London Bible show the most careful execution in
their repeated reliance on the accompanying text. This phenomenon
usually only occurs in an early version of a text, close to the date of the
genesis of a new recension. Since the vernacular Bibles in The Hague,
Brussels, and Munich are all securely dated between 1435 and 1439,[66]
we can postulate a date between 1425 and 1435 for the London Bible.

---

[64] Contemporary records fail to produce the name of Claes Brouwer enrolled in the
Utrecht gild. He is named from a series of payments to him recorded in the Brussels
Bible. See Byvanck and Hoogewerff, *La miniature hollandaise*, p. 16, and Vogelsang,
Holländische Miniaturen, p. 44.

[65] See Rickert, *Journal of the Walters Art Gallery*, pp. 79-108.

[66] The Brussels and Munich Bible are dated 1431 and 1439 by contemporary colophons, and Byvanck, *La miniature hollandaise*, p. 16, suggests that The Hague Bible must
predate the Brussels Bible, for the latter closely copies an initial from The Hague Bible.

Considering the vast number of illustrations in the London Bible, it is unlikely that its artists created an entirely new picture cycle. Although specific borrowings of entire scenes have not been found in contemporary illustration, it is still possible that the Dutch artists took over the basic structure of their compositions from any number of manuscripts–historical chronicles, literary texts, and spiritual writings. However, Dutch artists rarely slavishly copied their models.[67] And the amount of narrative material in the vernacular Bible miniatures seems only explainable as a creation of the Dutch workshop, which constituted an overlay to the original, probably borrowed, compositions. Examination of the other early vernacular Bibles provides further support for such intervention on the part of the artists. While the similarity in text, particularly in the breaks left for the miniatures, suggests that these manuscripts may all emanate from one workshop,[68] none of them seem to reuse miniatures from the other Bibles. Not only is there no correspondence in compositions, but often different episodes were substituted altogether, apparently at whim.[69] To my knowledge, only four Bible manuscripts contain miniatures which consistently either copy one another or the same model, a Bible in Amsterdam (Oudheidkundig Genootschap, Ms. 8) and one in London (British Library, Add. Ms. 15410), both containing shortened cycles,[70] and The Hague and Brussels Bibles. Even after a picture cycle for the vernacular Bible existed in the North in the London Bible, it was not copied by the next group of miniaturists for the Hague, Brussels, and Munich Bibles, nor by the final group in the Vienna Bible.

---

[67] This characteristic of Dutch illumination has been pointed out by Delaissé, *Dutch Manuscript Illumination*, p. 64.

[68] Although the subjects of the miniatures often change, the break left in the text for the illustration occurs in almost exactly the same position in all the manuscripts, excepting the Vienna Bible.

[69] One such example is the illustration of the Pharaoh's daughter speaking to Moses' mother in the London Bible, fol. 40v which is replaced by Moses found in the river in The Hague Bible, I, fol. 47r and in most of the remaining Bibles. Other examples of such substitutions are numerous.

[70] Miniatures preceding the following books correspond in the Amsterdam and London Bibles (British Library, Add. Ms. 15410): Exodus, Deuteronomy, and Numbers. In the Brussels and The Hague Bibles, the miniatures for the Legend of Alexander and the two books of Maccabees reproduce each other, both sets being executed by Byvanck's Master A. See Byvanck and Hoogewerff, *La miniature hollandaise*, pp. 14, 16. Ross, *Medieval Alexander Books*, p. 168ff., has studied the Alexander miniatures in these two manuscripts and found no iconographic parallels in other illustrated recensions of the legend, thereby supporting the theory that Dutch miniaturists may have created large cycles for texts previously unillustrated in The Netherlands.

Therefore, the theory that the artists of the London Bible borrowed compositions and individual figures, but significantly altered them to their own idiom, remains the most plausible explanation for the origins of its picture cycle.

Panel paintings portraying Old Testament themes were not common in fifteenth century Netherlandish art, but their occurrence seems to be restricted to the Dutch North where narrative cycles proliferated in Bible illustration. Scenes taken from the Octateuch occur in the work of Dirc Bouts and several of his followers. Bouts was active in Haarlem before establishing himself in the southern Netherlands where he executed the four Old Testament panels extant from his *oeuvre*.[71] Albrecht Bouts painted at least two Old Testament panels, one illustrating *Gideon's Fleece* and the other the *Meeting of Abraham and Melchizedek*.[72] And, the anonymous Master of the Gathering of Manna depicted two infrequently represented subjects, a *Gathering of Manna* panel, after which he is named and one of the *Offering of the Jews*.[73] Then, the little-known Master of the Joseph Sequence executed six roundels of the life of Joseph from Genesis,[74] a story which enjoyed a special popularity in the vernacular Bibles receiving many miniatures. Although the work of the Master of the Joseph Sequence has not been localized, the other artists were all associated with Haarlem in the northern Netherlands, a center which is known to have played an important role in fifteenth century painting.[75] In the sixteenth century two masters working in Amsterdam and Leiden continued the tradition of Old Testament illustration in panels. Jacob van Amsterdam's two works, representing *Saul and the Witch of Endor* and *David and Abigail*[76] and Lucas van Leyden's numerous prints and paint-

---

[71] On Dirc Bouts, see M. J. Friedländer, *Early Netherlandish Painting*, Vol. III: *Dirc Bouts and Joos van Ghent*, Leiden, 1968.

[72] *Ibid.*, pp. 38-42, Pl. 59.

[73] On the Master of the Gathering of Manna, see *Ibid.*, p. 83, Pls. 54-55, and E. Haverkamp-Begemann, "Een Noord-Nederlands Primitief," *Bulletin Museum Boymans Rotterdam* 11 (1951), pp. 51-57.

[74] On the Master of the Joseph Sequence, see Friedländer, *Early Netherlandish Painting*, Vol. IV, Pls. 70-71, where the six roundels depict episodes from the story commonly represented in the Dutch First History Bibles as well.

[75] On the Haarlem school see James Snyder, "The Early Haarlem School of Painting, *Art Bulletin* 42 (1960), pp. 39-55 and 113-32, with the more recent addendum, "The Early Haarlem School of Painting, Part III: The Problem of Geertgen tot Sint Jans and Jan Mostaert," *Art Bulletin* 53 (1971), pp. 445-466.

[76] See Friedländer, *Die Altniederländische Malerei*, Vol. XII: *Pieter Coeck und Jan van Scorel*, Pls. 25-251.

ings may be cited.[77] Lucas is often considered something of an anomaly in Netherlandish art, but his keen interest in and reliance on biblical themes links him securely with fifteenth century tradition of Bible illustration.

Only recently, the dependence of one Netherlandish master, Hieronymus Bosch, on the *Historia Scholastica* has been suggested. Gombrich discussed the importance of this commentary as a means of decoding Bosch iconography, using the artists' Madrid *Epiphany* and the much-discussed *Garden of Earthly Delights*.[78] In the case of the former painting, he suggested that the man standing in the doorway of the hut in the background may well be Herod, based in part on descriptions of Herod from the *Historia Scholastica*.[79] And he proposed that the *Garden of Earthly Delights* might be retitled *The Lesson of the Flood* as a result of the correspondence of its pictorial contents with the *Historia Scholastica's* description of the period just preceding the Deluge.[80] In addition, other themes deriving from the *Historia Scholastica* and popular in the Dutch *Eerste Historiebijbel* frequently occur in sixteenth and seventeenth century Netherlandish painting. An engraving done in 1524 by Lucas van Leyden illustrated *Lamech Kills Cain*.[81] *Moses Trampling the Crown* occurs in numerous examples, in a tapestry by an anonymous Brussels master done around 1560,[82] a drawing attributed to a Rembrandt follower,[83] and a panel variously attributed to L. Doomer and A. de Gelder,[84] to cite only a few. Similarly, the *Fall of the Idols* is portrayed as part of the Flight into Egypt by a number of artists including the Master of the

---

[77] M. J. Friedländer, *Lucas van Leyden*, Leipzig, 1925 (Meister der Graphik, 13).

[78] E. H. Gombrich, "The Evidence of Images," in C. S. Singleton (ed.), *Interpretation: Theory and Practice*, Baltimore, 1969, pp. 35-104, and E. H. Gombrich, "Bosch's Garden of Earthly Delights': A Progress Report," *Journal of the Warburg and Courtauld Institutes* 32 (1969), pp. 162-170.

[79] Gombrich, *JWCI*, p. 170.

[80] Gombrich in *Interpretation: Theory and Practice*, pp. 75-89.

[81] Friedländer, *Lucas van Leyden*. On Lucas' Bible prints see N. Beets, *De Houtsneden in Vorsterman's Bijbel van 1528; afbeeldingen der prenten van Jan Swart, Lucas van Leyden e.a.*, Amsterdam, 1915.

[82] H. C. Marillier, "Tapestries at St. John's College, Oxford," *Burlington Magazine* 49 (1926), pp. 205-210.

[83] Catalogued and illustrated in F. Lugt, *École hollandaise*, Vol. III: *Rembrandt, ses élèves, ses imitateurs, ses copistes*, no. 1227, p. 41, pl. LXVIII in *Musée du Louvre, Inventaire general des dessins des écoles du nord*, Paris, 1933.

[84] Now in the collection of the New York art dealer, Mr. Silberman, where it is attributed to A. de Gelder.

Evora Altarpiece[85] and the Master of Frankfort.[86]

While this brief survey is not intended to be exhaustive, it does point to the simultaneous existence particularly in the North of a tradition of painting using Old Testament subjects and themes from the *Historia Scholastica* in the fifteenth and sixteenth centuries. The interest in the text of the vernacular Bible and the creation of a cycle of illustrations for it must be considered as a source for this tradition. That the tradition was not extinguished in the North is suggested by Rembrandt's interest in narrative themes from the Old Testament.[87] And his preference for certain stories, for example those represented by the Tobias and Esther cycles, recalls the Dutch Bible artists' predilection for the same themes. One pen drawing in the Metropolitan Museum depicts *Tobias Praying at Sara's Bed*, a subject consistently included in miniatures for the book of Tobit in the vernacular Bibles and represented in the London Bible (British Library, Add. Ms. 10043) in a composition using the same iconographic elements as Rembrandt's drawing.[88] Some of Rembrandt's narrative themes may have been borrowed from an illustrated High German Flavius Josephus which he owned.[89] But Rembrandt's familiari-

---

[85] This episodes occurs on a wing of the sixteenth century Altarpiece of the Virgin located in Evora, Museu Regional, the central panel of which is copied after Hugo van der Goes', *Virgin Enthroned with Four Female Saints*, Benziger Collection, Solothurn. Both panels are catalogued and illustrated in M. J. Friedländer, *Early Netherlandish Painting*, Vol. IV. *Hugo van der Goes*, Leiden/Brussels, 1969, add. no. 146, p. 89, Pl. 121 and no. 36, p. 75, Pl. 43 respectively.

[86] The grisaille predella panel illustrating the *Flight into Egypt*, executed in about 1505 by the anonymous Antwerp Master of Frankfort belongs with his Altarpiece of the Holy Kindred in Friedländer, Vol. 7: *Quentin Massys*, 1971, no. 129, p. 76, Pl. 100. Other panels illustrating the fall of the idols include Henri met de Bles, Flight into Egypt, Copenhagen, Statens Museum for Kunst, catalogued by M. J. Friedländer, *Altniederländische Malerei*, Vol. 13: *Antonis Mor und seine Zeitgenossen*, Leiden, 1936, no. 63, p. 146. The motif appears as well in panels by Lucas Gassel, Collection of Fr. van Gardinge, Eindhoven, Holland; the Master of the Half Lengths, Vienna Museum; the Master of the Adoration of the Groote Collection, Bayerisches Staatsgemälde Sammlungen; and Melchior Broederlan's Dijon Nativity.

[87] See Christian Tümpel, "Studien zur Iconographie der Historien Rembrandts. Deutung und Interpretation der Bildinhalte," *Nederlands Kunsthistorisch Jaarboek* 20 (1969), pp. 107-198.

[88] Illustrated *Ibid.*, Pl. 56. On Rembrandt's interest in the book of Tobit, see Julius Held, "Rembrandt and the Book of Tobit," *Rembrandt's Aristotle and other Rembrandt Studies*, Princeton, 1969, pp. 104-129. Held mentions the parallel between Rembrandt's father's blindness and Tobit's blindness as a motivating factor in Rembrandt's fascination with the story, and in addition discusses contemporary religious sentiment. It is likely, however, that artistic tradition may also have been a motivating factor.

[89] Tümpel, *Nederlands Kunsthistorisch Jaarboek*, p. 109.

ty with fifteenth century Dutch Bible illustration may also have been first-hand, for his inventory records his possession of a pre-seventeenth century Bible.[90]

---

[90] *Ibid.*, and H.-M. Rotermund, "Rembrandts Bibel," *Nederlands Kunsthistorisch Jaar-boek*, 8 (1957), pp. 123-150.

CHAPTER THREE

PICTORIAL REALISM IN THE MINIATURE CYCLES

Pictorial "realism" in Dutch art is a much touted phenomenon, which has been used to denote many diverse aspects of fifteenth century painting. One of the most common characteristics, in fact almost the hallmark, of Dutch realism is the predilection for genre scenes as evidenced in the Zweder Master's seascapes[1] and the Hours of the Virgin miniatures of the Cleves Hours,[2] to cite only two instances. Frequently claimed as another feature of Dutch realism is a trend towards naturalistic detail, as occurs in the borders from the Master of the Morgan Infancy Cycle[3] and the Master of Catherine of Cleves ateliers. As a technical means of displaying the realistic contents, Lyna[4] noted the use around 1400 of three-dimensional picture frames for miniatures in Flemish, if not Dutch, manuscripts. Stylistic features cited as Dutch contributions to realistic painting are the use of naturalistic facial modelling and a painterly "impressionistic" technique, as well as an observation of psychological reactions and an attention to portraiture.[5] Executed around 1400, the unusually naturalistic female head[6] and the striking "group portrait" in the Gelre Armorial[7] betoken the precocious interest, and

---

[1] Particularly in the Breviary of Reinald of Gelders (New York, Pierpont Morgan Ms. M. 87) discussed by Dorothy Miner, "Dutch Illuminated Manuscripts in the Walters Art Gallery," *The Connoisseur Yearbook* (1955), pp. 66-77, and by Delaissé, *Dutch Manuscript Illumination*, pp. 22-24.

[2] Published by John Plummer, *The Hours of Catherine of Cleves*, New York, n.d., with blbliography, (1968).

[3] James Marrow, "Dutch Manuscript Illumination before the Master of Catherine of Cleves," *Nederlandse Kunsthistorisch Jaarboek* 19 (1968), pp. 51-114, has published some of these miniatures with their unusual borders from British Library, Add. Ms. 30003.

[4] F. Lyna, "Les miniatures d'un manuscrit du 'Ci nous dit' et le réalisme pré-eyckien," *Scriptorium* 1 (1947), pp. 106-118.

[5] These aspects of Dutch realism have been most thoroughly discussed by M. Rickert, *Journal of the Walters Art Gallery;* "Review of F. Gorissen 'Jan Maelwael und die Brüder Limburg'," *Art Bulletin*, 39 (1957), pp. 73-77; and *The Reconstructed Carmelite Missal*, Chicago, 1952.

[6] Noted first by Rickert, *Art Bulletin*, p. 74, and discussed in more detail by Delaissé, *Dutch Manuscript Illumination*, pp. 15-16. A facsimile of the Gelre Armorial has been published by V. Bouton, *Wapenboek ou armorial de 1334 à 1372, précedé de poésies héraldiques par Gelre, heraut d'armes*, 10 vols, Paris/Brussels, 1881-1905.

[7] Discussed and illustrated in F. Gorissen, "Jan Maelwael und die Brüder Limburg:

indeed the artistic proficiency in expressing this interest, in the accurate representation of the human face. Artists throughout the century explored the possibilities of a painterly technique which is found around 1400 in the miniatures of Dirc van Delft's *Tafel van den Kersten Ghelove*[8] and around 1475 in the Soudenbalch Master's Vienna Bible.[9] Similarly, efforts were made, throughout the century and with increasing ease, to depict psychological realism, from the tentative experiments of one anonymous master in the London Bible to the self-confident displays of the Soudenbalch Master in the Vienna Bible.

That each aspect discussed above is a characteristic of pictorial realism — Dutch or otherwise — cannot be denied. However, there has been little attempt to examine systematically the interrelationship of these aspects in order to define the Dutch attitude towards realism in the fifteenth century. With the possible exception of the Master of Catherine of Cleves,[10] neither the collected *oeuvre* of one artist nor a progression of related works have been studied with a view towards determining their contribution to realism. Realism in all its various facets can be shown to exist in works from the beginning of the century in the North Netherlands as the examples above demonstrate. And, in the single detailed attempt to discover a continuity in Dutch style, Delaissé[11] suggested that it is the inveterate interest in psychological realism which establishes an internal stylistic development in Dutch manuscript illustration. Are we then to assume that throughout the century there was a consistent linear development towards a *summa* of realistic expression involving all its aspects? Or, as is more likely, were different aspects more common at different points in time and in different types of illustrations, perhaps encouraging the development of

---

ein Nimweger Kunstlerfamilie um die Wende des 14. Jahrhunderts," *Vereeniging tot Beoefening van Geldersche Geschiedenis, Oudheidkunde en Recht, Bijdragen en Mededelingen* 54 (1954), pp. 153-221, and Delaissé, *Dutch Manuscript Illumination*, pp. 13-14.

[8] Rickert, *Journal Walters Art Gallery*, pp. 79-108.

[9] On the Soudenbalch Master see P. J. H. Vermeeren, "De Nederlandse Historiebijbel der Oostenrijkse Nationale Bibliotheek, Cod. 2771 en 2772," *Het Boek* 32 (1955), pp. 101-139; Delaissé, *Dutch Manuscript Illumination*, pp. 42-45, 47-48; and Byvanck and Hoogewerff, *La miniature hollandaise*, p. xxiii.

[10] K. G. Boon, "L'art hollandais et ses sources," *Connaissance des arts* 217 (1970), pp. 94-105, has attempted to place the realism of the Master of Catherine of Cleves within a European context.

[11] Delaissé, *Dutch Manuscript Illumination*, p. 63: "All these miniatures show the same consciousness of human life and emotion; progressively the artists seem to delve more deeply into them and to analyze them more thoroughly."

related aspects? The continuity and diversity in the Dutch attitude towards realism in one group of manuscripts can be appraised by an examination of the contents, style, and technique of the miniatures in the first Dutch vernacular Bibles dating from the first through the third quarters of the fifteenth century.

Interest in Genre Scenes

Realistic scenes of everyday life proliferate in the Dutch vernacular Bibles. The miniature in the London Bible accompanying the text in the book of Kings on the building of Solomon's temple (I Kings 8:65) depicts the activities of the workmen employed to execute this task (Fig. 28). On the left, two men with axes chop down trees, while two seated men hew large boulders, splitting them with hammers and chisels.[12] The temple, itself, is nowhere in sight. In the Lochorst Bible, the representation of *Bezaleel and Aholiab Fashioning Pillars for the Ark of the Tabernacle* (Exodus 37:15) resembles a snapshot of the local smithy (Fig. 29). Within the confines of a small wooden workshop, the smiths are engaged in forming the gold capitals for the pillars. Two completed pillars are propped against the wall of the shop on the left, while one smith sits at a bench in the center beating the gold capital with a metal instrument and the other stands holding the top of a pillar in the hot furnace on the right. Shelves lining the wall in the background display various tools of the trade — a metal square, a clamp, tongs, hammers — in a setting which is a precursor to that of Petrus Christus' *St. Jerome* (Detroit),[13] some two decades later. Like the preceding two miniatures, the *Making of Bricks from Straw* in the Lochorst Bible represents the mechanical process with one worker in the background pounding straw on a wooden table and another in the foreground transporting the completed bricks in a wheelbarrow to the table on the left (Fig. 30). On the right, the furnace used for their baking is depicted, while the dirt necessary as an ingredient for their construction is alluded to by the disordered ground and the nearby abandoned shovel.

---

[12] In the Italian Visconti Hours, the Building of Solomon's Temple is also represented with great attention to the everyday activities of the workmen. But here the temple itself is in view as well. See M. Meiss and E. Kirsch, *The Visconti Hours*, London, 1972.

[13] Discussed and illustrated in Friedländer, *Early Netherlandish Painting*, Vol. 1: *The Van Eycks and Petrus Christus*, Leiden, 1967, p. 104, Pl. 103.

Each of these miniatures represent themes common in biblical cycles, whose basic elements derive from the text of the Bible. But, the text has undergone a mental elaboration by the artist which the miniatures reflect. Some Bibles do indeed retain relatively static illustrations of these scenes, for example of Solomon's temple, the completed pillars for the Ark, or the bullying of the workers by the Pharoah's taskmasters,[14] each closer to the text itself. However, the miniaturists of the London and Lochorst Bibles have imaginatively infused these standard representations with new life, by depicting the activities of people involved in the bustle of their daily affairs. And, this process has transformed the original themes considerably.

Numerous themes, otherwise strictly biblical in content, reflect a love for additional genre details. One of the most delightful examples occurs in the *Birth of Samson* in the Lochorst Bible (Fig. 31). In a rustic, wood-beamed chamber Samson's mother lies in bed, holding a string which is attached to the child's cradle. By pulling the string the cradle rocks to and fro, while a nursemaid cooks the meal in an open hearth on the left and Manoah, Samson's father, approaches the chamber through the doorway in the background. The unassuming charm of this domestic scene is reminiscent of the Cleves Hours, in which one miniature illustrates Joseph building an additional wing to the peasant dwelling, as the Christ child makes his tentative first steps with the help of a medieval "walker."[15] The *Birth of Lot's Daughters' Children* in the London Bible (fol. 20r) might be more properly entitled *Lot Prepares a Meal* after the detail shown of the father cooking on an open hearth while his daughters lie incapacitated in bed with their infants. In the miniatures of *Herod's Attempted Suicide* (Fig. 27) from The Hague Bible and *Amnon and Tamar* in the Vienna Bible a "potty chair" adjacent to Herod's bed and a cat perched on Tamar's enhance the domesticity of the respective rooms.

Occasionally, this preoccupation with day-to-day activities resulted in the abandonment of traditional Bible subjects, in preference for less frequently illustrated sections of the text. The usual program of illustrations for the beginning of Joshua in an extensive biblical cycle represented sequentially Rahab lowering the spies, the priests bearing the ark to Jerusalem, Joshua setting up the twelve stones at Gilgal, the encounter

---

[14] The completed pillars and the bullying of the workmen are illustrated in the London Bible, fols. 62v and 43r.

[15] Illustrated in Plummer, *Catherine of Cleves*.

of Joshua and the angel at Gilgal, and the surrounding of Jericho by Joshua's people.[16] But in the London Bible, a substitution occurs for the scenes representing events at Gilgal. In place of Joshua and the twelve stones, symbolic of the twelve tribes of Israel, the London Bible illustrates the *Encampment at Gilgal* (fol. 114r). Joshua's men have only recently arrived at Gilgal and they are busily engaged in setting up camp. Two tents have already been pitched in the background, and a man in the foreground is hammering the final tent-pin of the third tent into the ground. The encounter between Joshua and the angel is supplemented by an illustration of Joshua's men eating fruit at Gilgal in the same miniature (Fig. 32). During a medieval "picnic", four men sit on the ground, with a white napkin on which fruit is laid spread before them. One man leaves the gathering to pick cherries from a tree. The ravenous appetite of the central figure is well portrayed as he hungrily opens his mouth to devour a morsel of fruit. A concession is made to traditional Bible iconography by the accompanying representation of Joshua and the angel. However, the dull, puppet-like motions of these figures are in marked contrast to the animated festivity of the men on the left, suggesting that the artist's real interest lay in the representation of the latter.

In their selection of realistic themes, the artists did not depart from the biblical text. They simply scanned the narrative for themes readily adaptable to the representation of an everyday activity. Where necessary the artists drew freely upon their own knowledge of the activities peculiar to various trades, as in the illustrations of *Bezaleel and Aholiab Fashioning Pillars*. Sometimes, they included genre details drawn also from their experience, such as the cat in the bedroom and the baby's cradle. We may well inquire into the reason for such a pervasive attention to realistic activities and details in the Bibles. Of course, the burgeoning interest in the realistic world characteristic of products of the International Style should not be overlooked, as it certainly contributed to Dutch style around 1400.[17] However, the peculiar nature of the Bibles themselves

---

[16] This sequence is depicted in five successive miniatures in The Hague Bible, I, fols. 132r, 132v, 133r, 133v, 134r and in the Nuremberg Bible on fols. 2r, 2v, 3r, 3v, 4r.

[17] The relation between Dutch fifteenth century art and the International Style is discussed peripherally by Panofsky, *Early Netherlandish Painting*, pp. 51-64. The migration of Netherlandish artists to Paris in the last quarter of the fourteenth century is well-known. However, the characteristics which Netherlandish artists imparted to Parisian styles, as well as the French elements in early Dutch art, have never been sufficiently defined.

may also have provided an impetus for the illustration of genre scenes. The statement of the Bible's aims in the prologue is particularly suggestive.[18] If an individual was to be encouraged to refer to the *historie* of the text for events which he could relate to his own spiritual life, the miniatures could facilitate this process by making the events easy to identify with. This was achieved not only through narrative clarity in the pictorial contents, but also through familiarity of narrative, as occurs in examples from the London and Lochorst Bibles. A representation of Solomon's temple undoubtedly would have appeared rather foreign — though nonetheless impressive — to the viewer, but the representation of the workmen hewing stones was immediately comprehensible.

Certain realistic details in the treatment of the figures demonstrate further efforts towards directness in the miniatures, towards what is familiar and understandable. In the illustrations for the sequence of episodes from David's life in the book of Kings in the London Bible, David appears first as a child when he is anointed by Saul (Fig. 33). Then, he plays the harp to Saul as a beardless adolescent, and later he smites the Philistines as a brown-bearded young man (Fig. 24). Finally, he woos Bathsheba as a white-haired old man (Fig. 14). The direct appeal of such a technique is obvious; David is not viewed as a remote historical personage, but an ordinary man subject to the fates of time, like all of us. David's red garment identifies him throughout the David story, again inspiring familiarity. This simple device is repeated, with few exceptions, for each principal participant in the London Bible, so that Tobias always wears a pink robe, Aaron a red one, and so forth. Only when a collaborating miniaturist takes over the illustration at the beginning of a new gathering does the costume of an individual character occasionally change within the story.[19]

Interest in Bizarre Subjects

There is not only in Dutch realism an interest in the ordinary, the mundane, albeit rendered with much ingenuity and resultant charm. The miniatures in the Bibles also reveal an acute interest in the unusual.

---

[18] See above, pp. 22-24.

[19] This occurs in the London Bible where David's costume and physical type changes on fol. 160v. in the illustration of Joab and Absalom before the King forming part of a new gathering by a different artist.

In the illustrations relating the story of the golden calf from the book of
Exodus both realistic strains are present. In place of the standard
illustration depicting *The Dance around the Golden Calf*, the Hague Bible
depicts *Aaron Molting Gold* (fol. 70v) which, like the miniature in the
Lochorst Bible of Bezaleel and Aholiab Fashioning Pillars, provides a
visual account of the ordinary activities of the participants preliminary
to the main event. On the other hand, the illustration of *Moses Punishes
the Israelites* in the Lochorst Bible represents a quite different type of
activity (Fig. 34). As a result of the idolatry committed by the Israelites
who worshipped Aaron's golden calf during Moses' absence on the
mountain, the Israelites were duly punished by Moses who forced them
to consume the golden powder of which the now-destroyed idol was
originally composed. Following this initial punishment, the idolators
were struck down. In extensive biblical cycles, and in the majority of
the Dutch Bibles, it is this latter episode, the *Slaying of the Israelites* which
is depicted.[20] However, the first punishment is quite explicitly rendered
in the Lochorst Bible, in which a wooden vat filled to its brim with
golden dust occupies the center of the composition while Moses stands
on the right holding a canteen to the mouth of a man on the left who
dutifully, though not willingly, drinks its contents. The other idolators
stand watching, awaiting their turns, in two groups on left and right.
No other illustrations exist, to my knowledge, of this bizarre event in
late Medieval and Netherlandish art, so its representation does not seem
to have been motivated by an existent pictorial tradition. Rather, it
seems that the artist took a peculiar interest in its bizarre eccentricity.

A similar bizarre event which attracted the imaginative faculties of
one miniaturist of the London Bible was the *Consumption of Blood before
Saul's Altar* (Fig. 35). After the Israelites had been commanded to fast
by Saul on the day of their battle against the Philistines, Jonathan's
men disobeyed and ate the blood and flesh of the spoils. In the miniature
one of the Israelites is depicted in the center before Saul's altar slaying
a sheep, while another in the foreground and a third in the background
grasp broken blood-stained bones on which they are gnawing. Several
men in the background gaze at the action in horrified surprise, a reaction
of which the central figure is apparently oblivious as he slaughters his
animal with abandoned relish. Although this incident is consistently

---

[20] Illustrations of the Slaying of the Israelites occur in the Munich Bible (fol. 66r) and
The Hague Bible (I, fol. 71r).

represented in the Dutch biblical cycles, only in the London Bible are the men actually depicted engaged in this odd activity.

This interest in the bizarre often acquired comical overtones in the Bible miniatures. For example, in the London Bible *David Feigning Madness before Achish* is illustrated (Fig. 36). After fleeing Saul's wrath to Achish, the King of Gath, David fears recognition and possible capture by Achish's men, and as a result feigns madness to escape detection. In the miniature, he is comically portrayed letting "his spittle fall down upon his beard" (I Samuel 21:13), while he stands awkwardly tilted forward, hands held tightly together before him. His charade does indeed appear amusing, to which the slight smiles and faint scorn on the faces of Achich's servants and the King himself attest. Almost laughable is the quite literal depiction of the *Choice of Gideon's Army* in the same Bible (Fig. 37). The miniature depicts the "trial by water" which Gideon used to reduce the number of his army volunteers. According to the Bible, those who "lappeth of the water with his tongue, as a dog lappeth" (Judges 7:5) were to be sent away, while those "that lapped, putting their hand to their mouth," (Judges 7:6) were to be retained. Thus, a river runs in the foreground of the miniature at which two groups of men are shown, one group kneeling awkwardly with their mouths to the water and the other group scooping up water with their hands. Gideon stands behind this highly comical sight.

A final variation of the interest in the unusual in the Dutch Bibles is a group of miniatures which betray a fascination with morbidity, particularly when it involves physical discomfort or torture. This occurs in several illustrations, for example one in the London Bible (fol. 188v) and one in the Brussels Bible (fol. 63r), representing women boiling their children for food. In the former, a passage from the book of Kings (II Kings 6:28-29) is depicted in which the king of Israel and a Samarian woman each boil their respective children for food during a famine. The miniature illustrates one woman stirring the huge iron kettle, in which an infant is seen, on the hearth on the right. Instead of the king, another woman holding her child by the hand awaits her turn on the left. In the Brussels Bible, a similar illustration represents two women boiling their children after the siege and famine related in the apocryphal Destruction of Jerusalem.

With great relish, the artist of the Munich Bible (fol. 139r) has illustrated the episode of the king's men cutting off Adonibezek's thumbs and toes (Judges 1:6-7), a subject commonly illustrated in the Dutch biblical cycles but without such conviction.[21] In an interior setting, Adonibezek lies under a table bleeding from both feet and one hand, the severed pieces of which are on the floor surrounding him. A man on the right holds a sword poised to cut off the thumbs of his left hand. Miniatures depicting similar unusual subjects in a realistic manner abound in the Bibles: Rechab and Banah's hands and feet are cut off in the Nuremberg Bible (fol. 51r); the Levite's concubine is delimbed in the London, The Hague, and Nuremberg Bibles (fols. 133r, 154r, and 25r, Fig. 38); and the king's sons' heads are presented to Jehu in three wooden trunks in the London Bible (Fig. 39).

But it is in the Vienna Bible that physical torture was most exploited in illustrations by the anonymous Master of Evart van Soudenbalch. The illustrations for the four books of Kings, Samuel and Kings in modern versions, complete an abbreviated cycle of only sixty illustrations in the Vienna Bible, compared to the eighty-five miniatures standard in the London, Hague, and Nuremberg Bibles which make up the other manuscripts illustrating this part of the text. Of these sixty illustrations more than a quarter of them depict mass slaughters and retaliatory murders, not only a far greater percentage than occurs in the other biblical cycles but an increased number of episodes as well. New representations were included for at least five episodes not illustrated in the other cyles, while all the episodes usual in the other Bibles retained their places in the Vienna Bible. Clearly, there was a selective process operative in the planning of this cycle which isolated such morbid episodes and assigned them an increased prominence.

This process occurred for the *Slaying of Jezebel* in the Vienna Bible (Fig. 40). Normally, Jezebel's death at the hands of Jehu in avengement of the house of Ahab was depicted in some manner in the Bibles. The miniature in the London Bible supplies the most narrative rendering of the episode (Fig. 41). Here, Jehu stands at the city walls instructing three eunuchs standing at a window above to toss Jezebel down. They are depicted lowering Jezebel's body from the window to the ground where three hungry dogs sit ready to devour her carcass. The miniature is, thus, a straightforward and explicit illustration of the text (II Kings 9:31-33). In the Nuremberg Bible Jezebel's appearance once at the window of a house and again on the ground below refers to the same incident. Whereas, the miniature in The Hague Bible (fol. 219r) illus-

---

[21] This occurs in the Nuremberg Bible (fol. 13v) and The Hague Bible (I, fol. 143r).

trates a succeeding verse in which the men go in search of Jezebel's body in order to give her a proper burial but find "no more of her than the skull, and the feet, and the palms of *her* hand," (II Kings 9 : 35) a phenomenon explained by the Lord's prophecy that "dogs shall eat the flesh of Jezebel" (II Kings 9 : 10, 36), related twice in this chapter.

In the miniature in the Vienna Bible (Fig. 40) it is the action described by this prophecy which is illustrated rather than the actual narrative of the event as it is depicted in the three other Bibles. All the elements in the narrative represented in the three other miniatures, the town, its city walls, Jehu, and the eunuchs, are absent. Only the imposing, buxom figure of the dead Jezebel huddled on the barren ground and mercilessly ravaged by dogs is depicted. Her proximity to the picture plane creating the illusion of great bulk and size, the dramatic foreshortening of her figure, and the omission of all other pictorial elements, including even a more foliated landscape, except Jezebel and the dogs, enhance the monstrosity of the event itself.

These techniques are repeatedly employed by the Master of Evart von Soudenbalch in his representations of morbid unusual events. *Lions Slaying the Assyrians* (fol. 224r) illustrating another episode from the book of Kings (II Kings 17:26), absent in the other cycles which possess no illustrations for this chapter, are depicted as huge fearsome beasts devouring the frightened people, both groups of which are pushed up close to the picture plane. Two similar miniatures from this Bible, previously described by Delaissé,[22] represent scenes which are common enough but render the episodes in a revolutionary way, utilizing stylistic techniques already noted in the *Slaying of Jezebel* and *Lions Slaying the Assyrians*. A tiny David slays the incredibly large Goliath (Fig. 42), while lifting his beard, the latter's head occupying a full one third the width of the miniature! And, in the illustration of *Samuel's Murder of King Agag* (Fig. 43), the beheaded, muscular king is placed on a wooden block diagonal to the picture plane, apparently being quartered as well as beheaded as blood gushes forth from his neck and the split extending a third of the way down his back. As Delaissé has observed, "the scene looks like a butcher's shop or a slaughterhouse."[23]

In selection of subjects, these two mainstreams of naturalistic expression — representation of the usual and the unusual — characterize

---

[22] Delaissé, *Dutch Manuscript Illumination*, pp. 43-44.
[23] *Ibid.*, p. 44.

the realism of the pictorial contents of the Dutch Bibles. They are, in
fact, closely related to each other. First, a close scrutiny of the narrative
of the biblical text was the direct inspiration for the themes in both
cases. Secondly, a keen observation of the external world provided the
artistic know-how necessary to execute the themes. Although we normally
consider that observation of reality results in a close depiction of ordinary
everyday details, such a visual process must inevitably have produced a
perception of the unusual as well. And thirdly, both types of illustrations
facilitated a closer contact between viewer and picture and viewer and
text, encouraging their use as moral example. Whereas this was achieved
by the familiarity of the representations in the first type of realistic
subjects discussed, the grotesque eccentricity of the second type probably
produced a similar result. If the viewer was to relate episodes in the
Bible narrative to his own spiritual life, they necessarily had to evoke a
response in him, as the *Women Boiling their Children* and the *Choice of
Gideon's Army* must certainly have done.

An indigenous Dutch love for unusual representations must not be
disregarded as a factor perhaps providing a catalyst for the choice of
these themes. Many examples of unusual scenes appear in miniatures
from a group of Flemish manuscripts around 1400 which are at once
provincial and innovational.[24] In the *Pèlerinage de la vie humaine* (Brussels,
Bibliothèque royale, Ms. 10176-78) a miniature of the Last Judgment
humorously depicts one of the damned transported on the back of a
camel towards Pluto's throne to receive judgment.[25] The frequently
discussed Wiesbaden *Rapiarium* shows a group of Jews about to stone
Christ,[26] a seldom represented scene of physical cruelty, which interestingly enough also occurs in one Bible.[27] More gruesome aspects of

---

[24] This group of manuscripts is discussed in Lyna, *Scriptorium*, pp. 106-118.

[25] The unusual features of this manuscript were first noted by Lyna, *ibid*. The manuscript was discussed in greater detail by L. M. J. Delaissé, "Les miniatures du 'Pèlerinage
de la vie humaine' de Bruxelles et l'archéologie du livre," *Scriptorium* 10 (1956), pp. 233-
250, who localized production of the extraordinarily realistic miniatures in Paris, executed around 1400, by an artist from the Lower Rhine who later established himself in
Rouen where he produced the miniatures in a Breviary in Baltimore (Walters Art
Gallery, Ms. 300).

[26] Wiesbaden, Staatsarchiv Ms. B 10. Illustrated in Delaissé, *Dutch Manuscript Illumination*, fig. 38; and catalogued with bibliography by Deschamps, *Middelnederlandse
Handschriften*, no. 88, pp. 243-246.

[27] Brussels Bible, fol. 50r, depicts Christ and three men in a temple, the former walking
towards a door on the right, while three men on the left pick up stones.

Christ's Passion,[28] such as the spike block attached from the waist so that it may gouge Christ's ankles as he walks bearing the cross, are illustrated in Dutch Passion texts and miniatures deriving from them, examples of which are the *Livre des meditacions de la vie de nostre Signeur Jhesucrist* (British Library, Royal Ms. 203 IV)[29] and the Brussels grisaille Hours.[30] It is true that each of these miniatures has a textual basis, usually within the manuscript that it illustrates which provided the "script" for the contents of the scene, but the choice of such an abundance of scenes depicting unusual events cannot be explained from their appearance in the text alone.

The Relationship of the Vienna Bible to the Earlier *Eerste Historiebijbels*

That examples from some Bibles appear more frequently than others in the preceding discussion of realism of contents is not accidental. In the latest Bible of the group, the Vienna Bible, the isolation and multiplication of scenes emphasizing physical torture has already been noted, as for example in the *Slaying of Jezebel* in this Bible. In the earliest manuscript, the London Bible, genre scenes and everyday details are far more abundant than in the Vienna Bible. The remainder of the Bibles, executed within several decades of the London Bible, are closer to it in their attention to genre scenes and details, although without the wholesale interest in such representations which resulted, for example, in the substitutions in the London Bible of the traditional iconographic cycle in the book of Joshua for the inclusion of everyday scenes.

We may inquire what the reasons are for this shift in interest away from genre scenes apparent in the development from the earlier Bibles to the latest. The varying composition of the cycles and the different relationship between the miniatures and their text may in part be responsible. In the Vienna Bible, the biblical cycle is significantly

---

[28] Pictorial representations deriving from Dutch vernacular Passion texts are discussed in F. Pickering, *Literature and Art in the Middle Ages*, London, 1970, pp. 281-285.

[29] This manuscript is discussed by Lyna, *Scriptorium*, pp. 106-118.

[30] Brussels, Bibliothèque royale, Ms. 21696. This manuscript and the group of Dutch Hours containing grisaille miniatures which relate to it have been extensively studied in an unpublished thesis by Gloria Konig Fiero, *Devotional Illumination in Early Netherlandish Manuscripts: A Study of the Grisaille Miniatures in Thirteen Related Fifteenth Century Dutch Books of Hours*, Florida State University, 1970.

different from those in the earlier Bibles. It is characterized by a condensation of the total number of miniatures utilizing only a third of the usual number of representations for the books of Genesis through Tobias.[31] The cycle from Genesis through Judges, that is up to the books of Kings, received only a bare minimum of attention, each book being represented by one, or at the most a group of three prefatory miniatures, as was common in the other type of illustrative cycle of the first Dutch vernacular Bible.[32] Moreover, in the books of Kings and in the remainder of the text which has miniatures inserted *within* it, there is no longer a consistently close relationship between the pictorial contents of the miniature and the narrative of the juxtaposed text.[33]

These features had several ramifications on the pictorial cycles, probably affecting the shift from genre scenes. Obviously, when only one miniature was to introduce a large section of the text, as in the beginning of the Vienna Bible, it was most logical that this miniature depict a well-known and representative scene. And, genre scenes were seldom amongst the most representative episodes of any chapter. As a result of the reduction of the total number of miniatures in other sections of the text, there was less opportunity for minaturists to elaborate the essential narrative sequence with supplementary genre scenes. Scenes emphasizing physical suffering generally were far more crucial than genre scenes to the dramatic action, such as the *Slaying of Jezebel*. Finally, the separation of miniature and text resulted in a more distant relationship between the contents of the pictures and that of the text, affecting the choice, as well as the contents, of subjects represented. As we have seen, the representation of genre scenes in the earlier Bibles was partially an end product of the close reading of the text, a process no longer followed in the planning of the Vienna Bible.

---

[31] Whereas the Vienna Bible has only 89 miniatures for these books, The Hague and London Bibles have 252 and 243 miniatures respectively. If the remaining early Bibles had been illustrated from Genesis to Tobias, they would also have had cycles of similar length, for the Munich and Lochorst Bibles have 114 miniatures each for the books of Genesis through Ruth alone.

[32] See above, p. 10.

[33] In the London Bible the passage illustrated by the miniature always appears in close proximity to the illustration. However, in the Vienna Bible, this is no longer always the case, as for example in the Birth of Samuel, illustrating I Kings 1 (20) but placed before I Kings 1 (1). In this context Ross' conclusions in *Medieval Alexander Books*, p. 180, on the independence of the Alexander cycles in the earlier First History Bibles and the Vienna Bible are significant. He has determined that the artists of the Alexander miniatures in the Vienna Bible did not follow one of the earlier Dutch models, whereas the Alexander miniatures in The Hague and Brussels Bibles are interdependent.

In this respect, the Vienna Bible represents a *terminus* in the development of the first Dutch vernacular Bible. Following a pattern of development common in illustrated texts, this version of the illustrated vernacular Bible as represented by the London Bible demonstrates, at its genesis, an intimate reliance on the text in the creation of its pictorial cycle. Not only were the miniatures in the earliest Bibles placed at the precise point in the textual passage which they illustrated, they also relied heavily on the text for their contents. Perhaps it is not an accident of preservation that the majority of illustrated vernacular Bibles which survive between 1440 and 1465,[34] that is between the first group of densely illustrated Bibles and the Vienna Bible, follow a different system of illustration. They use a single miniature prefacing each book, rather than contained within the text, a system which encouraged a greater disparity between miniature and text. As such, they are the immediate predecessors of the Vienna Bible, which combined their system of illustration and that employed in the group of manuscripts related to the London Bible.

Genre scenes seldom appear in this middle group of Bibles, whose miniatures betray a minimum of narrative content. Instead, there appears to be a greater attention to the stylistic treatment of the contents rather than an interest in the contents *per se*. Miniatures with interior settings, for example *Abisag before David* in the British Library Bible (Add. Ms. 15410, Fig. 44), show three-dimensional rooms receding convincingly, with tiled floors, wood-beamed ceilings, and panelled walls serving as perspectival aids. Compared to the *Feast of Joseph* (fol. 35r) in the London Bible where a tiled floor recedes to a patterned backdrop in a room whose walls and ceilings are not visible, the British Library miniatures present an accurate representation of a realistic setting. In the treatment of exterior settings, a foreground, middle-ground, and background are convincingly rendered in *Judith Slaying Holofernes* (Fig. 45) in the same British Library Bible. Here, the tent defines the foreground, and a slight incline with fortifications in the middle-ground provides a transition to the steep hill on which a city rests in the background. This is a marked development from the representation of foreground alone or foreground and background common in the earliest Bibles and exemplified by the *Making of Bricks from Straw* (Fig. 30) in the Lochorst Bible.

Even when genre scenes were depicted in the Vienna Bible, both their

---

[34] Listed on p. 10.

contents and treatment differed significantly from those in the earlier Bibles. A comparison of the two miniatures from the Vienna and Lochorst Bibles illustrating the *Making of Bricks from Straw* (Figs. 46 & 30) is telling. In the miniature from the Lochorst Bible (Fig. 30), each stage in the mechanical process is represented or alluded to — the excavation of the dirt, the grinding of the straw, the baking of the bricks, and their transport after completion to the finished pile. However, in the Vienna Bible (Fig. 46), only two men labor over a few bricks at imprecisely defined tasks. The furnace is represented on the right, but the other steps in the process are not depicted. Moreover, the treatment of the subjects varies strikingly. In the Lochorst Bible, the foreground is defined by two men working and the Pharaoh's taskmasters standing on the side-lines, while the furnace and the work shed fill the entire background in the same plane. Likewise, in the Vienna Bible two men working and the two taskmasters appear in the foreground, but here the similarity ends. A furnace defines the near middleground and a castle the far middle-ground with two men walking on a diagonal path towards the furnace, thereby establishing a visual connection between these two areas. In the background, a hilly landscape recedes from the far middleground to the distant background. Thus, there is a gentle spatial progression in the Vienna miniature which integrates the individual elements, the figures and the landscape. The primary concern with describing in detail the everyday activities in the Lochorst miniature has been subordinated to a fundamental concern with the pictorial aesthetics of the representation in the Vienna Bible.

This concern with pictorial aesthetics in the Vienna Bible led to an advance in realistic landscape painting in its miniatures. As in the miniature representing the *Making of Bricks from Straw*, there is a clear definition of spatial areas in the illustration of *Samuel Killing Agag* (Fig. 43). Each area is subtly differentiated from the others by the definition of its forms, variations in the brushwork, and coloristic gradations. The foreground is painted with broad brushstrokes which are lighter in tone than those used for the middleground. Several large flowers and blades of grass at the border of the frame remind the viewer of this area's closeness. Sketchily painted shrubbery rests on dark hills in the middle-ground; both the shadowy tone and indistinct details of this area imply its relative distance from the foreground. Similar means suggest the extreme distance of the background in which impressionistic dots and faint lines denote blurred greenery and architecture. The forms appear to dissolve in the distance because of the pale greenish-blue paint applied in what resembles a wash technique.

The realistic landscape painting in the Master of Evart von Soudenbalch's miniatures is all the more striking when compared with the treatment of the landscape in the earlier Bibles. Frequently, as in the Lochorst Bible's *Making of Bricks from Straw* (Fig. 30), any background landscape is eliminated altogether by the placement of buildings directly behind the figures extending from one edge of the picture frame to the other. Where a background landscape does occur, the horizon is lowered considerably so that the landscape terminates in the near middleground rather than in the distance. This technique is employed for example in *David Playing the Harp to Saul* in the Nuremberg Bible (Fig. 19). Even then, the landscape receives only a cursory treatment in which the single attempt to differentiate receding spatial areas is the use of diagonal parallel lines becoming denser towards the line of the horizon. And in the Passion Master's miniatures in the Brussels Bible, the landscape is treated simply as a broad carpet of green, identical in tone throughout. For the most part, miniatures in these Bibles use the landscape only as a necessary stage set for the figures; as such, they barely pay lip service to its naturalistic details.

Another aspect of realistic portrayal at which the Master of Evart van Soudenbalch excelled was psychological realism. The miniature of *Solomon and the Queen of Sheba* (Fig. 47) previously discussed by Delaissé[35] demonstrates well the subtlety of this miniaturist's depiction of human responses. In an otherwise conventional representation, Solomon embraces the Queen of Sheba, whose bodily stance and facial expression display a certain coquetry. It is to this that the three women on the right, possibly Solomon's wives, jealously react. The one on the far right has apparently just stepped forward, hands placed on her hips and face slightly contorted in a mood betraying outright indignation. The woman nearest to the couple gazes at them with a sad envy, while the perturbed countenance of the middle figure shows her equal displeasure at the event. These women are not mentioned in the biblical text which simply records the Queen of Sheba's visit to Solomon, his openness with her, and her admiration of his wisdom. This suggests that the artist chose to elaborate on the scene in this way as a result of his own interest in psychological detail, drawing on a story in which the elements of flirtation

---

[35] Delaissé, *Dutch Manuscript Illumination*, p. 43.

and jealousy were only implicit. Many other scenes in the Vienna Bible reveal a similar attention to psychological realism: The *Wedding of Cana* (fol. 21v) has been cited[36] for the diverse attitudes of the attending guests; and Joseph's sons in *Jacob Blessing the Sons of Joseph* (fol. 49v) gaze at each other with expressions betraying at once youthful playfulness and sibling rivalry.

This interest in psychological realism is not altogether new in the Vienna Bible, for it also appears in the London Bible, the earliest Bible of the group. In the London Bible's miniature of the *Making of Bricks from Straw* (fol. 43r) there is considerable variety in the attitudes of those present. On the left, the faces of the Israelites who are seated cutting straw under the supervision of the taskmasters display a resigned sadness, while those of the taskmasters show harsh frowns. The Pharaoh stands self-confident and authoritative on the right despite the questioning of a man beside him who gazes at the Israelites with blatant disapproval simultaneously pointing towards the Pharaoh. In the same Bible, in the *Stoning of the Blasphemer* (Fig. 48), the pain suffered by the stoned man is portrayed on his face, contrasting with the sadistic sneer of one of his torturers and the disappointed sadness of Moses. In these scenes, neither the subtlety of expression nor complexity of response have yet been attempted. Surely the complex responses of jealousy and competitive rivalry as depicted in the Vienna Bible required more consummate skill than the representations of sadness or disapproval in the London Bible. Yet if the earlier artists were not sufficiently competent to represent subtle human emotions, they were nevertheless interested in scenes which would entail their depiction. For in the London Bible, the miniaturist substituted a representation of the Pharaoh's daughter approaching Moses' mother (fol. 40v) for the more standard illustration of the *Finding of Moses*.[37] Here, the two women confront each other, the former asking the latter to nurse her own child, in a scene whose contents was perhaps inspired by an interest in the instinctual gratitude of the natural mother at the favor bestowed on her.

In the earlier Bibles the realism of contents, noted particularly in the depiction of genre scenes and bizarre events, has yielded to a realism in style, apparent in the treatment of the landscape and psychological

---

[36] *Ibid.*, pp. 44-45.

[37] The *Finding of Moses* is illustrated in the following Dutch Bibles: London Bible, fol. 74v; The Hague Bible, fol. 47r; and Munich Bible, fol. 45v.

responses of the figures in the Vienna Bible. This change may in part be explained by different artists' work and different dates of execution. For instance, it is not surprising that the Master of Evert van Soudenbalch's style is more sophisticated than that of the anonymous masters of the London Bible. He worked in the third quarter of the fifteenth century when many of the earlier stylistic innovations had already been assimilated. Moreover, as an artistic personality he was more interested in the elements of landscape setting and human response than the London Bible miniaturist whose concerns rested primarily with the external elements of the narrative. These considerations are not without a certain validity, for individual artistic idioms and the general stylistic development undoubtedly affected differences in the Bible miniatures.

Nevertheless, there may also be an integral relationship between the realism of contents early in the century and the later psychological realism. As we have observed, the primary concern of the earlier miniatures was to provide a continuous visual narrative accompanying the text. Both the representation of genre scenes and the supplementary use of everyday details conformed to this intention. Genre scenes expanded the story in an easily comprehensible fashion, by representing ordinary individuals involved in mundane activities. The use of everyday details satisfied the external requirements for separate episodes by supplying the "stage props" either necessary to or common during their occurrence. This visual recreation of daily events, as occurs in the London Bible, perhaps facilitated the subsequent depiction of psychological realism in the Vienna Bible. In the process of narrative illustration, a complete reconstruction of the trappings of any given situation certainly expedited the study of individual responses to their surroundings and to each other in that situation.

But the study of psychological character also served as one additional means of completely realizing the narrative which has been shown to be the governing motivation in both text and pictures. It is inherent in the concept of narrative illustration and was, thus, a natural area of pursuit in the process of enhancing the story. In the Bible miniatures, its development may be followed from the initial hesitant forays of the London miniaturist to the complex character studies of the Vienna artist. In the earliest Bibles psychological realism remained subservient to the narrative trappings, though an interest in human psychology has been noted in these miniatures. Whereas in some miniatures in the Vienna Bible narrative trappings have been shed in favor of compelling character portrayals. The vocabulary of human responses increases during the century. Basic emotions, such as anger, joy, and sadness to simple stimuli occur in the earliest Bibles, while an interest in responses produced by the interpersonal dynamics of complex situations is apparent in the later miniatures. This exploration of an interpersonal situation in a narrative context with the concomitant diminution of the naturalistic surroundings, found in its initial stages in the Vienna Bible, receives its fullest exploitation two centuries later in Rembrandt's work.[38] But it is not surprising that, in the fifteenth century, essays at psychological realism occurred most frequently in Bible illustration, which interestingly enough contains many of the same themes used in Rembrandt's psychological studies.[39] The narrative nature of the biblical text provided the most opportunities for a type of illustration which enhanced the story, whereas devotional texts, including Books of Hours, generally produced a more iconic imagery.

Secondary Decoration

It was in the areas of subject content and psychological portrayal that the Bible miniatures were most adventurous. Other features of the illustration, notably the frames and their borders,[40] are characterized by a marked conservatism. Essentially three types of frames closely related to one another, are employed in the early group of Bibles: two sketched parallel lines (Fig. 7), a simple gold band joining all four sides (Fig. 42), and a gold band to which are juxtaposed on each side alternating red and blue bars through which a white line is drawn (Fig. 1). The middle group of Bibles employs the second and third method;[41] the disappearance of the first type probably is due to the absence of Bibles containing pen-and-ink miniatures for which it was used, rather than to its abolition from the repertory. And the final Bible, the Vienna Bible, consistently uses only the second method, the gold band. The source of

---

[38] Rembrandt's study of psychological reactions has been discussed in Jacob Rosenberg, *Rembrandt*, Cambridge, 1968 (2nd edition), with bibliography.

[39] Biblical themes treated in this way by Rembrandt include episodes from the Tobias story, David's life, and Esther's life. New Testament episodes occur as well, but their portrayal is not so frequent as the Old Testament ones. See Tümpel, *Nederlands Kunsthistorisch Jaarboek*, pp. 184-194.

[40] The secondary decoration of the Dutch Bibles has never been fully studied. See the brief comments by Byvanck and Hoogewerff, *La miniature hollandaise*, pp. xxi-xxii.

[41] See p. 10 for a list of these Bibles.

these methods of framing is in French manuscripts, generally associated with Paris and executed in the last quarter of the fourteenth century. Of the numerous examples, the *Terence des Ducs* (Fig. 49), executed around 1400 for the Duke of Berry, may be cited.[42]

The use of somewhat *retardataire* frames in Bibles around 1425 is not too surprising, for Dutch manuscript illustration was still in its early stages of development during which it was likely to borrow from more established traditions rather than its own sparse indigenous practices. But the continuing use of these frames in 1475 in the Vienna Bible deserves some explanation. By 1475 in The Netherlands there was a persisting tradition, albeit sporadic, of experimentation with realistic framing techniques. A group of devotional manuscripts executed around 1400 possesses miniatures whose frames simulate those of wooden panel painting.[43] This technique was then adopted in the North where it was employed consistently for the well-known grisaille miniatures produced perhaps in Delft for insertion in Books of Hours.[44]

The Bible miniaturists probably were familiar with these traditions, but their conservatism in the face of it was influenced by several factors. First, such a large number of miniatures in any one book necessitated the use of simple techniques to speed their production. Devotional manuscripts generally possessed shorter illustrative cycles, thereby permitting more time for all the features of their illustration. Secondly, the narrative content of biblical miniatures was probably considered the most important facet of their decoration. A naturalistic rendering of the frames

---

[42] Executed by three artists, one of whom was the Bedford Master. See Jean Porcher, *French Miniatures from Illuminated Manuscripts*, London, 1960.

[43] This group of manuscripts is discussed by Lyna, *Scriptorium*, pp. 106-118. Bohemian illumination provides the closest parallels for these manuscripts. Like the *Ci nous dit* manuscript, Bohemian books frequently employed simulated wooden frames, as for example in the virtually unknown astrological treatise for King Wenceslas (Vienna, Oesterreichische Nationalbibliothek, Ms. 2352). Here, the frames form broad window boxes receding three dimensionally on which the figures actually perch. This manuscript has been studied by Josef Krása, "Astrolgické Rukopisy Vaclava IV," *Umění* 12 (1964), pp. 466-486 (English summary), and Bohemian manuscripts of this era are fully treated in an important monograph by Josef Krása, *Die Handschriften König Wenzels IV*, Vienna, 1971.

[44] It is perhaps significant that this group contains the only examples of realistic frames in the North Netherlands. Even when realistic styles were employed, borrowed perhaps from Bohemian manuscripts, Dutch artists generally did not adopt their framing techniques, suggesting that the adoption of simulated wooden frames in the grisaille miniatures may have fulfilled a function in relation to the images. Their iconic quality would have been enhanced by these frames.

would not particularly have enhanced the narrative, though it would not have detracted from it, whereas naturalistic frames for devotional miniatures served an actual function for the viewer in relation to the image.[45] They created a subjective transition between the viewer's space and the picture space facilitating identification with the imagery which was, after all, the basic function of an iconic image.

Like the frames, the accompanying border decoration remained relatively conservative. A number of types, again basically similar, occur in the Bibles. In the Nuremberg Bible (Fig. 12), spindly fernlike rinceaux to which tiny green flowers are attached predominate. The Brussels, Hague, and London Bibles (Figs. 27 & 32) use pen-drawn rinceaux with green teardrop leaves on them ending in gold trilobes, ovals, or triangles. In the British Library Bible (Fig. 45) and in one in the Meermanno-Westreenianum in The Hague, this second type of border decoration is elaborated by bold acanthus leaves used for a few miniatures. Few of the Bibles consistently employ border decoration for each miniature; many limit its use to select miniatures such as those prefacing each book. And in the Munich Bible only the eight miniatures in the style of the Master of Catherine of Cleves are accompanied by border decoration,[46] closest in type to that in the Nuremberg Bible.[47] In the Vienna Bible, many miniatures also appear without border decoration and those which possess it do not elaborate on the earlier types, with the few exceptions of the full-page marginal illustration which includes several grotesques.[48]

This use of border decoration also demonstrates a persistent clinging to old traditions, for the border decoration has its sources in the same group of French manuscripts which provided the models for the frames.[49] Their outmoded style is difficult to reconcile with the fact that their place

---

[45] The phenomenon of naturalistic frames and their relation to devotional imagery in the North has been fully discussed by Sixton Ringbom, *Icon to Narrative. The rise of the dramatic close-up in fifteenth century devotional painting*, Åbo, 1965 (Acta Academiae Aboensis, Series A, Vol. 31, nr. 2).

[46] These miniatures are all contained in the second gathering: fols. 9v, 10v, 11v, 13v, 14v, 15v, 16v.

[47] Compare Byvanck and Hoogewerff, *La miniature hollandaise*, Pls. 85 and 109 (Munich and Nuremberg Bibles). Closer still to the Munich borders are those in a Prayerbook in The Hague (Museum Meermanno-Westreenianum, Ms. 10 E 1) in Byvanck and Hoogewerff, *La miniature hollandaise*, Pls. 25, 26, 27. Like the Munich Bible, this manuscript contains miniatures in the style of the Master of Catherine of Cleves.

[48] Grotesques are employed, for example, on fols. 47r and 113r.

[49] The *Terence des ducs* (Bibliothèque de l'Arsenal, Ms. 664); Paris Breviary (Chateauroux, Ms. 2); and *L'épitre d'Othéa à Hector* (Paris, Bibliothèque Nationale, ms. fr. 606).

of execution was the geographical area which perhaps contributed most to the development of realistic border decoration. During the first quarter of the fifteenth century, the Master of the Morgan Infancy Cycle produced the borders for a British Library Book of Hours which contains surprisingly naturalistic renderings of flowers and animals.[50] These demonstrate the existence of naturalistic border decoration previous to the Master of Catherine of Cleves' famous experiments,[51] in which bird cages, mussels, archery equipment, and coins are amongst only a few of the objects linked in the margins. The final experiments with border decoration in the last quarter of the century from the atelier of the Master of Mary of Burgundy probably also sprung from Dutch origins.[52] Yet, even the borders accompanying the Master of Catherine of Cleves' illustrations in the Bibles are strikingly *retardataire*. And the reason for this must be due again partly to the large number of miniatures accompanying the text. In addition, the type of book did not lend itself to hidden symbolism, which many of the above borders in Books of Hours contain,[53] primarily because of the strictly narrative content.

Conclusions

The pictorial realism displayed in the early group of Dutch Bibles was subservient to the narrative of both text and picture. Free rein was given to the expression of realism, but it was primarily in the realm of choice

[50] Add. Ms. 30003. On this and related manuscripts see J. Marrow, *Nederlands Kunsthistorisch Jaarboek*, pp. 51-114.

[51] *Ibid.*, pp. 100-102. Marrow has suggested that the borders in the British Museum Hours may actually have provided the inspiration for some in the Cleves Hours, such as those containing acorns and oak leaves and those with peapods. Compare *ibid.*, figs. 25-26 with Plummer, *Catherine of Cleves*, Pls. 137, 3.

[52] It is difficult to determine whether the Dutch characteristics of the Master of Mary of Burgundy's style derive from his early training, possibly in Holland, or his association with Lieven van Latham in Flanders, the latter a one-time collaborator with the Master of Catherine of Cleves. The classic monograph on the Master of Mary of Burgundy remains Otto Pächt, *The Master of Mary of Burgundy*, London, 1948, but see in addition the more recent study, G. I. Lieftinck, *Boekverluchters uit de omgeving van Maria van Bourgondie, ca. 1475-ca. 1485*, Brussels, 1969 (Verhandelingen van de Koninklijke Vlaamse Academie voor Wetenschappen, Letteren en Schone Kunsten van België, Klasse der Letteren, 31, nr. 66).

[53] No comprehensive study of border symbolism in Dutch manuscripts exists. On the borders in the Cleves Hours, see Plummer, *Catherine of Cleves*, with bibliography, and on those in British Library, Add. Ms. 30003, see Marrow, *Nederlands Kunsthistorisch Jaarboek*, pp. 51-114.

of subjects and details which remained closely bound to the textual contents of the Bibles. Basically, such themes owe their existence to the planning of extensive miniature cycles which, through their large number of illustrations, provided scope for the complete pictorial exposition of a story in microscopic detail. It has been suggested that the inclusion of everyday activities in miniatures was intentional and that it corresponded to the aims of the text implied in the prologue.[54] Here, the anonymous translator stated that the biblical stories provided all that it was necessary to know with reference to one's spiritual state. As the emphasis on narrative in the illustrations conformed to this interest in the *historie* of the text, so perhaps realistic subjects were chosen to facilitate the process of learning referred to in the prologue. As mentioned earlier, realistic subjects were easy to identify with, thereby enabling the viewer to gain insight into the narrative which could then serve as moral example.

Certain products of the International Style show a similar use of realism. The Limbourg Brothers Calendar pages of the *Très Riches Heures* (Chantilly, Musée Condée, Ms. 65)[55] display an analogous use of realistic subject matter which Pächt[56] has related to early Italian nature studies. Both the January feast scene and the February snowscape are notable depictions of individuals involved in their daily routines. Yet, while some of the calendar pages demonstrate the existence of one precedent for the realistic subject matter in the Bibles, the whole group differs in two fundamental respects. First, the scenes of everyday life in the calendar are accompanied by a group of miniatures which depict the artificial and highly stylized surroundings of courtly activities, a feature totally absent in the Bibles where even kings and queens reside in humble domestic dwellings.[57]

Secondly, the subjects of the calendar miniatures go beyond their function in relation to the text. Traditionally miniatures accompanying a calendar portrayed activities characteristic of each month in differentiated settings which denoted the various seasons. Thus, they narrated pictorially the progression from month to month. However, the calendar pages in the *Très Riches Heures* demonstrate the pursuit of realistic por-

---

[54] See above, p. 77.

[55] A recent facsimile of this manuscript has been published by J. Longnon with R. Cazelles and M. Meiss, *The 'Très Riches Heures' of Jean, Duke of Berry*, New York, 1969.

[56] Otto Pächt, "Early Italian Nature Studies and the Early Calendar Landscape," *Journal of the Warburg and Courtauld Institutes* 13 (1950), pp. 13-47.

[57] As in the London Bible's settings for King Solomon on fols. 167r to 175v.

trayal for its own sake. For example, the detail of the peasants' exposing themselves as they are warmed by the fire in the February miniature[58] is completely superfluous to the identification of that particular month. On the other hand, the Bible miniaturists included genre scenes and details only when they served the demands of the text. This is not to deny that they also had a genuine interest in the depiction of nature; however, such an interest was rarely expressed in the Bibles when it was not intimately connected with the text.

Bohemian art around 1400 has often been cited as one of the fore-runners of European realism.[59] Wenceslas and his court commissioned a number of extensively illustrated Bibles, including one in the vernac-ular,[60] which we may examine for their possible contributions to Dutch realism. For example, the Antwerp Bible (Antwerp, Museum Plantin-Moretus, Ms. 15.1)[61] contains a few rather unusual subjects and details whose *raison d'etre* is probably an interest in pictorial realism rather than iconographic peculiarities. One such theme depicts the *Preparation of Curtains for the Tabernacle* (fol. 98v), a miniature which shows the Israelites busily tearing up old garments for their use as curtains on the completed tabernacle in the background. This miniature shows an everyday activi-ty — the tearing up of old cloth for re-use — in illustration of a section of the text which even the Dutch Bible miniaturists treated with a more standard subject, the completed tabernacle with its curtains.[62] The use

---

[58] Longnon, *Très Riches Heures*.

[59] The relation of Bohemian art to European realism has been treated by E. Dostàl, *Přispěvky k Dějinám Českého Illuminátorského Umění Na Sklonku XIV*, Stoleti, 6, *Contributions to the History of Czech Art of Illumination about the Year 1400* (Opera Facultatis Philosophicae Universitatis Masarykianae Brunensis, Cislo 26), Brno, 1928; and Josef Krasa, "Huma-nistische und Reformatorische Gedanken in der Höfischen Kunst Wenzels IV," *Acta Historiae Artium Academiae Scientiarum Hungaricae* 8 (1967), pp. 197-203.

[60] On illumination in general at the court of Wenceslas, see M. Dvorak, "Die Illumina-toren des Johann von Neumarkt," *Jahrbuch der Kunsthistorischen Sammlungen des allerhöch-sten Kaiserhauses* 22 (1901), pp. 35ff; Julius von Schlosser, "Die Bilderhandschriften König Wenzels I," *Jahrbuch der Kunsthistorischen Sammlungen des Allerhochsten Kaiserhauses* 14 (1893), p. 214ff; and Herman Sharon, "Illuminated Manuscripts of the Court of King Wenceslas IV of Bohemia," *Scriptorium* 9 (1955), pp. 115-124, with bibliography. The vernacular Bibles, the most important of which is a four-volume German copy in Vienna (Oesterreichisches Nationalbibliothek, Mss. 2759-2764), have never been studied as a group.

[61] Described and illustrated in M. Vermeiren, "La Bible de Wenceslas du Musée Plantin-Moretus à Anvers," *De Gulden Passer*, 31 (1953), pp. 191-229.

[62] The completed tabernacle is depicted in the Munich Bible (fol. 71r), the Hague Bible (I, fol. 75v), and the London Bible (fol. 63v). In the Hague Bible (I, fol. 73v) the making of the curtains is illustrated with other activities in a miniature depicting the Building of the Altar.

of this miniature in the Bohemian Bible is similar to the use of other genre
scenes in the Dutch Bibles where an everyday activity *closely tied to the
text* fills out the narrative.

But the miniature of the *Preparation of the Curtains for the Tabernacle* is
unusual in the Antwerp Bible. Generally, the realism in this manuscript
is not so closely bound to the accompanying text. The depiction of the
Plague of Locusts (Fig. 50) might be termed extra-narrative. True, it shows
a startling image of about a dozen large and naturalistic locusts occupying
the entire picture space. But their representation relates far less of the
actual story than the corresponding subject from the Lochorst Bible. In
the latter manuscript the miniature shows Aaron and Moses warning the
Pharaoh of the Plague which is evidenced by the Locusts surrounding
them (Fig. 51). In the Antwerp Bible, the viewer must elaborate for
himself the narrative details missing in the miniature — Moses and
Aaron's warning to the Pharaoh and their subsequent sending of the
locusts. Realism in the narrative has, thus, been subordinated to the
realistic nature study which was of more interest to the artist. The locusts,
in fact, may have been traced from a North Italian sketchbook of nature
studies[63] or even a late medieval bestiary.

The use of realistic subject matter in devotional manuscripts executed
around 1400 provides a closer parallel to the Dutch Bibles. As aids to
private worship, Books of Hours often contained realistic miniatures
which supplemented the prayers and facilitated identification with
religious personages. The more immediately comprehensible an image
was, the easier this process of identification became. Several examples of
such realistic subjects occur in the DeBuz Book of Hours (Cambridge,
Harvard University Library Ms. 42).[64] One of the illustrations for the
Matins prayers of the Hours of the Virgin depicts the *Virgin at the Loom*
(Fig. 52). The Virgin, represented as a young innocent girl clad in

---

[63] One example of such a book is the sketchbook of Giovanni de Grassi in Bergamo,
published in fascmile: *Taccuino di disegni, Codice della Biblioteca Civica di Bergamo*, Milan
Milan, 1961.

[64] See Millard Meiss, *French Painting in the Time of Jean de Berry. The Limbourgs and
their contemporaries*, 2 vols., New York, 1974; A. Heiman, *Der Meister der 'Grandes Heures
de Rohan' und seine Werkstatt*, Hamburg, 1930 (unpublished doctoral dissertation),
subsequently published as "Der Meister der 'Grandes Heures de Rohan' und seine
Werkstatt," *Städel-Jahrbuch* 7-8 (1932), pp. 1-62. See also Jean Porcher, *The Rohan Book
of Hours*, London, 1959; and on the DeBuz Hours themselves, E. Panofsky, "The deBuz
Book of Hours. A New Manuscript from the Workship of the Grandes Heures de Rohan,"
Harvard Library Bulletin 3 (1949), pp. 163-182.

white, sits on a low stool before her loom. She is surrounded by various realistic details which suggest a humble domestic setting — a washstand and towelrack on the left, a dog in the foreground, and a box of weaving implements at her feet. The ordinary character of her surroundings is offset only slightly by the tesselated background and domed ceiling. In another charming miniature illustrating the prayer "Je te salve, Maria," (Fig. 53) the Virgin and Christ child both stand, the former supporting the latter's arms as he learns to walk. The domestic appeal of such a subject is obvious, and it is certainly reminiscent of the miniature in the Cleves Hours about two decades later illustrating Christ learning to walk with the aid of a medieval "walker."[65]

While a genre element in the Debuz Hours is certainly present, the miniatures are not without symbolic significance. Each is juxtaposed to a central, more traditional representation which is in turn accompanied by a third miniature: the *Virgin at the Loom* accompanies the *Annunciation* in the center with the *Offerings of Joachim and Anne* represented below (Fig. 54); and the *Christ Child Learning to Walk* accompanies a central *Pieta Madonna* with the *Virgin Adoring the Christ Child* below it (Fig. 55). In the first instance, the *Virgin at the Loom* illustrates an episode from the apocryphal youth of Mary before the Annunciation, as does the *Offering of Joachim and Anne* below the *Annunciation*. And, the miniature of the *Christ Child Learning to Walk* shows us the earth-bound Madonna next to the heavenly *Pietà Madonna*. Not only does the physical context of the miniatures suggest their symbolic import, but individual details as well imply a significance beyond their use as genre scenes. As Panofsky has pointed out,[6] the *Virgin at the Loom* contains Marian symbolism alluding to the Virgin's purity — the towel rack, the washstand, and perhaps even the dog.

Nevertheless, these two realistic miniatures must have served as reminders of Mary's earthly qualities. Standard liturgical representations of which the *Annunciation* and the *Pietà Madonna* are examples, were undoubtedly awesome, for their subject matter was generally outside the realm of the spectator's everyday experience. For example, while we may assume that an annunciation was an event outside the realm of experience of the fifteenth century housewife, what housewife had not participated in weaving and teaching her children to walk! These genre-

---

[65] Plummer, *Catherine of Cleves*.
[66] Panofsky, *Harvard Library Bulletin*, p. 171.

like scenes probably suggested to the viewer of the book that the activities of holy personages were not so far removed from the humble pursuits of mortal man. It is even possible that the combination of three miniatures which included one realistic subject in the DeBuz Hours was executed with this dichotomy in mind, although all the illustrated pages in this manuscript do not display this same combination of images.[67] One other page of the manuscript lends support to such an interpretation. In illustration of Sect, the *Adoration of the Magi* (Fig. 56) is depicted in the center while two smaller miniatures on the right and below show the magi's servants attending and watering the kings' horses as they wait for them. Again, the care of horses must have been a common sight to which the ordinary man was accustomed.

Certain miniatures in the DeBuz Hours, therefore, contain a use of subject matter similar to the Dutch Bibles. As the ordinary man could identify with Mary's daily pursuits and the grooms' activities in the DeBuz Hours, so were persons and activities in the Bibles easily comprehensible. David appears first as clean-shaven; then he grows a beard; and later his hair turns white. The Israelites construct bricks from straw using all the implements common to the fifteenth century brick-making trade, as Bezaleel and Aholiab use tools common to the goldsmiths. Similar examples may be found in abundance in the Bibles.

This use of realistic subject matter in pictures as an aid to devotion seems to be a new feature in works of art around 1400. However, it occurs relatively infrequently in works associated with Paris such as the DeBuz Hours. Such subject matter is more characteristic of the North Netherlandish milieu of which the Hours of Catherine of Cleves is the most striking, though not an isolated, example. That it apparently appears first in devotional manuscripts is not too surprising. These were

---

[67] For example, on fol. 82r the Crucifixion of Christ is illustrated in the central miniature and the Crucifixion of the Thieves appears in the two lateral miniatures. Nevertheless, other northern Hours similarly employ one genre-like scene on the folio opposite a more standard illustration. In the Hours of Engelbert of Nassau (Oxford, Bodleian Library, Ms. Douce 219-220), Joseph and Mary are refused asmission to the inn opposite the Visitation, and Mary walks off to tell Elizabeth of the News opposite the Annunciation, as J. J. G. Alexander has noted in *The Master of Mary of Burgundy A Book of Hours for Engelbert of Nassau*, London, 1970, Pls. 73, 76. The British Library Hours (Add. Ms. 30003) from the workship of the Master of the Morgan Infancy Cycle employs a similar iconographic layout, with one full-page miniature facing an initial, the latter often representing a genre scene, illustrated in Marrow, *Nederlands Kunsthistorisch Jaarboek*, pp. 55-114.

the books which laymen traditionally used on a daily basis for devotion; and the subjects of their miniatures were thus brought within the layman's comprehension. A similar use of realistic subjects in the Dutch Bibles is attributable, at least in part, to a similar use of the manuscripts themselves. It would not be invalid to regard the Dutch *Eerste Historiebijbel* as a type of devotional text for the layman. The stories in the text provided moral examples on which to meditate in order to correct the reader's spiritual state. And the narrative of the text was full of everyday occurrences on which to form genre-like scenes, understandable to the layman.

One feature in the Dutch Bibles — psychological realism — finds little parallel in earlier art. As discussed earlier, the depiction of psychological reactions was intimately linked with narrative illustration. Since devotional manuscripts generally possessed miniatures with well-defined subjects of long-standing artistic tradition, these did not present much ground for experimentation. But the extensive narrative programs in Dutch vernacular Bibles provided a hitherto relatively untapped ground. And with the emphasis on a system of illustration in which the activities of the lofty were recognizable reconstructions of the pursuits of ordinary man, the study of man's psychological reactions must have been a natural avenue of exploration.

CHAPTER FOUR

THE RELIGIOUS AND HISTORICAL BACKGROUND

Whether the interests expressed in the text of the First History Bibles were a response to religious concerns of the day is a problem which must be examined. In approaching this problem several questions may be posed. First, can the actual use of these books be discerned from internal evidence from the manuscripts themselves? Patronage, original provenance, and contemporary written notations all provide some clues to the fifteenth century history of the manuscripts. Secondly, is there any evidence for an interest in this type of book — a vernacular Bible — in contemporary primary sources?

Internal Evidence in the Manuscripts

Evidence of patronage in the illustrated First History Bibles is varied though sparse. Only five of the fourteen illustrated exemplars contain colophons or heraldry identifying the original owners of the book (see Appendix I). Two of the five manuscripts (London, British Library, Add. Mss. 10043 and 38122) belonged to a member of the Lochorst family, a well-known Utrecht family whose arms are displayed in both codices.[1] Byvanck and Hoogewerff have assumed that the second of these was commissioned by Herman van Lochorst (died 1438), deacon of Utrecht Cathedral,[2] and there seems little reason to doubt this assumption. Another Bible manuscript was also commissioned by a Utrecht ecclesiastic. The Vienna Bible bears the arms of Evert van Soudenbalch (died 1503), a canon of Utrecht Cathedral, as well as his donor portrait.[3] Two other manuscripts seem to have been written probably for members of the bourgeoisie, whose names do not appear in other primary sources of the period. The Brussels Bible contains a short inscription stating that it was written for Claes Peterszoon. And, a Bible in The Hague (Museum Meermanno-Westreenianum, Ms. 10A18-19) has a

---

[1] See above, p. 1.
[2] Byvanck and Hoogewerff, *La miniature hollandaise*, p. 13.
[3] See above, p. 1.

colophon stating that it belonged to Joffer Alijt Lauwers, who in turn gave it to the Convent of St. Agnes near Nijmegen.

Only the last of these five illustrated Bibles was eventually destined for monastic use, a fact which is understandable since few monasteries could afford the luxury of illuminations. However, the majority of the unillustrated codices which possess clues to their provenance did belong to monasteries and cloisters. Two manuscripts (Utrecht, Bibliotheek der Rijksuniversiteit, Ms. 5 E 6 and The Hague, Koninklijke Bibliotheek, deposit K. A. XXXII) belonged to the house of St. Margaret, an Augustinian nunnery at Gouda. Two additional manuscripts also belonged to monastic houses connected with Windesheim, one probably to the Rooklooster near Groenendaal (The Hague, Koninklijke Bibliotheek Ms. 128 C 2) and another to Marienborch at Nijmegen (The Hague, Koninklijke Bibliotheek, Ms. 75 E 7), both Augustinian monasteries. At least one other exemplar testifies to monastic ownership; a Bible in the Hague belonged to the cloister of St. Margaret in Haarlem (The Hague, Koninklijke Bibliotheek, Ms. 129 C 3).

Whether these manuscripts were, in fact, products of monastic scriptoria is another question. Some certainly were not written in the monasteries to which they belonged, but were gifts like the Hague Bible of Alijt Lauwers (Museum Meermanno-Westreenianum, Ms. 10A18-19) and one of the Gouda Bibles (The Hague, Koninklijke Bibliotheek, deposit K. A. XXXII) mentioned above. Although most of the colophons simply state ownership by a cloister, two colophons actually imply monastic execution: a manuscript in The Hague was either written at Groenendaal or copied from an exemplar written there (The Hague, Koninklijke Bibliotheek, Ms. 129 C 2); and one in Brussels (Bibliothèque royale, Ms. II 3398) was also actually written in a cloister. Although all the unillustrated First History Bibles were not written in monastic scriptoria, some were written there. And the presence of exemplars in monastic libraries would suggest their use within the confines of the foundations.

Then, if some of the First History Bibles were used in the cloisters, for what purpose were they employed? The manuscripts, themselves, are not completely silent on this question. De Bruin[4] noted the presence in several codices of notations which clearly suggest that the text of the First History Bible was used for daily readings in the refectory. This may

---

[4] de Bruin, *NAK*, 48, p. 53.

have been the case also with an example in Brussels (Bibliothèque royale, Ms. II 2409) whose margins are marked with notations, such as *en leest niet* and *dese scholastica en sal men niet lesen*.[5] Interspersed throughout the story of Lot and his daughters, such notations may have been simply a means of distinguishing the appropriate verses designated for oral recitation. However, another reason for their existence is also possible. We know that many monasteries maintained libraries of Netherlandish translations, in addition to their collections of Latin texts.[6] And these Netherlandish books were designated as the *studierboeken* or "study books."[7] It is possible that notations forbidding the reading of certain sections of the Bible were to be used as guides during private study. This suggestion is particularly tempting for the Brussels manuscript where the reading restrictions apply primarily to the more "racy" sections of the story of Lot and his daughters.

While it seems likely that the unillustrated copies of the First History Bible were used for oral readings and private study, it is somewhat difficult to determine the use made of the more lavish illustrated exemplars. Most of these are completely void of any notations. But the copy in London (British Library, Add. Ms. 10043) which probably belonged to Herman van Lochorst has letter and number notation inscribed in red in the margins of the text of Genesis. These notations which use capital letters "A" through "D", followed by the small lower case numbers, one to four, may indicate the correspondence of certain passages with those in a Latin Bible. Thus, they may relate to the readings of Bible passages for the Mass, and their presence in a Dutch Bible could have constituted a cross-reference system to another, probably liturgical, book.[8]

Internal evidence from the manuscripts provides little other data concerning patronage, original provenance, or use, although several other manuscripts reveal the names and cities of origin of the scribes. For example, one of the illustrated Bibles (London, British Library, Add. Ms. 16951) was written by a surgeon, Hughe Gherijtz at Noirtich; and

---

[5] Fol. 38v.

[6] K. O. Meinsma, *Middeleeuwsche Bibliotheken*, Amsterdam, 1902. The list of Dutch books survives for the St. Barbara cloister at Delft and for the Rooklooster near Groenendaal.

[7] *Ibid.*

[8] Such notations appear throughout early Dutch printed Bibles, such as in the Vorsterman Bible produced in Antwerp from 1522-1548.

another unillustrated copy was written by Gherardus Wessel of Deventer (The Hague, Koninklijke Bibliotheek, Ms. 69 B 10). However, contemporary records have failed to produce any further information on their identity or place of activity. The place of origin of one further manuscript, the illustrated Hague Bible, may be assumed as the bishopric of Utrecht from the presence of a large number of Utrecht saints in the apocryphal Letters of the Saints.[9] And the patronage of two other manuscripts (The Hague, Koninklijke Bibliotheek Ms. 78 D 39 and Brussels, Bibliothèque royale, Ms II 3398) may eventually be determined through an identification of their heraldry.

Even when evidence of patronage, provenance, and use is absent in the manuscripts, the date of completion of the manuscripts is usually inscribed. From these dates, execution of the unillustrated and illustrated manuscripts alike may be placed securely within the middle two quarters of the fifteenth century. The earliest dated unillustrated manuscript was executed in 1423 (Leiden, Bibliotheek der Rijksuniversiteit, Ms. Ltk. 234), whereas the earliest dated illustrated exemplar dates from 1431 (Brussels, Bibliothèque royale, Ms. 9018-9023). The latest dated manuscript is an illustrated London Bible (British Library, Add. Ms. 16951) which was completed in 1474. While a few manuscripts may predate or postdate these limits, all the dated copies are spread throughout the limits — 1423, 1431, 1439, 1440, 1443, 1462, 1468, 1474 — with the emphasis falling towards the second quarter of the century. But, in order to understand more fully the possible reasons behind the production during these years of the First History Bibles during these years, it is necessary to turn from the manuscripts to a study of the interest in the Bible and in vernacular texts in the fifteenth century.

The Devotio Moderna's Interest in the Bible and Vernacular Texts

References to the *Devotio Moderna's* interest both in the Bible and in vernacular texts occur frequently in literature on this religious movement. It is de Bruin who is perhaps most outspoken on the role of the *Devotio Moderna* in Dutch scriptural translations.[10] He has maintained that the sixteenth century Protestant and Catholic biblical translators

---

[9] Byvanck and Hoogewerff, *La miniature hollandaise*, p. 16, cite the following Utrecht saints: Sts. Pancrace, Willebrord, Servais, Odulphe, Bavon, Elizabeth, Lebuin, Martin.

[10] de Bruin, *CSSN, Series Minor*, I, pp. xviii-xxii, and *NAK* 48, pp. 44-52.

owe the most to fifteenth century translators who were almost exclusively connected with the *Devotio Moderna*.[11] Hyma[12] and Deschamps[13] both support de Bruin's views, and it is perhaps significant that both have published editions of the single most important work attesting to an overriding emphasis in the *Devotio Moderna* on the vernacular Bible, Gerard Zerbolt's (1367-1398) *Super modo vivendi devotorum hominum simul commorantium*.[14] In addition, Hyma makes continual references to the importance of the Bible in devotional practices of the movement.[15] And, Deschamps gives further weight to the theory of a translation movement instigated by members of the *Devotio Moderna* in his researches on Dirc van Herxen (1381-1457), another member of the movement.[16]

Few works on Geert Groote (1340-1384), the spiritual leader of the *Devotio Moderna* and founder of the Brothers and Sisters of the Common Life, fail to mention his interest in monastic and lay religious education.[17] His heavy reliance on the Bible and other early Church writings and his itinerant preaching, often in the vernacular, have been rightfully stressed. Other religious leaders of the movement have received detailed monographic treatment as well, and in each case the same concerns recur. John Cele (died 1415),[18] rector of the school at Zwolle, was Groote's closest friend. He patterned his life closely on his mentor's, mirroring Groote's spiritual concerns with the Bible and vernacular preaching. Another contemporary of Groote, Gerard Zerbolt,[19] was the movement's first apologist on its methods of private devotion. Zerbolt's

---

[11] de Bruin, *CSSN, Series Minor*, I, p. xxi, and *De Statenbijbel en zijn voorgangers*.

[12] In A. Hyma, "The 'De Libris Teutonicalibus' by Gerard Zerbolt of Zutphen," *Nederlandsch Archief voor Kerkgeschiedenis* 17 (1924), pp. 42-70.

[13] J. Deschamps, "De Dietse kollatieboeken van Dirc van Herxen (1381-1457) rektor van het Zwolse fraterhuis," *Handelingen van het xxiii-e Vlaams Filologencongres*, Brussels, 1959, pp. 186-193, and "Middelnederlandse vertalingen van Super modo vivendi (7e hoofdstuk) en De libris teutonicalibus van Gerard Zerbolt van Zutphen," *Handelingen der Koninklijke Zuidnederlandse Maatschappij voor Taal- en Letterkunde en Geschiedenis* 14 (1960), pp. 67-108.

[14] The Latin edition of the seventh chapter on Dutch books was published by Hyma, *NAK*, 17, pp. 42-70, and the Dutch translations of this chapter by Deschamps, *Handelingen Koninklijke Zuidnederlandse Maatschappij*, pp. 67-108.

[15] Hyma, *The Christian Renaissance*, pp. 3, 19, 56, 67-73, 93, 96, 117, 199.

[16] Deschamps, *Handelingen van het xxiii-e Vlaams Filologencongres*, pp. 186-193.

[17] See in particular, Épiney-Burgard, *Gerard Grote*, pp. 224-247, 297-298.

[18] A biography of John Cele has yet to be written. See the introduction to the publication of his sermons by Thomas De Vries, *Duutsche sermoenen door magister Joan Cele Rektor der Zwolse school gehouden tot zijn clerken 1380-1415*, Zwolle, 1947.

[19] The most recent complete study on Gerard Zerbolt is J. van Rooy, *Gerard Zerbolt van Zutphen. I. Leven en geschriften*, Nijmegen, 1936.

chief treatise devotes an entire chapter to the necessity of vernacular translations of the Scripture for this end.[20] Two later writers, Dirc van Herxen[21] and Johannes Schutken[22] demonstrate that the early concerns of the movement continued with similar vigor in the fifteenth century.

A continuing interest in the Bible and in vernacular texts in the late fourteenth and fifteenth centuries is well documented in the chronicle of the monastery of the Augustinian Canons Regular at Windesheim. Written in the late fifteenth century by Johannes Busch, the *Chronicon Windeshemense*[23] records first Geert Groote's translations of scriptural books for the laity in the late fourteenth century.[24] Then, the Windesheim revision of the Vulgate executed in that monastery receives detailed coverage.[25] Next, Busch relates the continuation of Groote's translation activity by Johannes Schutken while the latter was librarian of the cloister and director of the scriptorium.[26] And, finally we learn of a sixteenth century trilingual Bible, the Netherlandish part of which was completed by Nicolas van Winghe, a Canon Regular of the Windesheim congregation at Louvain.[27]

Yet, despite the published evidence in favor of *Devotio Moderna* interest in the Bible and in vernacular texts, in the most recent monograph on this movement Post[28] carefully avoids any emphasis on the movement's role in vernacular Bible translations. Marrow[29] has interpreted Post's statements as a flat denial of any such activity. But this is not exactly the case. Post discusses the Windesheim revision of the Vulgate in some detail.[30] However, he attributes the motivation behind this activity to an interest in ritualistic uniformity rather than in the Bible text itself: the monks "were not interested in the correct text of the Bible or in its meaning; but in uniformity at the choir service and in reading aloud."[31]

---

[20] Published by Hyma, *NAK*, 17, pp. 42-70.

[21] On Dirc van Herxen see P. J. H. Knierim, *Dirc van Herxen*, Leiden, 1926.

[22] See J. Acquoy, *Het Klooster te Windesheim en zijn invloed*, I, pp. 280-289.

[23] Edited by K. Grube, *Des Augustinerpropstes Iohannes Busch Chronicon Windeshemense und Liber de Reformatione Monasteriorum*, Halle, 1886 (Geschichtsquellen der Provinz Sachsen und angrenzender Gebiete, 19).

[24] *Ibid.*, p. 109.

[25] *Ibid.*, pp. 311-313.

[26] *Ibid.*, p. 191.

[27] Acquoy, *Klooster te Windesheim*, II, pp. 269-271.

[28] Post, *Modern Devotion*.

[29] Marrow, *Medium Aevum*, p. 254.

[30] Post, *Modern Devotion*, pp. 304-308.

[31] *Ibid.*, p. 307.

Both factors may, in fact, have provided the inspiration for a correction of the Vulgate. The *Devotio Moderna's* interest in the Bible and in vernacular translations is not discussed elsewhere in Post's monograph. It is likely that this omission is intentional, reflecting Post's opinion as Marrow has assumed, for when Post mentions Groote's extensive references to the Bible, he quickly adds that such familiarity with the Scriptures was very much in line with other medieval theologians.[32]

But, it would be unfair to discredit Post's study. In his introduction, he clearly sets forth his objections to previous scholarship, and his own methodology derives in part from his assessment of past scholarly misjudgements. He states that scholars on the *Devotio Moderna* have paid little attention to the contributions of other equally significant religious movements, which also played a role in devotionalism,[33] and have tended to write "only in superlatives"[34] on the *Devotio Moderna*. Moreover, he criticizes scholars' often exclusive use of late fourteenth century writers to deduce characteristics of the *Devotio Moderna* into the late fifteenth century.[35] And, finally, he cautions against the indiscriminate use of primary sources by religious writers during the period as reflections of a universal spiritual piety characteristic of the *Devotio Moderna*.[36] Thus, Post's study is a cautious work, perhaps a much-needed one, given the grandiose achievements often claimed for the *Devotio Moderna*.

None of the above works provide a complete account of the *Devotio Moderna's* role in the translation of the Bible or their interest in the Bible. References to this activity are found only in snatches in various accounts. Nor is there any general assessment of the *Devotio Moderna's* role. If it did indeed play a part, was the movement an active participant or simply the spiritual inspiration? Were vernacular texts for use by members of the movement or for use by the laity whom the movement hoped to reach?

The validity of examining the *Devotio Moderna's* connection with the Bible and with vernacular texts is suggested not only by scholarship on the movement and primary sources such as the *Chronicon Windeshemense* but also by the manuscripts themselves. The movement's connection with the Windesheim revision of the Vulgate, the *Tweede Historiebijbel,*

---

[32] *Ibid.*, p. 169.
[33] *Ibid.*, p. 17.
[34] *Ibid.*, p. 49.
[35] *Ibid.*, p. 16.
[36] *Ibid.*, p. 17.

and Erasmus has already been pointed out. Moreover, the fact that several exemplars of the First History Bible originally belonged to Augustinian cloisters of the Windesheim congregation deserves some explanation. In dealing with this problem, first, the work of three spiritual leaders in the fourteenth century will be examined: Geert Groote, John Cele, and Gerard Zerbolt. Secondly, the contributions of their fifteenth century spiritual heirs will be discussed to determine whether the original goals of the movement did, in fact, continue into the period which produced the First History Bibles. In each instance an attempt will be made to assess just how representative the views of such writers were, and whether they acquired any widespread popularity. Finally, other evidence of an interest in the Bible and vernacular texts will be presented. This includes documentation from cloister libraries and monastic rules.

Groote's frequent quotations from the Bible have often been noted,[37] and it is clear that he must have read thoroughly both the Old and New Testaments, as well as their commentaries. The importance of the Bible is stressed in Groote's treatise, *Conclusa et proposita*,[38] which constitutes his statement on the spiritual ideal, containing religious recommendations for his disciples. In the chapter entitled "De sacris libris studendis," he states that the Gospels are the "staff of all study" and "the mirror of life," for in them the life of Christ is contained.[39] Next in order are the Epistles of Paul and the Acts of the Apostles.[40] Following a short list of works by early Church Fathers and medieval theologians,[41] concentrating on saint's lives and biblical commentaries, the Bible reappears. First, the books of the Old Testament which are excerpted frequently in the liturgy are recommended: Proverbs, Ecclesiastes, Ecclesiasticus, and the Psalms.[42] And, secondly, biblical books for historical reading are suggested, with their relevant commentaries from the Church Fathers: the Pentateuch, Joshua, Judges, Kings, the Prophets.[43] The emphasis on biblical books over other exegetical writings in *Conclusa et proposita*

---

[37] In Hyma, *The Christian Renaissance*, pp. 17, 19; Épiney-Burgard, *Gérard Grote*, pp. 57-63; Post, *Modern Devotion*, pp. 168-169; and Van Zijl, *Gerard Groote*, pp. 107-108.

[38] Published in M. I. Pohl (ed.), *Thomae Hemerken a Kempis opera omnia*, Fribourg, 1922, Vol. VII, pp. 87-107.

[39] *Ibid.*, p. 97.

[40] *Ibid.*, p. 97.

[41] *Ibid.*, p. 98.

[42] *Ibid.*, p. 98.

[43] *Ibid.*, p. 98.

suggests that the Bible was, in fact, considered by Groote as the single most important book.

Did Groote expect that Bible reading should be in Latin or was the vernacular considered acceptable? The treatise *Conclusa et proposita* was written in Latin, but this was probably because it was essentially designed as a guide to Latin-reading disciples, not to a more general lay audience. But in much of Groote's other work, he clearly hoped to reach the laity. The Book of Hours, traditionally a private devotional manual specially for the laity, was translated into Dutch by Groote.[44] And, Groote must have preached frequently in the vernacular. Although most surviving sermons are Latin texts, accounts of Groote's activity as a preacher record his popularity as an itinerant preacher to crowds in various towns. That Dutch texts[45] of these sermons have not survived is not particularly surprising;[46] they would not have been copied so frequently as the Latin ones for use within religious communities.

In two works Groote's views on the relative value of Latin and vernacular texts are expressed quite explicitly. The first is the *Dictamen rigmicum* or the Hymn of Windesheim[47] which was written at Windesheim probably to celebrate community festivals. In one section of this rhymed *vita*, Groote's epithet is given as the *magistrum humillimum qui non spernit theutonicum* or "the most humble master who did not spurn Dutch."[48] And later he is described as an individual who judged books on the merits of their contents regardless of whether they were in Latin or Dutch.[49] The second work is a treatise on meditation, *Tractatus de quatuor generibus meditationum sive contemplationum*.[50] Here, Groote discusses the ways in which images — literal, visual, and aural — can aid meditation. The Bible, he states, acquires a freshness and newness if read in the vernacular, thereby suggesting that vernacular reading is in some ways preferable.[51] For, if

---

[44] van Wijk, *Getijdenboek*.

[45] Épiney-Burgard, *Gérard Grote*, pp. 182-193.

[46] The only Dutch sermon by Groote which has survived is published by W. Moll, "Dit sijn de vijf poente die meester Geert de Grote den volke tUutrecht predicte," *Studien en Bijdragen op 't gebied der historische theologie*, 1 (1970), pp. 404-411.

[47] Edited by T. Brandsma, "Twee berijmde levens van Geert Groote," *Ons Geestelijk Erf* 16 (1942), pp. 5-51.

[48] *Ibid.*, p. 33.

[49] *Ibid.*

[50] Edited by A. Hyma, "Het Tractatus de quatuor generibus meditationum sive contemplationum or Sermo de nativitate Domini," *Archief voor de Geschiedenis van het Aartsbisdom Utrecht*, 49 (1924), pp. 296-326.

[51] *Ibid.*, pp. 313-314.

this text is read in Latin, Groote tells us, the human memory recalls numerous other references related to the biblical text which detract from the devotional aids which can be gained from the Bible text alone.[52]

In the *Tractatus de quatuor generibus*, Groote's view of the Bible reveals several points of contact with that of the anonymous "translator of 1360." Both writers recommend vernacular Bible study. Moreover, both writers suggest that the literal meaning of the stories of the Bible is alone sufficient. Groote's statement particularly eschews commentaries, although his interest in biblical commentaries is known from other sources;[53] and the translator uses the commentary only to elucidate the obscure sections of the Bible, retaining the importance of the literal meaning in the text. And finally, both Groote and the "translator of 1360" suggest that the literal meaning of the vernacular Bible serves as an aid to devotion. In these respects, the "translator of 1360" and Geert Groote are kindred spirits, as the First History Bibles in the fifteenth century also mirror both the fourteenth century translator's and Groote's views.

Groote's interest in vernacular Bible study was pursued further by other early leaders associated with the *Devotio Moderna*. One such person was John Cele, Groote's closest friend and disciple, who became rector at the city school of Zwolle in 1374 or 1375 and remained there until his death in 1415. Neither a Brother of the Common Life nor an Augustinian cleric, Cele may still be treated as a sympathetic affiliate of the *Devotio Moderna* for two reasons.[54] First, his close friendship with Groote produced more than a strong emotional bond; a community of ideas and goals is also obvious. Secondly, Cele's work at Zwolle brought him into close contact with the Brothers of the Common Life in that town, who established a house there and shared the rector's zeal for educational reform.[55]

It was Cele's position as rector at Zwolle which enabled him to put into practice many of the educational views held by Groote. In this context, Groote's strong disapproval of Cele's proposal to abandon his rectorship and enter a Franciscan monastery is meaningful.[56] Cele was

---

[52] *Ibid.*

[53] For example, from the *Conclusa et proposita*, see above, p. 108.

[54] Post, *Modern Devotion*, p. 16, objects to the treatment of Cele as a member of affiliate of the *Devotio Moderna* because the school of Zwolle was not a brethren school.

[55] An account of the activities of the Zwolle house may be found in M. Schoengen (ed.), *Jacobus Traiecti alias de Voecht narratio de inchoatione domus clericorum in Zwollis*, Amsterdam, 1908, and the most complete study of the school at Zwolle is M. Schoengen, *Die Schule von Zwolle von ihren Anfängen bis zu dem Auftreten des Humanismus*, Freiburg, 1898.

[56] van Zijl, *Gerard Groote*, pp. 192-193.

very much Groote's apostle to the lay world, as represented by the school-boys whom Cele instructed. As Groote's apostle, Bible study was the focus of Cele's educational program. He recommended study of the entire Bible, and to facilitate private study oral readings from the Bible took place three times a day.[57] In the mornings, the Epistles were read; in the afternoons the Gospels; and in the evenings the Old Testament.[58] During each reading, students were advised to write down parts of the Bible which seemed relevant to them, as a means of compiling a collection of individually significant passages into their personal meditation books for private use.[59] Hyma [60]has seen this exercise as the origin of the *rapiarium*, defined as a collection of excerpts of personal importance for private devotion. The *Imitatio Christi*[61] is one such book, and *rapiaria* are generally viewed as characterizing the form of personal piety for which the *Devotio Moderna* became known. That such texts had their origin as devotional exercises on the Bible suggests the considerable importance attached to the Bible for private meditation.

Not all Bible study in the school at Zwolle was conducted in Latin. In fact, students were taught to pray in both Dutch and Latin.[62] More-over, some sessions in the school were conducted entirely in the vernacular, primarily for the benefit of the inhabitants of Zwolle who were invited to attend Cele's "weekend classes."[63] Cele urged farmers and townspeople to read the Bible in their own tongue, and difficult passages would then be elucidated during his discourses.[64] And the majority of Cele's sermons, probably directed towards the townspeople which have survived are in Dutch.[65] In Cele's work, then, Groote's theoretical views and individual practice became established on a wider scale. The Bible was the most important study book; its reading in the vernacular was not only tolerated but encouraged; and the end of this study was a form of private devotion.

---

[57] Hyma, *The Christian Renaissance*, p. 93.

[58] *Ibid.*

[59] Grube (ed.), *Chronicon Windeshemense*, p. 207.

[60] Hyma, *The Christian Renaissance*, p. 96. The *Chronicon Windeshemense*, p. 207, does in fact term the study books compiled by Cele's students as rapiaria.

[61] Translated and edited by George Maine, *Thomas à Kempis The Imitation of Christ*, London, 1957.

[62] Grube (ed.), *Chronicon Windeshemense*, p. 214. Two versions — one Dutch and one Latin — of a prayer recited by Cele's students are given in the chronicle.

[63] Hyma, *The Christian Renaissance*, p. 94.

[64] *Ibid.*

[65] Published in de Vries, *Duutsche sermoenen*.

Groote's theoretical views on vernacular Bible study and Cele's practical execution of these undoubtedly represent a fundamental and widespread characteristic of the *Devotio Moderna* during its first quarter century of existence. But, they were not without opposition. In fact, opposition had haunted the movement and its leaders almost from the beginning. In 1383, the Bishop of Utrecht, Florent van Wevelinckhoven, issued an edict prohibiting Groote's preaching in the bishopric.[66] Much of the opposition was based at least ostensibly on the assumption that the communities of the *Devotio Moderna* were unlawful, like those of the Beguines and Beghards before them, since they had no official religious affiliation. Opposition continued until 1418 when a Dominican, Mathew Grabow, presented a long treatise to the Council of Constance attacking the movement.[67] Among Grabow's criticisms was one directed towards the use of vernacular scriptural texts within the movement. In 1418, Grabow was censured by the Council, and the *Devotio Moderna* was granted official sanction by the Church,[68] sanction which encompassed their use of vernacular Bibles.

The support of the Council was not won without effort, and it was with a view to winning their approbation that Gerard Zerbolt of Zutphen wrote his treatise on the Brothers of the Common Life, one chapter of which defends the use of vernacular books.[69] Gerard's treatise, *Super modo vivendi*, is a stylized, extremely erudite, well-reasoned argument which reads as though written for an unsympathetic audience. Each point is supported by a statement from an authority corroborating its validity. Most frequent among the authorities are the Bible, but Augustine, Jerome, Hugh of St. Victor, and Canon Law are also quoted with regularity. Only one Latin manuscript of this text has survived,[70] a fact which also suggests a very specific and learned audience for Gerard's original treatise.

The arguments set forth in the treatise in favor of vernacular translations of the Bible are extensive. Throughout the work, Gerard cites Church Fathers who permitted, even encouraged, the reading of the

---

[66] The edict did not specifically ban Groote; it simply restricted preaching to priests, excluding deacons, which Groote was. The opposition to Groote and the reasons for it are discussed by van Zijl, *Gerard Groote*, pp. 293-328.

[67] *Ibid.*, p. 298.

[68] *Ibid.*, pp. 298, 333.

[69] Published by Hyma, *NAK*, 17, pp. 42-70.

[70] Nuremberg, Stadtbibliothek, Ms. Centuria II, no. 10.

Bible. Furthermore, he cites a passage from Canon Law where heretics are urged to read the Bible in order to mend their ways.[71] That such reading may be in the vernacular is deduced by Gerard from historical factors. Since the entire Bible, with the possible exception of the Epistles of Paul, was written in a language other than Latin, what possible reason, Gerard asks, can there be for stipulating that only a Latin reading is permissible now.[72] Moreover, he points out that in the early stages of Christianity the Hebrews had a Hebrew Bible, the Greeks a Greek one, and so forth.[73] And, all early missionaries translated the Bible into the language of the people whom they hoped to convert.[74] There is not, Gerard reasons, an original tradition of only a Latin Bible, so therefore a prohibition against Dutch Bibles is invalid.[75] Gerard also goes to great length to refute an accusation that the Dutch Bibles contain *novitates et curiositates*, assuring his reader that they are strictly canonical.[76] And, he argues that the laity should, in fact, be exhorted to read the vernacular Bible, for if they were forbidden to read it, they might in fact read none at all, like the heathens whom the missionaries attempted to convert.[77]

However, Gerard did not consider the entire Bible suitable for reading by the laity, for he felt that it contained too many difficult sections. While the birth, life, and death of Christ was readily comprehensible to the layman, the simple man did not possess sufficient knowledge to understand the books of the Old Testament, the Prophets, and the Apocalypse.[78] Nevertheless, such passages were not to be censored, but rather accompanied by explanatory glosses. Although the identity of such a commentary suitable for the layman is not given, Petrus Comestor's *Historia Scholastica* would be a likely candidate. Contained in the *Super modo vivendi*, then, is an explicit statement not only of the importance of the vernacular Bible for laymen but also of the necessity of accompanying the vernacular scriptures with a Dutch commentary. And the biblical sections considered difficult to understand by Gerard are those very ones which do indeed appear with their appropriate commentaries in the First History Bibles.

---

[71] Hyma, *NAK*, 17, p. 47.
[72] *Ibid.*, pp. 55-56.
[73] *Ibid.*, pp. 57-58.
[74] *Ibid.*
[75] *Ibid.*, p. 56.
[76] *Ibid.*, pp. 62-63.
[77] *Ibid.*, p. 58.
[78] Deschamps, *Handelingen Koninklijke Zuidnederlandse Maatschappij*, 14, p. 90.

Gerard's views on vernacular Bible translations continued to circulate throughout the fifteenth century, though not in Latin and not even precisely in their original form. Many extant manuscripts commonly called the *Super modo vivendi* are simply translated excerptions from the treatise of the chapter on vernacular books;[79] the remaining defense on the Brothers of the Common Life is omitted. And some translations, like one in Vienna (Oesterreichische Nationalbibliothek, Ms. 13708),[80] have been discovered inserted between other vernacular texts. The Vienna manuscript contains Dutch texts of Groote, Ruysbroec, and Maerlant, in addition to the translation from *Super modo vivendi* and Hyma[81] has suggested that this inclusion was an attempt by the copyist to justify to his readers the reading of vernacular sacred writings.

The sanction received from the Council of Constance in 1418 must not have dispelled all doubts on the permissability of reading the Scripture in Dutch. One translation of Gerard's chapter, dated as late as 1445,[82] introduces the treatise with the remarks that since doubts still persist on the use of vernacular texts, the writer has gathered together diverse texts in support of their reading. The existence of numerous other fifteenth century Dutch translations of this chapter from *Super modo vivendi* suggests that the production, ownership, and reading of vernacular Bibles remained a fundamental concern of the *Devotio Moderna* during this period. And its translation into Low German and repeated copying in Germany[83] probably reflects the *Devotio Moderna's* activity in that country as well, for we know that the most extensive influence of the movement outside The Netherlands was in Germany.[84]

Alterations and modifications made in the fifteenth century translations of Gerard's treatise are suggestive of the audience for whom this translation was made, as well as that for whom the vernacular Bibles

---

[79] C. G. N. de Vooys, "De Dietse tekst van het traktaat: 'De libris teutonicalibus,'" *Nederlandsch Archief voor Kerkgeschiedenis* 4 (1907), pp. 117-134, and Deschamps, *Handelingen Koninklijke Zuidnederlandse Maatschappij*, 14, pp. 67-108.

[80] Published by de Vooys, *NAK*, 4, pp. 117-134.

[81] A. Hyma, "Is Gerard Zerbolt of Zutphen the Author of the 'Super modo vivendi'?" *Nederlandsch Archief voor Kerkgeschiedenis* 16 (1921), pp. 107-128.

[82] Utrecht, Bibliotheek der Rijksuniversiteit, Ms. 3 L 6 in Deschamps, *Handelingen Koninklijke Zuidnederlandse Maatschappij*, 14, p. 99: "Want sommige twivel maken of et behoerlic si dat leke lude die heilige scrifte lesen ende of et gheoerloft si die in duytscher tale te hebben."

[83] Hyma, *The Christian Renaissance*, p. 116.

[84] On the *Devotio Moderna* in Germany see I. Crusius, *Die Brüder vom gemeinsamen Leben in Deutschland*, Göttingen, 1956.

were intended. The *Super modo vivendi* referred generally to the laity as those who should be encouraged to read the Bible in the vernacular.[85] But in the fifteenth century, the categories of readers were specified more fully. Most of the manuscripts refer to both the "laity and the unlearned,"[86] suggesting another group of readers who are not specifically laity. This group may, in fact, have been the schoolchildren whose reading of vernacular Bibles is used as a justification for the use of such books in the introduction to one of the translations executed by Dirc van Herxen (Nijmegen, Bibliotheek van het Berchmanianum, M. IIa).[87] Another translation of the treatise suggests a use by lay sisters attached to a convent. This manuscript (Utrecht, Universiteits Bibliotheek, Ms. 3L6),[88] dated 1445, belonged to the cloister of St. Agatha in Amersfoort. The additions in it to Gerard's text contain historical references to the use of vernacular texts by other lay personages, such as the hermits in the wilderness addressed by Augustine.[89]

The existence of these fifteenth century translations of Gerard Zerbolt's treatise not only testifies to the continuing use of vernacular scriptural texts within the Netherlands, but also to their use by schoolchildren and lay brothers and sisters. That scriptural translation activity to fill this need did not cease in the fifteenth century is suggested by the work of Johannes Schutken (died 1423), librarian at Windesheim.[90] The *Chronicon Windeshemense* praises Schutken as a fine and active copyist, a learned student of the Holy Scripture, and an outstanding translator in the vernacular.[91] Furthermore, we learn that Schutken translated the Epistles and Gospels for the whole year, in other words the Pericopes, the Psalter, and numerous other works of the Church Fathers.[92] Two reasons are presented in the chronicle for Schutken's translation interests. First, in his position as head of the scriptorium he desired uniform texts for the purpose of copying manuscripts in the scriptorium.[93] And, secondly, in his role as *consilarius* to the monks and lay brothers, he hoped to enhance their understanding of the scripture.[94]

---

[85] Hyma, *NAK*, 17, p. 45.

[86] Deschamps, *Handelingen Koninklijke Zuidnederlandse Maatschappij*, p. 78.

[87] *Ibid.*, p. 77.

[88] *Ibid.*, pp. 99-108.

[89] *Ibid.*, p. 100.

[90] Acquoy, *Klooster te Windesheim*, I, pp. 280-289.

[91] Grube (ed.), *Chronicon Windeshemense*, p. 192.

[92] *Ibid.*

[93] *Ibid.*

[94] *Ibid.*

Like other members of the *Devotio Moderna*, Schutken viewed the role of scriptural books as the most important factor in personal devotion. Before him, Cele had once remarked that the church would have perished long ago if it had not been for good books or Sacred writings.[95] And, according to Hyma,[96] Gerard Zerbolt went so far as to state that the reading of good books was more profitable than the use of the sacraments or listening to sermons.

While the writings of leaders of the *Devotio Moderna* suggest a continuing interest in vernacular Bible reading from the late fourteenth through the fifteenth centuries, documentary evidence testifies to the actual possession and use of such books. Composed shortly after 1409, the *Consuetudines*[97] of the Zwolle house of the Brothers of the Common Life designate the time and manner of Bible reading there:

> Festivis diebus, postquam divina officia in ecclesia fuerint de vespera expleta, de bona consuetudine consuerent ad domum nostram venire scholares et alii boni, viri causa spiritualis instructionis, quibus legeretur in teutonico aliquis passus Sacre Scripture de materia plana, que ad emendationem vite eos poterit provocare, videlicet de viciis, de virtutibus, de contemptu mundi, de timore Dei et similibus.[98]

According to the *Consuetudines* students, who are perhaps school boys, and other good men came to the house on Sundays and feast days to hear passages of the Bible read in Dutch. Another document records the possession in monasteries of vernacular Bibles as late as 1508. The printed Constitutions of the Augustinian Canons Regular[99] specify ownership in monastic libraries of a vernacular Bible with the commentary from the *Historia Scholastica*,[100] a description to which the text of the First History Bible conforms.

The presence and use of vernacular Bibles in the houses of the lay Brothers of the Common Life is not too surprising. Educational reform tended to be a chief interest in these houses, and education of the laity was achieved by the Brothers through their schools and their copying

---

[95] Hyma, *The Christian Renaissance*, p. 96.

[96] Hyma, *NAK*, 17, p. 44.

[97] Published by Schoengen (ed.), *Jacobus Traiecti*, pp. 243-248.

[98] *Ibid.*, p. 247.

[99] *Constitutiones fratrum heremitarum sancti Augustini*, Venice, 1508, and Joannes Staupitz, *Constitutiones fratum heremitarum sancti Augustini*, 1505.

[100] *Constitutiones fratrum heremitarum sancti Augustini*, Venice, 1508, c. xxxvii and *Constitutiones fratrum heremitarum sancti Augustini*, 1505, c. 37, f.e. vii, r, cited by Axters, *Vroomheid*, III, p. 353.

and dissemination of manuscripts.[101] Moreover, the Brothers of the Common Life, themselves, were lay; they were never officially affiliated with a monastic order, although they maintained a sympathetic rapport with the Windesheim Congregation's monasteries of the Augustinian Canons Regular.

But, the possession and use of vernacular Bibles in monastic houses are somewhat more surprising. It has already been mentioned that many monastic libraries maintained a separate Netherlandish collection, the manuscripts of which were designated as *studierboeken*. And, some monasteries had two distinct positions available in the library: a librarian of Dutch books and one of Latin books.[102] Such collections were probably maintained for the lay brothers affiliated with the monasteries, for the monks themselves could undoubtedly read Latin. Some clarification is provided by the monastic Constitutions of Windesheim which designated that oral recitation *alta voce teutonice* of the seven penitential psalms was to be conducted for the lay brothers and the converts.[103] The collections of Dutch books probably fulfilled the same function as Dutch recitation; they were provided for the spiritual edification of these lay groups.

Conclusions

From a consideration of the evidence surrounding the *Devotio Moderna*, it seems probable that the extensive copying of vernacular Bibles, to which the number of extant manuscripts attests, was a response to the religious concerns of that movement. Certainly, the possession of unillustrated exemplars of the First History Bible by Windesheim monasteries and cloisters is explainable by the *Devotio Moderna's* interest in the education of lay monks and nuns and religious converts. Such exemplars include the Bible written at Groenendaal (The Hague, Koninklijke Bibliotheek, Ms. 129 C 2) and the one from Marienborch at Nijmegen (The Hague, Koninklijke Bibliotheek, Ms. 75 E 7). Other copies of the First History Bibles which do not contain clues to their original prove-

---

[101] On the Brothers' role in education in The Netherlands see R. R. Post, *Scholen en onderwijs in Nederland gedurende de Middeleeuwen*, Utrecht, 1954.

[102] Meinsma, *Middeleeuwsche Bibliotheken*, p. 147. Johannes Schutken, for example, was *librarius librorum teutonicorum* at Windesheim according to Grube (ed.), *Chronicon Windeshemense*, p. 192.

[103] Cited in W. Moll (ed.), "Geert Groote's Dietsche vertalingen," *Verhandelingen der Koninklijke Akademie van Wetenschappen, Afd. Letterkunde* 13 (1880), p. 33.

nance may well have belonged to the houses of the Brothers of the Common Life, particularly those which ran schools.

Just how widespread the influence of the *Devotio Moderna's* interest in the vernacular Bible was is difficult to assess. It seems to have reached monasteries beyond the confines of the Windesheim Congregation, as possession of vernacular Bibles by non-Windesheim foundations suggests. The cloister of St. Margriet in Gouda which owned two vernacular Bibles (Utrecht, Bibliotheek der Rijksuniversiteit, Ms. 5 E 6 and The Hague, Koninklijke Bibliotheek, deposit K. A. XXXII) was an Augustinian foundation, so it is not surprising that some of its practices correspond with those of the Augustinian Windesheim foundations. Moreover, the cloister was located in Gouda, a town where much *Devotio Moderna* activity took place primarily through the efforts of the Brothers of the Common Life who had a brethren house and ran an active school there.[104] The ownership by non-Windesheim cloisters of two other exemplars of the First History Bible suggests that the use of vernacular Bibles in such foundations was not restricted to *Devotio Moderna* ones, although it did originate there.

Other manuscripts of the First History Bible were owned by the laity and we do not know, for the most part, whether these owners had any particular connections with the *Devotio Moderna*. But in the case of the Lochorst family who seem to have been the patrons of two illustrated First History Bibles,[105] there are demonstrable connections with the *Devotio Moderna* affiliated monastery of the Oude Gracht in Utrecht. In 1415, following a battle over the Utrecht Schism, Herman van Lochorst, deacon of the Cathedral, and his brother Gijsbrecht sought refuge within the walls of the monastery.[106] Herman maintained his ties with the Augustinians, for in 1431 when he refused to accept an order from the Council of Basel to tone down his behavior, the monks attempted to persuade him to comply.[107] Finally, in 1432, at the request of the monks, he met the Council's demands and retrieved his position as deacon of Utrecht Cathedral until his death in 1438.[108]

Herman van Lochorst's ownership of vernacular Bibles suggests that

---

[104] A brief discussion of the origin and development of the house in Gouda is found in Post, *Modern Devotion*, pp. 403-406.

[105] See above, p. 100.

[106] L. Schmedding, *De regeering van Frederik van Blankenheim*, Leiden, 1899, p. 87.

[107] *Nieuw Nederlandsch Biografisch Woordenboek*, Leiden, 1912, II, pp. 830-831.

[108] *Ibid.*, p. 831.

their ownership, if not their reading, may have been relatively common. It is true that his connections with the *Devotio Moderna* may have inspired his commissioning of such books, but his position does not qualify him under any of the general categories of the population for whom vernacular Bible reading was recommended. He was lay, but his university education and ecclesiastical position certainly required a reading knowledge of Latin. Other lay owners of the vernacular Bibles, particularly the more luxurious illustrated ones, may have held positions in society similar to Herman van Lochorst's, such as Claes Peterszoon. The *Devotio Moderna*, then, seems to have been responsible for a general religious milieu responsive to vernacular scriptural texts. School children, lay affiliates of Windesheim monasteries, and religious converts — all connected with the *Devotio Moderna* — did possess and use such texts. However, it seems their ownership and reading extended to laity outside the immediate circle of the *Devotio Moderna*. This phenomenon witnesses the establishment of a general religious climate in the North Netherlands influenced, at least in regards to vernacular Bible reading, by the spiritual sentiments of the *Devotio Moderna*.

CHAPTER FIVE

CONCLUSIONS

This investigation of the illustrated vernacular Dutch First History Bibles has demonstrated that both text and illustration acted as inter-related units in each manuscript. In the text of these vernacular manu-scripts the literal meaning of the Scripture was emphasized by the choice of Petrus Comestor's *Historia Scholastica* as the accompanying commen-tary. The close correspondence in contents between the text and the miniatures certainly suggests that the illustrations were conceived as pictorial restatements of the biblical text and its commentary. More-over, the particular system of illustration used in the Bibles further en-hanced the importance of the literal meaning of the Scripture. In narra-tive illustrations, the biblical stories were recounted fully and accurately without apocryphal intrusions. Realistic features, an emerging charac-teristic of contemporary European art, were introduced freely into the Bible miniatures so that the stories in the text would be more readily comprehensible to the readers.

The extensive popularity of the First History Bible, as evidenced by the large number of extant manuscripts, is attributable to *Devotio Moderna* activity. Affiliates of the Windesheim Congregation and schools of the Brothers of the Common Life rank high among the documented users of the First History Bibles. And, the textual and pictorial contents of the manuscripts conform to the ideals of this religious movement. The Bible itself was the "study book" most frequently prescribed as devotional reading material by members of the movement, and commentaries were recommended only to elucidate unclear portions of the biblical narra-tive. Realistic narrative illustrations served the purpose, in part, of familiarizing readers with otherwise remote historical events and per-sons. The fact that production of these manuscripts ceased after 1475 does not imply that the text fell into disuse. Rather, their printing after this date filled a continuing need for these texts in the North Nether-lands, a need still at least partially within circles of the *Devotio Moderna*.

A similar investigation of the relation between text and illustration would certainly be useful when applied to other types of texts produced in The Netherlands. Illustrated Books of Hours, Passion texts, and apoc-

alyptic cycles all contain unusual iconographic features often characterized as "Dutch." Yet, little is known about the origin of such features.

In Dutch Books of Hours, the Hours of the Virgin are frequently
illustrated with events from the Passion, rather than the life of the Virgin
which was more common elsewhere.[1] Moreover, one standard religious
illustration is often juxtaposed to an everyday scene on the facing folio,
as occurs in the Hours of Engelbert of Nassau (Bodleian Library, Douce
Ms. 219-220)[2] and in a British Library Hours (Add. Ms. 30003).[3] In
Passion texts, representations such as the spike-block hanging from
Christ's waist, in addition to other details of physical cruelty, often
occur.[4] Periodically, these details appear in Books of Hours, transposed
from their original placement in Passion texts. And Dutch apocalyptic
cycles, like the Paris Picture Book Apocalypse (Bibliothèque nat., fonds
néerl. 3) and the Brussels Bible apocalypse[5] have been cited as containing
unusual iconographic features.

A detailed analysis of the texts in these types of books might demonstrate that such books were conceived with a thoroughly integrated system
of text and illustration, as were the Dutch First History Bibles. Marrow's
exploratory investigations along these lines have indeed pointed to a
close relation between text and illustration. He has demonstrated that
John the Baptist's attribute of the lantern, another characteristically
"Dutch" feature appearing in Books of Hours, Breviaries, and even panel
paintings, does have a textual basis.[6] And its textual source exists in both
the Dutch Breviary and Book of Hours, those very manuscripts which
contain John the Baptist with a Lantern miniatures. In addition, Marrow has shown that the peculiar features of Dutch Passion iconography
derive from Dutch Passion texts some with accompanying miniatures.[7]
Further studies of the relation between text and illustration, for example

---

[1] Delaissé, *Gatherings in Honor of Dorothy E. Miner*, p. 210.

[2] Alexander, *Hours of Engelbert of Nassau*, Pls. 73-76.

[3] Marrow, *NKJ*, pp. 55-114.

[4] Mentioned in Pickering, *Literature and Art*, pp. 281-285, and examined in detail by
J. Marrow, *From Sacred Allegory to Descriptive Narrative: Transformations of Passion Iconography in the Late Middle Ages*, Columbia University, 1974 (unpublished doctoral dissertation).

[5] The peculiarities of this apocalyptic cycle are mentioned by Delaissé, *Dutch Manuscript Illumination*, pp. 35-36, who further states that it is clear that the miniatures betray
a close reading of the accompanying text.

[6] James Marrow, "John the Baptist, Lantern for the Lord: New Attributes for the
Baptist from the Northern Netherlands," *Oud Holland* 83 (1968), pp. 3-12.

[7] Marrow, *NKJ*, pp. 55-114.

involving a close perusal of the apocalypse commentaries or the prayers contained in various Hours, may well yield more evidence of this relation.

The reason for this close relation between text and illustration in Dutch books — Hours, Passion texts, and Breviaries, as well as vernacular Bibles — may well be found in the devotional aims and practices of the *Devotio Moderna*. While the recent trend in scholarship has been to minimize this movement's effect on manuscript production in The Netherlands,[8] it now seems that the role it played, at least in Bible production and use, was significant. Certainly, vernacular Books of Hours from the North Netherlands must have been vehicles for reaching the laity, as were the Bibles. Recent research has proved that the majority of extant Books of Hours follow as "use of Windesheim" formerly thought to be "use of Utrecht."[9] If, in fact, such books were tools of the Windesheim Congregation and the Brothers of the Common Life, it is likely that their systems of illustration would have features in common with the Dutch vernacular Bibles. Given the aims of the movement discussed above, it is particularly probable that the illustrations would serve similarly as restatements of the text.

It has not been the purpose of this study to explore fully questions of localization and number of workshops, the identity and separation of miniaturists, and the relation of the vernacular Bibles to other Dutch manuscripts. These three important questions require a complete codicological study of the manuscripts before conclusions can be advanced. Nevertheless, information contained in parts of this study and data found in the Appendix does throw some light on these intriguing questions. Thus, certain preliminary observations can be presented which hopefully may facilitate future research.

Codicological data, which can best be used to determine the number of workshops, are strikingly diverse. Physical features of the manuscripts, such as material, size, and format, vary from book to book. (See Appendix I) While the pen-drawn Munich Bible, for example, is executed on paper, the pen-drawn Lochorst Bible is on parchment, as are the majority of the illustrated exemplars. Some unillustrated codices are even executed on both parchment and paper, with leaves of either material used

---

[8] Particularly in Marrow, *Medium Aevum*, pp. 251-255, and Post, *Modern Devotion*.

[9] F. Gorissen, "Das Stundenbuch im rheinischen Niederland," *Studien zur klevische Musik und Liturgiegeschichte. Beiträge zur rheinischen Musikgeschichte* 75 (1968), pp. 63-109.

apparently randomly throughout the manuscripts. Likewise, the size of
the manuscripts are infinitely varied; no two books have uniform mea-
surements. Moreover, three types of gothic script commonly used during
the period are employed in the Bibles. The Munich Bible uses a *cursiva*
script; the Lochorst, Nuremberg, and The Hague Bibles use *hybrida*; and
the London Bible uses *textualis*.[10]

Normally, some standardization of production, evident in the consistency of the secondary features of the manuscripts, may be expected
in a prolific workshop. This is the case, for example, in Burgundian
centers of production and in many French ones of the period.[11] However,
such variations in the First History Bibles do not necessarily imply that a
different workshop was responsible for each manuscript. Dutch manuscript production has been proven to be less systematic and regularized
than its European counterparts.[12] And the advertising placard of Herman Strepel, a professional scribe, stating his proficiency in three types
of script, proves that one atelier or individual could easily master diverse
techniques.[13]

There is one feature of the Bibles which argues for the possibility of a
small number of workshops, namely their format which is similar in
three respects. First, they all utilize two columns to the page with illustrations inserted within the text. Secondly, the break in the text for
insertion of the miniatures occurs at approximately the same position in
various groups of manuscripts. And, thirdly, the number of illustrations
is uniform in various groups of manuscripts.

Detailed analysis of the textual breaks for the mniniatures and of the
number of miniatures permits more precise speculation on the number of
workshops. On the basis of the number of illustrations used for a com-
parable portion of the text, the Bibles divide into three groups. The first
group is made up of the Munich and Lochorst Bibles which have 114 and

---

[10] The nomenclature followed is that proposed by G. I. Lieftinck in "Pour une
nomenclature de l'écriture livresque de la période dite gothique," *Nomenclature des écri-
tures livresques du IXe au XVIe siècle. Premier Colloque International de Paléographie Latine*, Paris,
1953, pp. 15-34 (Colloques internationaux du Centre national de la recherche scientifi-
que. Science humaines, 4).

[11] The Burgundian centers are discussed in Delaissé, *Le siècle d'or*, and the French ones
in Delaissé, *Gatherings in Honor of Dorothy E. Miner*.

[12] Delaissé, *Dutch Manuscript Illumination*, pp. 20-22.

[13] B. Kruitwagen, "De Munstersche schrijfmeester Herman Strepel (1447) en de
schriftsoorten van de Broeders van het Gemeene Leven en de Windesheimers, *Het Boek*
22 (1934), pp. 209-230, 23 (1935), pp. 1-54.

113 miniatures respectively for the biblical books from Genesis through Ruth. The second group is made up of The Hague, London, Brussels, and Nuremberg Bibles, which have denser cycles of illustration. The London and The Hague Bibles, for example, possess 147 and 154 illustrations for this section of the Bible, so their cycles are almost half again as lengthy. Similar comparisons prove a consistency in the number of illustrations in the other two Bibles. The third group consists only of the Vienna Bible which stands apart from the others in its number of illustrations, possessing only 21 miniatures illustrating Genesis through Ruth and containing a similarly shortened cycle for the remainder of the Bible.

The comparative number of illustrations suggests three Bible workshops, but further examination of the specific physical relation between text and illustration may indicate only two. Where the same portions of the text occur in the manuscripts belonging to group two — The Hague, London, Brussels, and Nuremberg Bibles — the break in the text for the insertion of the miniature occurs consistently in the exact same position. For example, the miniature of the *Slaying of Eglon by Ehud* occurs in The Hague, London, and Nuremberg Bibles (fols. 144v, 124v, and 15r) illustrating a passage from the book of Judges (3:21-24). In each of these three manuscripts the same sentence (Judges 3:27) is interrupted. Comparisons of miniature placement in the New Testament text of The Hague and Brussels Bibles supports the inclusion of the latter codex in this group.

A similar close relation exists between the Munich and Lochorst Bibles. The illustration of *Lamech Killing Cain* (Genesis 4:8) occurs in the middle of one sentence (Genesis 4:11) in both Bibles (fols. 10v and 17r respectively). The same subject occurs in every manuscript of both groups. Furthermore, its placement in the text in The Hague and London Bibles (fols. 10v and 9r) is within the same or a closely adjacent verse (Genesis 4:13 and 4:14). The *Lamech Killing Cain* is not an isolated case; miniatures in group one are found in group two in the same location with statistical frequency.

Therefore, it is possible that all manuscripts from groups one and two follow a single workshop exemplar. The Munich and Lochorst Bibles possess fewer miniatures but *every* miniature in them occurs at a position in the text which is also illustrated in the Bibles from the second group These two Bibles may simply be "economy editions" from the same workshop, possessing only two thirds the number of miniatures and executed for a less wealthy clientele. The fact that both books contain sketchy pen-and-ink drawings rather than painted miniatures further supports the possibility of their being more economical productions though they are by no means of inferior quality.

That a single Dutch workshop could have had enough diversity in production to execute two models of the same book — an economy and a luxury one — is further supported by the discrepancy in miniature subjects in the Munich and Lochorst Bibles. As mentioned above, both Bibles seem to emanate from one workshop, possessing near-identical texts, number of illustrations, and physical formats. Yet, frequently their subjects differ, with one manuscript illustrating a slightly preceding or following verse in the same location in the text. For example, in the Lochorst Bible in illustration of the book of Genesis (2:7), the miniature of the *Creation of Eve* (fol. 9v) replaces that of *God Enthroned* (fol. 6r) in the Munich Bible. Similarly, *Adam Naming the Animals* (fol. 12r) in the Lochorst Bible replaces the *Introduction of Adam and Eve* (fol. 7v) in the Munich Bible, both illustrating the same verse (Genesis 2:23). The extent to which miniatures with different subjects were substituted is great: the total number of subjects represented in all the Bibles exceeds by a denominator of two that contained in a complete Dutch Bible.

Whether such diversity in production techniques was due to the artists' own initiative, the overseers' directions, or the patrons' requests is an important question, but one which as yet is unanswered. Related to this is the identity or profession of the overseer. We still do not know whether a layman or an ecclesiastic directed and planned the miniature cycles; and, we also need to discover whether the workshops themselves were lay or monastic.

A discussion of the workshops and their procedure inevitably brings up the problem of the Bible artists, itself something of a "Pandora's box." Some of the miniaturists seem to have been regular employees of the workshops which produced the Bibles. These include Master "A" of the London Bible who appears also in the Brussels Bible, the so-called Claes Brouwer and the Alexander Master of the Brussels and The Hague Bibles, and one miniaturist of the Nuremberg Bible who worked on The Hague Bible as well. However, the work of others appears less frequently. The Master of Catherine of Cleves executed only eight superb miniatures in the second gathering of the Munich Bible, which was then ecompleted by a second-rate craftsman who it seems was only a one-time contributor. And the Lochorst Bible contains miniatures related to the style of the Master of Catherine of Cleves. Then, the Soudenbalch

Master executed the majority of illustrations in the Vienna Bible, though his work is found in none of the other manuscripts.

This breakdown of the more significant Bible miniaturists and the apparent division of their labor has certain ramifications for any theory on the number of workshops. It again suggests the possibility of three distinct ateliers. Artists who worked on The Hague, London, Brussels, and Nuremberg Bibles are interrelated. They parcelled out the execution of the miniatures to the point where the Alexander Master repeats his own compositions in both The Hague and Brussels Bibles. The Munich and Lochorst Bibles were illustrated by artists who took no part in the illustration of the preceding four Bibles, again suggesting the separation of these two from the other four. And, the fact that the style of the Master of Catherine of Cleves appears in both further supports a link between them. In all respects, the Soudenbalch Master's Vienna Bible remains separate from the other two groups, but the question of the precise relation between the other two groups remains open.

One further difference between the miniaturists working on each of the Bible groups is their degree of specialization. The artists of The Hague, London, Brussels, and Nuremberg Bibles were strictly Bible miniaturists; to my knowledge, their hands can be identified in no other manuscripts. On the other hand, both the Master of Catherine of Cleves and the Soudenbalch Master were responsible primarily for minaitures in manuscripts other than Bibles. The Master of Catherine of Cleves did the illustrations for the famous Cleves Hours and a Book of Hours in Leiden (Universiteitsbibliotheek, Ms. B. P. L. 224), to mention only a few examples; and the Soudenbalch Master is perhaps most renowned for his illustrations in the Hours of Mary of Vronensteyn.[14]

This brings up questions concerning the relation of the Bible miniatures to those in other Dutch manuscripts. To what extent are miniatures in the first group of manuscripts isolated expressions of individual compositions and particular styles? What stylistic and compositional elements did the Master of Catherine of Cleves already have in his artistic *repertoire* when he began work on the Munich Bible, and what did he borrow from Bible manuscripts for his later products? While some borrowings must have occurred, their exact nature has yet to be defined. Nevertheless, the fact that Breviaries and Books of Hours, such as the Breviary

---

[14] L. M. J. Delaissé, "Le livre d'Heures de Mary von Vronensteyn, chef-d'oeuvre inconnu d'un atelier d'Utrecht achevé en 1460," *Scriptorium* 3 (1949), pp. 230-245.

of Renald of Guelders and the Cleves Hours, possess cycles of illustration whose miniatures utilize primarily biblical episodes makes a search for such borrowings mandatory. For example, there appears to be an equal attention to and a similar use of literal-narrative biblical illustrations in the Cleves Hours, which in their context acquire more sophisticated iconographic meanings.

The problems of the Bible workshops, miniaturists, and manuscript interrelationships still present considerable difficulties. However, some of these problems, like the number of workshops, can be elucidated through a study of the relation between text and illustration. Moreover, it is hoped that a detailed characterization of the Dutch Bibles as integrated written and illustrated books and an explication of the religious milieu which produced them provides a more solid historical framework in which to deal with such problems. Other texts, such as Books of Hours, Breviaries, Passion tracts, and apocalyptic cycles, might well benefit from a similar approach. Eventually, the treatment of Dutch manuscripts as integrated books in their historical setting may be coupled with a consideration of the more conventional art historical problems to develop a complete history of Dutch manuscript production.

APPENDIX

LIST AND DESCRIPTION OF MANUSCRIPTS

Amsterdam, Koninklijk Oudheidkundig Genootschap, Ms. 9
Brussels, Bibliothèque royale, Mss. 9018-19, 9020-23
Brussels, Bibliothèque royale, Ms. II 2409
Brussels, Bibliothèque royale, Ms. II 3398
Ghent, Bibliotheek der Rijksuniversiteit, Ms. 429
Ghent, Bibliotheek der Rijksuniversiteit, Ms. 430
The Hague, Koninklijke Bibliotheek, Ms. K.A. XXXII
The Hague, Koninklijke Bibliotheek, Ms. 78 D 38
The Hague, Koninklijke Bibliotheek, Ms. 78 D 39
The Hague, Koninklijke Bibliotheek, Ms. 75 E 7
The Hague, Koninklijke Bibliotheek, Ms. 128 C 2
The Hague, Koninklijke Bibliotheek, Ms. 129 C 3
The Hague, Koninklijke Bibliotheek, Ms. 133 D 31
The Hague, Museum Meermanno-Westreenianum, Ms. 10 A 18-19
Leiden, Bibliotheek der Rijksuniversiteit, Ms. Ltk. 232
Leiden, Bibliotheek der Rijksuniversiteit, Ms. Ltk. 234
Leiden, Bibliotheek der Rijksuniversiteit, Ms. Ltk. 1128
London, British Library, Add. Ms. 10043
London, British Library, Add. Ms. 15310-11
London, British Library, Add. Ms. 15410
London, British Library, Add. Ms. 16951
London, British Library, Add. Ms. 38122
London, Dutch Church, Austin Friars, Ms. 9
Middelburg, Zeeuws Genootschap voor Wetenschappen
Munich, Bayerische Staatsbibliothek, Cod. germ. 1102
Munich, Bayerische Staatsbibliothek, Cod. germ. 5062
Munich, Bayerische Staatsbibliothek, Cod. germ. 5150-51
Nijmegen, Museum van Oudheden, Ms. 12
Nuremberg, Stadtbibliothek, Ms. Solger 8⁰
Oxford, Bodleian Library, Ms. Add. B 26
Paris, Bibliothèque nationale, Ms. néerl. 38
Rotterdam, Gemeentebibliotheek, Ms. 96 B 2-3
Utrecht, Bibliotheek der Rijksuniversiteit, Ms. 5 E 6
Utrecht, Bibliotheek der Rijksuniversiteit, Ms. 4 E 3
Utrecht, Bibliotheek der Rijksuniversiteit, Ms. 2 B 13
Vienna, Oesterreichische Nationalbibliothek, Ms. 2771-72

Amsterdam, The Netherlands
Koninklijk Oudheidkundig Genootschap, Ms. 9

General Informaton
First History Bible (Genesis, Exodus, Leviticus, Numbers, Deuteronomy, Joshua,
    Judges, Ruth, I-IV Kings)

1 volume (205 fols)
parchment
ca. 1445
Utrecht
12 miniatures

Provenance
Gift to the Oudheidkundig Genootschap from D. Henriquez de Castro

*Bibliography**
Ebbinge Wubben, *Middelnederlandsche vertalingen*, no. 8, p. 16
Byvanck and Hoogewerff, *La miniature hollandaise*, no. 61, pp. 29-30

Brussels, Bibliothèque royale, Mss. 9018-19, 9020-23

General Information
First History Bible (I: Legend of Alexander, Maccabees I-II, Jean Hyrcan,
    Destruction of Jerusalem, Cyrus, Judith, Esther, Job, Proverbs, Ecclesiastes,
    Song of Songs, Book of Wisdom, Ecclesiasticus; II: Ezekiel, Daniel, Habak-
    kuk, Gospels, Acts, Letters, Apocalypse, The Prophets, Psalter)
2 volumes (126 and 181 fols.)
parchment
1431
Utrecht
243 miniatures (96 and 147)

Provenance
fol. 126v (I): Claes Peterszoon 1431
fol. 1r (I and II): Ce volume, enlevé de la Bibliothèque royale de Bourgogne
    après la prise de Bruxelles en 1746, et qui depuis lors a été placé dans la
    Bibliothèque du Roi à Paris, a été restitué par la France et replacé à
    Bruxelles dans la Bibliothèque de Bourgogne le 7 juin 1770

Bibliography
J. van den Gheyn, *Catalogue des manuscrits de la Bibliothèque royale de Belgique*, Vol. I:
    Écriture sainte et liturgie, Brussels, 1901, no. 108, pp. 52-55
Ebbinge Wubben, *Middelnederlandsche vertalingen*, no. 16, pp. 27-28
Byvanck and Hoogewerff, *La miniature hollandaise*, no. 29, pp. 16-17

Brussels, Bibliothèque royale, Ms. II 2409

General Information
First History Bible (Prologue, Genesis, Exodus, Leviticus, Numbers, Deuterono-
    my, Joshua, Judges, I-IV Kings)

---

* Bibliographical entries include only references to the manuscripts in the collection
catalogues and in the chief philological and art historical sources which contain catalogue
entries.

1 volume (438 fols.)
parchment
1412
South Netherlands
no illustrations

Provenance
fol. 354v: Dese voerscreven boec der bibelen wert volscreven int jaer ons Heren
doen men screef xiiii^c ende xii opten xiii^{en} dach in december, ende hi hoert
toe den beslotenen cloester van der derder regulen sinte Franciscus ghe-
heeten Syon binnen die stat van Liere.
Flyleaf: Purchased 1900 from Martin Nijhoff

Bibliography
van den Gheyn, *Catalogue des manuscrits*, no. 109, pp. 55-56
Ebbinge Wubben, *Middelnederlandsche vertalingen*, no. 2, pp. 10-11

Brussels, Bibliothèque royale, Ms. II 3398

General Information
First History Bible (Genesis, Exodus, Leviticus, Numbers, Deuteronomy)
1 volume (303 fols.)
parchment
1462
North Netherlands
no illustrations

Provenance
fol. 303r: Int jaer des heyligher gheboert ons liefs Heren Jesu Christi doe men
screef dusent vierhundert ende twe ende sestich doe waert dit boeck volscreven op sinte Remeys avont
fol. 303r: Anno 1462
fol. 1r: Capucinorum Trajectensium Dono Consul im Domini Henrici Stas 1704
fol. 1r: Ad usum p.p. Capucinorum Munster-blisiensium
fol. 2r: unidentified shield over which *hubrecht* is written

Bibliography

Ghent, Bibliotheek der Rijksuniversiteit, Ms. 429

General Information
First History Bible (Prologue, Genesis, Exodus, Leviticus, Numbers, Deuteronomy, Joshua, Judges, Ruth, I-IV Kings, Prayer of Manasses, Tobias,
Ezekiel, Daniel, Habakkuk)
1 volume (314 fols.)
paper
ca. 1400

South Netherlands
no miniatures

Provenance
Flyleaf: Memoria fratris Gisleni Baelde quam reliquit Bibliothecae Augustinia-
nae Gandensi, 11ᵃ januarii 1648

Bibliography
Jules de Saint-Genois, *Catalogue méthodique et raisonné des manuscrits de la Ville et de
l'Université de Gand*, Ghent, 1849-1852
Ebbinge Wubben, *Middelnederlandsche vertalingen*, no. 1, pp. 8-9

Ghent, Bibliotheek der Rijksuniversiteit, Ms. 430

General Information
First History Bible (I-III Maccabees, Gospels, Acts, Letters, Apocalypse,
Prophets, Letters of the Saints, Destruction of Jerusalem, Table of Contents,
Psalter)
1 volume (292 fols.)
paper
1468
Utrecht
38 miniatures

Provenance
fol. 206v: Ende dit boec wert begost te scriven des derden daghes na sunte Luci
ende geeyndet op Onser Vrouwen Avent daernaest komende in den vasten
doe men screef dusent CCCC ende lxviii
Flyleaf: Nov. Test. Cum gl., Ms. Monastien[se] 1418
collection M. L. van Gobbelschroy, sold 15 december 1851, lot 14, to the University Library

Bibliography
Saint-Genois, *Catalogue méthodique*, no. 430, pp. 311-314
Ebbinge Wubben, *Middelnederlandsche vertalingen*, no. 7, pp. 15-16
Byvanck and Hoogewerff, *La miniature hollandaise*, no. 111, pp. 50-51

The Hague, Koninklijke Bibliotheek, Ms. K. A. XXXII

General Information
First History Bible (Isaiah, Jeremiah, Lamentations)
1 volume (144 fols.)
paper
ca. 1400-1450
North Netherlands
no miniatures

Provenance
Flyleaf: Dit boec hoert toe den cloester der nonnen regulierissen van sunte
    Augustijns oerde wonende ter Goude in sunte Margrieten huus, welc hem
    ghegheven heeft voer een testament Volqwijn vander Wederhorst voer hem
    ende voer sijn wijf.

Bibliography
Ter Horst, *Koninklijke Bibliotheek*, p. 18
Ebbinge Wubben, *Middelnederlandsche vertalingen*, no. 29, pp. 39-40

The Hague, Koninklijke Bibliotheek, Ms. 75 E 7

General Information
First History Bible (Table of Contents, I-IV Kings, Tobias, Ezekiel, Daniel,
    Habakkuk, Cyrus, Judith, Esdras, Esther, Job, Ecclesiastes, Legend of
    Alexander)
1 volume (295 fols.)
paper
ca. 1400
North Netherlands
no miniatures

Provenance
Inserted paper: Toe Nymegen toe Marienborch. Tot sente Elyzabeth bynnen
    Hussen is gestorven op sente Nycolas dach onse lief suster Beel Grobben
    professijt, die onsen lieven Here oetmoedelick gedient heeft XLVI jaer, voer
    wier ziel wy begeren u devoete gebet om Gods wil.

Bibliography
Catalogus Codicum Manuscriptorum Bibliothecae Regiae, Vol. I: *Libri Theologici*,
    The Hague, 1922, no. 20, p. 4
Ebbinge Wubben, *Middelnederlandsche vertalingen*, no. 17, pp. 28-29

The Hague, Koninklijke Bibliotheek, Ms. 78 D 38

General Information
First History Bible (I: Genesis, Exodus, Leviticus, Numbers, Deuteronomy,
    Joshua, Judges, Ruth, I-IV Kings, Tobias, Ezekiel, Daniel, Habakkuk
    Psalter; II: Cyrus, Judith, Esdras, Esther, Job, Proverbs, Ecclesiastes, Song
    of Songs, Book of Wisdom, Ecclesiasticus, Legend of Alexander, I-III
    Maccabees, Destruction of Jerusalem, Gospels, Acts, Letters, Apocalypse,
    Prophets, Letters of the Saints)
2 volumes (291 and 298 fols.)
parchment
ca. 1430
Utrecht
491 miniatures

Provenance
Flyleaf (I): Hoc opus Bibliorum Teutonicorum duobus constans voluminibus ego
   subscriptus approbavi. Hac 19 Januarij Anno 1589. H. Cuyckius, Sacrae
   Theologiae Lovanii doctor et pontificius ac regius librorum censor.

Bibliography
Catalogus Codicum Manuscriptorum, I, no. 15, p. 3
Ebbinge Wubben, *Middelnederlandsche vertalingen*, no. 14, pp. 22-25
Byvanck and Hoogewerff, *La miniature hollandaise*, no. 25, pp. 13-14

The Hague, Koninklijke Bibliotheek, Ms. 78 D 39

General Information
First History Bible (Table of Contents, Prologue, Genesis, Exodus, Leviticus,
   Numbers, Deuteronomy, Joshua, Judges, Ruth, I-IV Kings, Tobias, Daniel,
   Habakkuk, Cyrus, Judith, Esdras, Esther, Job, Proverbs, Ecclesiastes, Book
   of Wisdom, Song of Songs, Ecclesiasticus, Legend of Alexander)
1 volume (389 fols.)
paper
1468
Utrecht
35 miniatures

Provenance
fol. 8v: Shield of the Gruther family many of whom lived in Utrecht in the
   fifteenth century (Ebbinge Wubben, p. 14)

Bibliography
Catalogus Codium Manuscriptorum, I, no. 19, p. 3
Byvanck and Hoogewerff, *La miniature hollandaise*, no. 110, p. 50

The Hague, Koninklijke Bibliotheek, Ms. 128 C 2

General Information
First History Bible (Table of Contents, Job, Psalms, Proverbs, Ecclesiastes, Song
   of Songs, Book of Wisdom, Ecclesiasticus, Legend of Alexander, I-II
   Maccabees, Gospels, Acts, Letters, Apocalypse, Destruction of Jerusalem)
1 volume (301 fols.)
parchment
ca. 1450
South Netherlands
2 miniatures

Provenance
fol. 180v: gescreven bi Jan Rusbroec int closter van Groenendal.
fol. 301r: Dit werck eindic van Latine in Duusche te makenne int jaer ons Heren
   doe men screef mccc ende lx op sinte Jans Baptisten avonde als alle kerstene

in vroeden ende in bliscippen pleghen te wesenen in die eere sijnre ghe-
boorten. Vanden beghinne der werlt waren leden tot desen daghe v^m jare
ende vi^c ende viii jare ende ix maent

Bibliography
Catalogus Codicum Manuscriptorum, I, no. 18, p. 3.
Ebbinge Wubben, *Middelnederlandsche vertalingen*, no. 12, pp. 19-20

The Hague, Koninklijke Bibliotheek, Ms. 129 C 3

General Information
First History Bible (Prologue, Genesis, Exodus, Leviticus, Numbers, Deuteronomy, Joshua, Judges, Ruth, I-IV Kings, Esdras, Tobias, Judith, Esther,
Job, Proverbs, Ecclesiastes, Song of Songs, Book of Wisdom, Ecclesiasticus,
Ezekiel, Daniel, Habakkuk, I-III Maccabees, Hircanus)
3 volumes (197, 168, and 204 fols.)
paper
ca. 1450
North Netherlands
no miniatures

Provenance
first and last fols. (each volume): Dit boec hoert toe closter sinte Margarieten toe
Haerlem

Bibliography
Catalogus Codium Manuscriptorum, I, no. 17, p. 3
Ebbinge Wubben, *Middelnederlandsche vertalingen*, no. 25, pp. 35-36

The Hague, Koninklijke Bibliotheek, Ms. 133 D 31

General Information
First History Bible (Joshua, Judges, Ruth, Job, Proverbs, Ecclesiastes, Book of
Wisdom, Ecclesiasticus)
1 volume (231 fols.)
paper
1440
North Netherlands
no miniatures

Provenance
fol. 90v: mccccxl
Flyleaf: De Boeken Josua, Rechteren, Ruth, Job, Parabolen, Ecclesiastes,
Sapientiae, ende Ecclesiasticus zeer schoon op Papier geschreven in het
Jaar 1440. Siet voor het boek van Job, het Eynde van Ruth

Bibliography
Catalogus Codium Manuscriptorum, I, no. 16, p. 3
Ebbinge Wubben, *Middelnederlandsche vertalingen*, no. 22, p. 34

The Hague, Museum Meermanno-Westreenianum, Ms. 10 A 18-19

General Information
First History Bible (I: Table of Contents, Genesis, Exodus, Leviticus, Numbers,
    Deuteronomy, Joshua, Judges, Ruth; II: I-IV Kings, Tobias, Ezekiel,
    Daniel, Habakkuk, Cyrus, Judith, Esdras, Esther, Job)
2 volumes (156 and 132 fols.)
parchment
ca. 1435
Utrecht
21 miniatures (9 and 12)

Provenance
Flyleaf (I) and fol. 132v (II): Dese duyssche bibel heeft joffer Alijt Lauwers
    ghegeven ... den convent van sunte Agneten buten Nymegen ... int jaer
    ons heren MCCCC ende drie en vijftich
Sale by P. van Damme in 1764 when it was lot 1250

Bibliography
P. J. H. Vermeeren and A. F. Dekker, *Koninklijke Bibliotheek.*
    Inventaris van de handschriften van het Museum Meermanno-Westreenianum,
    The Hague, 1960, no. 33, p. 14
Ebbinge Wubben, *Middelnederlandsche vertalingen*, no. 11, pp. 18-19
Byvanck and Hoogewerff, *La miniature hollandaise*, no. 32, p. 18

Leiden, Bibliotheek der Rijksuniversiteit, Ms. Ltk. 232

General Information
First History Bible (Table of Contents, Prologue, Genesis, Exodus, Leviticus,
    Numbers, Deuteronomy, Joshua, Judges, Ruth, I-IV Kings, Job, Tobias,
    Daniel, Jonah, Jeremiah, Judith, Esther)
1 volume (274 fols.)
parchment and paper
ca. 1450-1500
North Netherlands
no miniatures

Provenance
No indications

Bibliography
G. I. Lieftinck, *Codices Manuscripti Bibliotheca Universitatis Leidensis*, Leiden, 1948,
    Vol. V, Pars I, p. 47
Ebbinge Wubben, *Middelnederlandsche vertalingen*, no. 20, pp. 31-32

Leiden, Bibliotheek der Rijksuniversiteit, Ms. Ltk. 234

General Information
First History Bible (Psalter, Ezekiel, Daniel, Job, Proverbs, Ecclesiastes, Song of
    Songs, Book of Wisdom, Ecclesiasticus)
1 volume (286 fols.)
paper
1473 or 1483
North Netherlands
10 miniatures

Provenance
C. G. Hultman collection, sold to Leiden in 1821

Bibliography
Lieftinck, *Codices Manuscripti*, vol. V, Pars I, p. 12

Leiden, Bibliotheek der Rijksuniversiteit, Ms. Ltk. 1128

General Information
First History Bible (Table of Contents, Prologue, Genesis, Exodus, Leviticus,
    Numbers, Deuteronomy, Table of Contents, Tobias, Judith, Esther,
    Esdras, Nehemias, Legend of Alexander, I-III Maccabees)
1 volume (318 fols.)
paper
ca. 1425-1450
North Netherlands
no miniatures

Provenance
Flyleaf: Abrahamus Costerus Antwerpianus jure permutationis sibi vendicat
    A° 1601, 12 Apr.
Flyleaf: Isaac Jacobsz Bred   1656
Flyleaf: Cornelis de Gelder his boucke. — Bought in the jaere A° 1664

Bibliography
Leiden Bibliotheek der Rijksuniversiteit Handschriften Letterkunde 1085-2045, n. d.
    (Typescript)
Ebbinge Wubben, *Middelnederlandsche vertalingen*, no. 21, pp. 33-34

London, British Library, Add. Ms. 10043

General Information
First History Bible (Prologue, Genesis, Exodus, Leviticus, Numbers, Deutero-
    nomy, Joshua, Judges, Ruth, I-IV Kings, Tobias)
1 volume (209 fols.)
parchment
ca. 1435

Utrecht
243 miniatures

Provenance
fol. 112v: Lochorst family arms in upper margin
fol. 136v: the motto *Nul bien sans pane* is written in the margin
Flyleaf: Purchased in 1836, Hebers Sale, Lot 329

Bibliography
List of Additions to the Manuscripts in the British Museum in the Years MDCCCXXXVI-
     MDCCCXL, London, 1843, p. 6 (reprint 1964)
K. de Flou and E. Gaillard, "Beschrijving van Middelnederlandsche en andere
     handschriften die in Engeland bewaard worden," *Verslagen en Mededeelingen*
     der Koninklijke Vlaamsche Academie voor Taal- en Letterkunde, 1 (1895), pp. 19-22
R. Priebsch, *Deutsche Handschriften in England*, II: *Das British Museum mit einem*
     Anhang über die Guildhall-Bibliothek, Erlangen, 1901, p. 100.
Ebbinge Wubben, *Middelnederlandsche vertalingen*, no. 15, pp. 25-27
Byvanck and Hoogewerff, *La miniature hollandaise*, no. 35, pp. 19-20

London, British Library, Add. Ms. 15310-11

General Information
First History Bible (I: Prologue, Genesis, Exodus, Leviticus, Numbers, Deutero-
     nomy, Joshua, Judges, Ruth, I-II Kings; II: III-IV Kings, Tobias, Ezekiel,
     Job, Proverbs, Ecclesiastes, Song of Songs, Book of Wisdom, Ecclesiasticus,
     Daniel, Habakkuk, Esdras, Esther, Judith, I-II Maccabees)
2 volumes (209 and 183 fols.)
parchment
1460-1462
Hasselt
no miniatures

Provenance
fols. 1r and 183r (I and II): Dit boeck hoert toe den susteren int besloeten
     cloester sinte Katherinendael binnen der stat van Hasselt.
Flyleaf: Purchased of Tho. Thorpe 13 Aug. 1844
Inside cover: exlibris Augustus Frederick, Duke of Sussex

Bibliography
Catalogue of Additions to the Manuscripts in the British Museum in the Years MDCCCXLI-
     MDCCCXLV, London, 1850, list of additions to the department of manu-
     scripts 1844, p. 125 (reprint 1964)
De Flou and Gaillard, *Vlaamsche Academie*, I, pp. 13-19
Priebsch, *Deutsche Handschriften*, II, no. 153, p. 133
Ebbinge Wubben, *Middelnederlandsche vertalingen*, no. 3, pp. 11-12
Deschamps, *Middelnederlandse Handschriften*, no. 50, pp. 152-156

London, British Library, Add. Ms. 15410

General Information
First History Bible (Table of Contents, Prologue, Genesis, Exodus, Leviticus
Numbers, Deuteronomy, Joshua, Judges, Ruth, I-IV Kings, Tobias,
Ezekiel, Daniel, Habakkuk, Cyrus, Judith, Esdras, Esther)
1 volume (301 fols.)
parchment
ca. 1440
Utrecht
27 miniatures

Provenance
fols. 2v-3r: entries by Peter Oris in 1611-12, stating that he purchased the book
from Gheereyn Janssens, a printer, for 16 guilders
fol. 301v: Ick Peeter Oris hebbe dezen bybel wt gelezen van vore tot achter toe
den 26 Juli anno 1616
Front cover: arms of the Duke of Sussex
Flyleaf: Purchased of Tho. Rodd 18 June 1845 (Lot 113 of Sussex Sale)

Bibliography
Catalogue of Additions to the Manuscripts in the British Museum in the Years MDCCCXLI-
MDCCCXLV, London, 1850, list of additions to the department of manu-
scripts, 1845, p. 3 (reprint 1964)
De Flou and Gaillard, *Vlaamsche Academie*, I, pp. 9-12
Priebsch, *Deutsche Handschriften*, II, no. 154, pp. 133-4
Ebbinge Wubben, *Middelnederlandsche vertalingen*, no. 9, pp. 16-17
Byvanck and Hoogewerff, *La miniature hollandaise*, no. 60, pp. 28-29

London, British Library, Add. Ms. 16951

General Information
First History Bible (Genesis, Exodus, Leviticus, Numbers, Deuteronomy,
Joshua, Judges, Ruth)
1 volume (265 fols.)
parchment
1473-1474
Noirtich
39 miniatures

Provenance
fol. 265v: Dit bouc ende bibele is ghescreven uut devocien ende minnen in tijt-
cortinghe van enen gheheten meester Huge Gherijtz, surgijn tot Noirtich,
ende is begonnen int jair ons Heren duysent vierhondert ende drie ende
tseventich op sinte Cosmas Damianus avont ende is voleyndt des daghes
nae onser vrouwen dach Nativitas int jair van vier ende tseventich. Wilt
den Heer voir hem bidden om zalicheit sijnre zielen. Amen
fol. 265v: the initials V.P. appear and underneath the date 1666

fol. 265v: Ploos van Amstel, J.C., in Amsterdam 1772 with *ex libris*
fol. 1r: Purchased of Tho. Rodd, 22nd May 1847
fol. 1r: Ex illius donatione J. Hinssen

Bibliography
Catalogue of Additions to the Manuscripts in the British Museum in the Years MDCCCXLVI-MDCCCXLVII, London, 1864, p. 330 (reprint 1964)
De Flou and Gaillard, *Vlaamsche Academie*, I, (1895), pp. 22-24
Priebsch, *Deutsche Handschriften*, II, no. 180, p. 162
Ebbinge Wubben, *Middelnederlandsche vertalingen*, no. 23, pp. 34-35
Byvanck and Hoogewerff, *La miniature hollandaise*, no. 129, p. 57

London, British Library, Add. Ms. 38122

General Information
First History Bible (Genesis, Exodus, Leviticus, Numbers, Deuteronomy, Joshua, Judges, Ruth, I-IV Kings, Esdras, Tobias)
1 volume (379 fols.)
parchment
ca. 1435
Utrecht
120 miniatures

Provenance
fols. 29v, 73v, 112v, 156r, 158r, 174v, 214v, 238r: arms of the Lochorst family and city of Utrecht
fols. 379r-381r: death entries of the Van Zuylen van Nyvelt family from 1517-1558
Inside cover: Alfred Henry Huth *ex libris*

Bibliography
Catalogue of Additions to the Manuscripts in the British Museum in the Years MDCCCCXI-MDCCCCXV, London, 1925, no. 38122, pp. 22-23
Byvanck and Hoogewerff, *La miniature hollandaise*, no. 26, pp. 12-13

London, Dutch Church, Austin Friars, Ms. 9

General Information
First History Bible (I: I-IV Kings, Prayer of Manasses, Tobit, Ezekiel, Daniel, Habakkuk; II: Letters, Apocalypse)
2 volumes (260 and 305 fols.)
parchment and paper
ca. 1450
North Netherlands
no miniatures

Provenance
fol. 305v: Hier gaet wt de eerste partie van der byblen, die na onzer ordinancien
vulmaect was in Duutsche int jaer ons Heeren doe men screef M.CCC ende
LX upten vii^en maendt van Brachmaent. Deo gratias

Bibliography
Priebsch, *Deutsche Handschriften*, II, no. 328, pp. 324-25
Ebbinge Wubben, *Middelnederlandsche vertalingen*, no. 19, p. 31
Catalogue of the Dutch Church Library, Austin Friars, London, 1879, p. 156-157

Middelburg, Zeeuws Genootschap voor Wetenschappen (destroyed)

General Information
First History Bible (Esdras, Tobias, Judith, Esther, Daniel, Habakkuk, Ezekiel,
Psalter, Job, Song of Songs, Proverbs, Ecclesiastes, Book of Wisdom,
Ecclesiasticus, Legend of Alexander, I-III Maccabees, Destruction of
Jerusalem)
1 volume (164 fols.)
parchment
ca. 1445
18 miniatures

Provenance
1579: property of Maria Hupperts, widow of Wilhelm Radermacher, at Aachen
1580: property of Maria's son, Johan Radermacher and later of Daniel Radermacher
Finally, passed to Radermacher-Schorer and the Schorer families who in 1911
gave it to the Zeeuws Genootschap

Bibliography
Byvanck and Hoogewerff, *La miniature hollandaise*, no. 62, p. 30

Munich, Bayerische Staatsbibliothek, Cod. germ. 1102

General Information
First History Bible (Genesis, Exodus, Leviticus, Numbers, Deuteronomy, Joshua,
Judges, Ruth)
1 volume (154 fols.)
paper
1439
Utrecht
117 miniatures

Provenance
fol. 154v: Deo gratias finitum A° 1439, vicesimo septimo die Julij
Binding: ex libris Bibliotheca Palatina [of Mannheim]

Bibliography
Catalogus Codicum Manuscriptorum Bibliothecae Regiae Monacensis, Tomus V-VI:
    Codicum Germanicorum Partem Priorem et Posteriorem Complectens, Wiesbaden,
    1972, no. 1102
Ebbinge Wubben, *Middelnederlandsche vertalingen*, no. 30, p. 40
Byvanck and Hoogewerff, *La miniature hollandaise*, no. 42, pp. 22-23

Munich, Bayerische Staatsbibliothek, Cod. germ. 5150-51

General Information
First History Bible (Genesis, Exodus, Leviticus, Numbers, Deuteronomy, Joshua,
    Judges, Ruth)
2 volumes (171 and 193 fols.)
paper
1445
North Netherlands
no miniatures

Provenance
fol. 1r: Dit boec hoert toe den cloestere der nonnen regulierissen van sunt
    Augustijns oerde, wonende ter Goude in sunte Margrieten huus, welc hem
    ghegheven heeft voer een testament Volquyn van der Wederhorst voer hem
    ende voer sijn wijf

Bibliography
Catalogus Codicum Manuscriptorum, V-VI, nos. 5150-51, p. 532
Ebbinge Wubben, *Middelnederlandsche vertalingen*, no. 28, p. 39

Munich, Bayerische Staatsbibliothek, Cod. germ. 5062

General Information
First History Bible (Joshua, Judges, Ruth, I-IV Kings)
1 volume (179 fols.)
paper
ca. 1450
North Netherlands
no miniatures

Provenance
Flyleaf: Item dit boeck hier toe Clar Verdel
Flyleaf: Claer Pieterdochter dochter van der Del
fol. 177v: Hier eyndet dit boec, ende in dit boec staet eerst van Josue ende
    daerna dat Rechter boec ende die vier Coninghen, gheeyndet bi Meynert
    Henrycszoen op sinte Francius die heylighe confessoers dach. Bidt voer hem
    om die mynne van Gode, want hi hevet wel te doen. Jhesus Maria Jeronimus.
    Amen Amen Amen

Bibliography
Catalogus Codicum Manuscriptorum, V-VI, no. 5062, p. 521
Ebbinge Wubben, *Middelnederlandsche vertalingen*, no. 26, pp. 37-38

Nijmegen, Museum van Oudheden, Ms. 12

General Information
First History Bible (Table of Contents, Genesis, Exodus, Leviticus, Numbers, Deuteronomy, Joshua, Judges, Ruth)
1 volume (310 fols.)
paper
1477
North Netherlands
2 miniatures

Provenance
fol. 302v: Dit boeck heeft gescreven Johan Siberts soen van Balgoy int jaer ons Heren MCCCC ende LXXVII begonnen had beloken paesschen ende geeyndet des dynxdages voir sunte Victoer ende doe wesende oeck een secundarius to Nymegen ende wonende met Henrick Niborger Engel Nyborgers soen.
fol. 1r: J. A. D. Rengers van Sleeburgh

Bibliography
Ebbinge Wubben, *Middelnederlandsche vertalingen*, no. 10, pp. 17-18

Nuremberg, Stadtbibliothek, Ms. Solger 8°

General Information
First History Bible (Joshua, Judges, Ruth, I-IV Kings, Tobias, Daniel, Habakkuk, Judith, Cyrus, Esdras, Esther, Job, Proverbs, Ecclesiastes, Song of Songs, Book of Wisdom, Ecclesiasticus)
1 volume (198 fols.)
parchment
ca. 1435
Utrecht
188 miniatures

Provenance
No indications

Bibliography
Karin Schneider and Heinz Zirnbauer, *Die Handschriften der Stadtbibliothek Nurnberg*, Vol. I: *Die deutschen mittelalterlichen Handschriften*, Wiesbaden, 1965, pp. 465-471
Ebbinge Wubben, *Middelnederlandsche vertalingen*, no. 13, pp. 20-22
Byvanck and Hoogewerff, *La miniature hollandaise*, no. 34, p. 19

Oxford, Bodleian Library, Ms. Add. B. 26. Now ms. Marshall 90

General Information
First History Bible (Joshua, Tobit, Ruth, Judith, Esther)
1 volume (82 fols.)
paper
ca. 1440
North Netherlands
no miniatures

Provenance
fol. 1r: Dit bueck hoert toe den besloten susteren tot sinte Marienborn in Willem Oeskens straet

Bibliography
F. Madan, H. Craster, and N. Denholm-Young, *A Summary Catalogue of Western Manuscripts in the Bodleian Library at Oxford*, Oxford, 1937, Vol. II, Part II, no. 5294, p. 1001
Priebsch, *Deutsche Handschriften*, I, no. 160, pp. 160-161
Ebbinge Wubben, *Middelnederlandsche vertalingen*, no. 4, p. 12

Paris, Bibliothèque nationale, fonds néerl. 38

General Information
First History Bible (Leviticus, Numbers, Deuteronomy, Joshua, Judges, Ruth, Esther, Judith, Proverbs, Van der phisionomie der menschen)
1 volume (255 fols.)
paper
ca. 1450
North Netherlands
no miniatures

Provenance
No indications

Bibliography
G. Huet, *Catalogue des manuscrits néerlandais de la Bibliothèque Nationale*, Paris, 1886, p. 43
Ebbinge Wubben, *Middelnederlandsche vertalingen*, no. 31, pp. 40-41

Utrecht, Bibliotheek der Rijksuniversiteit, Ms. 2 B 13

General Information
First History Bible (Table of Contents, Letters, Acts, Apocalypse, Prophets, Letters of the Saints, Gloss on the Apocalypse)
1 volume (220 fols.)
paper and parchment
ca. 1400-1450

North Netherlands
no miniatures

Provenance
Flyleaf: Ex dono Jo. van de Water Icti 1708

Bibliography
Catalogus Codicum Manuscriptorum, Bibliothecae Universitatis Rheno-Trajectinae,
    Utrecht, The Hague, 1887, no. 1008, p. 245

Utrecht, Bibliotheek der Rijksuniversiteit, Ms. 4 E 3

General Information
First and Second History Bible (Table of Contents, Prologue, Genesis, Exodus,
    Leviticus, Numbers, Deuteronomy, Joshua, Judges, Ruth, I-IV Kings,
    Habakkuk, Tobias, Ezekiel, Daniel, Cyrus, Judith, Esdras, Esther, Legend
    of Alexander, I-II Maccabees, Destruction of Jerusalem)
1 volume (518 fols.)
paper
ca. 1425-50 "saec. XV-XVI" (Cat.)
North Netherlands
no miniatures

Provenance
No indications

Bibliography
Catalogus Codicum Manuscriptorum, no. 1006, p. 243

Utrecht, Bibliotheek der Rijksuniversiteit, Ms. 5 E 6

General Information
First History Bible (Proverbs, Ecclesiastes, Song of Songs, Book of Wisdom,
    Ecclesiasticus)
1 volume (144 fols.)
paper
ca. 1400-1450
North Netherlands
no miniatures

Provenance
fol. 57r: Dit boec hoert toe den nonnen op die goude
Flyleaf: Dit boec hoert toe den regularissen tot sunte Marien ter Goude op de
    Goude

Bibliography
Catalogus Codicum Manuscriptorum, no. 1007, p. 244
Ebbinge Wubben, *Middelnederlandsche vertalingen,* no. 24, p. 35

Vienna, Oesterreichische Nationalbibliothek, Ms. 2771-72

General Information
First History Bible (I: Table of Contents, Prologue, Genesis, Exodus, Leviticus,
  Numbers, Deuteronomy, Joshua, Judges, Ruth, I-V Kings, Tobias, Ezekiel,
  Daniel, Judith, Esther, Job, Proverbs, Ecclesiastes, Song of Songs, Book of
  Wisdom, Ecclesiasticus, Legend of Alexander; II: Table of Contents,
  Gospels, Acts, Letters, Apocalypse, Prophets, Letters of the Saints, I-III
  Maccabees, Destruction of Jerusalem, Psalter)
2 volumes (343 and 261 fols.)
parchment
ca. 1450-1460
Utrecht
265 miniatures (154 and 111)

Provenance
Evert van Soudenbalch
ex libris Prinzen von Savoyen

Bibliography
*Tabulae codicum manuscriptorum praeter Graecos et Orientales in bibliotheca Palatina
  Vindobonensi Asservatorum,* Vienna, 1868, Vol. II, nos. 2771-72, p. 130
Ebbinge Wubben, *Middelnederlandsche vertalingen,* no. 5, pp. 13-14
Byvanck and Hoogewerff, *La miniature hollandaise,* no. 102, pp. 45-47
Pächt and Jenni, *Die illuminierten Handschriften und Inkunabelen der Österreichischen
  Nationalbibliothek. Holländische Schule,* 2 vols Vienna, 1975, pp. 43-85

BIBLIOGRAPHY

Acquoy, J. G. R., *Het Klooster te Windesheim en zijn invloed*, 3 vols. Utrecht, 1875-1880.

Anderson-Schmitt, M., "Über die Verwandtschaft der Alexandersagen im Seelentrost und in der ersten niederländischen Historienbibel," *Münstersche Beeiträge zur Niederdeutschen Philologie*, 1960, pp. 78-104 (Niederdeutsche Studien VI).

Axters, S., *Geschiedenis van de Vroomheid in de Nederlanden*. 3 vols. Antwerp, 1953.

Berger, Samuel, *La bible française au moyen age. Étude sur les plus anciennes versions de la bible écrites en prose de langue d'oïl*. Paris, 1884 (reprint 1967).

Boon, K. G., "L'art hollandais à ses sources," *Connaissance des arts* 217 (March 1970), pp. 94-105.

Bouton, V., *Wapenboek ou armorial de 1334 à 1372, précedé de poésies heraldiques par Gelre, héraut d'armes*, 10 vols., Paris/Brussels, 1881-1905.

Brandsma, T. (ed.), "Twee berijmde Levens van Geert Groote," *Ons Geestelijk Erf* 16 (1942), pp. 5-51.

Bruin, C. C. de, *De Statenbijbel en zijn voorgangers*. Leiden, 1937.

Bruin, C. C. de, "Bespiegelingen over de 'Bijbelvertaler van 1360.' Zijn milieu, werk en persoon," *Nederlands Archief voor Kerkgeschiedenis* 48 (1968), pp. 39-59, 49 (1968), pp. 135-154, 50 (1969), pp. 11-27, 51 (1970), pp. 16-41.

Bruin, C. C. de (ed.), *Corpus Sacrae Scripturae Neerlandicae Medii Aevi. Series Maior*. Leiden, 1969-.

Brussels, Bibliothèque Royale, *De Gouden Eeuw der Boekverluchting in de Noordelijke Nederlanden* (catalogue of an exhibition), Brussels, 1971.

Brussels, Bibliothèque Royale, *Middelnederlandse Handschriften uit Europese en Amerikaanse Bibliotheken* (catalogue of an exhibition by Jan Deschamps), Brussels, 1970.

Byvanck, A. W., "Aanteekeningen over handschriften met miniaturen. VII: Het atelier der Utrechtsche miniaturen," *Oudheidkundig Jaarboek* 9 (1929), pp. 136-145.

Byvanck, A. W., *De Middeleeuwsche boekillustratie in de noordelijke Nederlanden*. Antwerp, 1943.

Byvanck, A. W., *La miniature dans les Pays-Bas septentrionaux*. Paris, 1937.

Byvanck, A. W. and Hoogewerff, G. J., *La miniature hollandaise et les manuscrits illustrés du XIVe au XVIe siècle aux Pays-Bas septentrionaux*. The Hague, 1922-26.

Byvanck, A. W., "Noordnederlandsche Miniaturen der XVe eeuw in Handschriften van den Bijbel," *Bulletin van den Nederlandschen Oudheidkundigen Bond* 2e serie, 10 (1917), pp. 260-275.

Byvanck, A. W., "Utrechtsche miniaturen," *Het Gildeboek* 6 (1923-24), pp. 1-11, 63-80, 106-107, 179-195.

Campbell, M. F. A. G., *Annales de la typographie néerlandaise au XVe siècle*. The Hague, 1874.

Catalogus Codicum Manuscriptorum Bibliothecae Regiae, Vol. I: *Libri Theologici*. The Hague, 1922.

Catalogus Codicum Manuscriptorum Bibliothecae Regiae Monacensis, Tomus V-VI: *Codicum Germanicorum Partem Priorem et Posteriorem Complectens*. Wiesbaden, 1972.

Catalogus Codicum Manuscriptorum Bibliothecae Universitatis Rhenotrajectinae, Utrecht/The Hague, 1886.

Cockerell, S. C. and Plummer, John, *Old Testament Miniatures. A Medieval Picture Book with 283 Paintings from the Creation to the Story of David*. London, 1969.

Daniels, L. M., *Meester Dirc van Delf, O.P., Tafel van den Kersten Ghelove*. 4 vols., Antwerp/Nijmegen/Utrecht, 1939.

David, J., *Rijmbijbel van Jacob van Maerlant*. 3 vols., Brussels, 1858-59.

Delaissé, L. M. J., *A Century of Dutch Manuscript Illumination*. Berkeley/Los Angeles, 1968.

Delaissé, L. M. J., "Les miniatures du 'Pélerinage de la vie humaine' de Bruxelles et l'archéologie du livre." *Scriptorium*, 10 (1956), pp. 233-250.

Delaissé, L. M. J., "The Importance of Books of Hours for the History of the Medieval Book," *Gatherings in Honor of Dorothy E. Miner*, (eds. Ursula McCracken, Lilian M. C. Randall, and Richard H. Randall, Jr.). Baltimore, 1974, pp. 203-225.

Denucé, J., *Museum Plantin-Moretus. Catalogue des Manuscrits*. Antwerp, 1927.

Deschamps, Jan, "De dietse kollatieboeken van Dirc van Herxen (1381-1457) rektor van het zwolse fraterhuis," *Handelingen van het XXIIIe Vlaams Filologencongres*, Brussels, 1959, pp. 186-193.

Deschamps, Jan, "Middelnederlandse Bijbelhandschriften uit het klooster St. Catharina-dal te Hasselt," *Liber amicorum aangeboden aan Magister Jan Gruyters*. Hasselt, 1957, pp. 193-233.

Deschamps, Jan, "Middelnederlandse vertalingen van super modo vivendi (7de hoofd-stuk) en de libris teutonicalibus van Gerard Zerbolt van Zutphen," *Handelingen der Koninklijke Zuidnederlandse Maatschappij voor Taal- en Letterkunde en Geschiedenis* 14 (1960), pp. 67-108.

Dostal, E., *Příspěvky k Dějinám Českého Illuminátorského Umění Na Sklonku XIV*, Stoleti. 6. *Contributions to the History of Czech Art of Illumination about the Year 1400*, (Opera Facultatis Philosophicae Universitatis Masarykianae Brunensis. Cislo 26) Brno, 1928.

Druten, H. van, *Geschiedenis der Nederlandsche Bijbelvertaling*. Vol. 1: *Geschiedenis der Neder-landsche Bijbelvertaling tot het jaar 1522*. Leiden, 1895.

Dvořák, Max, "Die Illuminatoren des Johann von Neumarkt," *Jahrbuch der Kunsthisto-rischen Sammlungen des allerhöchsten Kaiserhauses* 22 (1970), p. 35ff.

Fiero, Gloria Konig, *Devotional Illumination in Early Netherlandish Manuscripts: A study of the Grisaille miniatures in thirteen related fifteenth century Dutch Books of Hours*. Florida State University, 1970 (unpublished doctoral dissertation).

Flou, Karl de and Gaillard, Edward, "Beschrijving van Middelnederlandsche Hand-schriften die in Engeland bewaard worden," *Verslagen en Mededeelingen der Kon. Vlaamsche Academie voor Taal- en Letterkunde* (Ghent), series 1 (1895), pp. 31-263.

Ebbinge Wubben, C. H. van, *Over Middelnederlandsche vertalingen van het Oude Testament*. The Hague, 1903.

Épiney-Burgard, G., *Gérard Grote (1340-1384) et les débuts de la Dévotion Moderne*. Wies-baden, 1970.

Gelder, H. A. Enno van, *The Two Reformations in the 16th Century. A Study of the religious aspects and consequences of Renaissance and humanism*. The Hague, 1961.

Gheyn, J. van den, *Catalogue des Manuscrits de la Bibliothèque Royale de Belgique*. Vol. I: *Écriture Sainte et liturgie*. Brussels, 1901.

Gorissen, F., "Jan Maelwael und die Bruder Limburg: ein Nimweger Kunstlerfamilie um die Wende des 14. Jahrhunderts." *Vereeniging tot beoefening van Geldersche Ge-schiedenis, Oudheidkunde en Recht, Bijdragen en Mededelingen* 54 (1954), pp. 153-221.

Greiteman, N., *De Windesheimse vulgaatrevisie in de vijftiende eeuw*. Hilversum, 1937.

Grube, K. (ed.), *Des Augustinerpropstes Iohannes Busch Chronicon Windeshemense und Liber de Reformatione Monasteriorum*. Halle, 1886.

Gumbert, J. P., *Die Utrechter Kartäuser und ihre Bücher im frühen fünfzehnten Jahrhundert*. Leiden, 1974.

Harderwijk, J. van, *Verslag van een handschrift, bevattende Jacob van Maerlants Nederduitsche prozaische bijbelvertaling met aanteekeningen en bijlagen*. The Hague, 1831.

Held, Julius S., "Rembrandt and the Book of Tobit," *Rembrandt's Aristotle and Other Rembrandt Studies*. Princeton, 1969, pp. 104- 129.

Hindman, Sandra, "Fifteenth-Century Dutch Bible Illustration and the 'Historia Scholastica'," *Journal of the Warburg and Courtauld Institutes* 37 (1974), pp. 131-144, Pls. 30-32.

Hindman, Sandra, "The Transition from Manuscripts to Printed Books in the Netherlands: Illustrated Dutch Bibles," *Nederlands Archief voor Kerkgeschiedenis*, 1975, LVI, pp. 189-209.

Hintzen, J. D., "De geïllimuneerde handschriften der Utrechtsche Universiteitsbibliotheek," *Het Boek* 10 (1921), pp. 1-13, 263-4.

Hoogewerff, G. J., *De Noord-Nederlandsche Schilderkunst*, 4 vols., The Hague, 1936-1947.

Huét, G., *Catalogue des Manuscrits Néerlandais de la Bibliothèque Nationale*. Paris, 1886.

Hyma, A., *The Christian Renaissance*. Hamden (Conn.), 1965.

Hyma, A. (ed.), "The 'De Libris Teutonicalibus' by Gerard Zerbolt of Zutphen", *Nederlandsch Archief voor Kerkgeschiedenis* 17 (1924), pp. 42-70.

Hyma, A., "Is Gerard Zerbolt of Zutphen the Author of the 'Super Modo Vivendi?'" *Nederlandsch Archief voor Kerkgeschiedenis* 16 (1921), pp. 107-128.

Hyma, A., *The Life of Desiderius Erasmus*. Assen, 1972.

Hyma, A. (ed.), "Het tractatus de quatuor generibus meditationum sive contemplationum of sermo de nativitate Domini," *Archief voor de Geschiedenis van het Aartsbisdom Utrecht*, 49 (1924), pp. 296-326.

James, M. R., "The Pictorial Illustration of the Old Testament from the Fourth to the Sixteenth Centuries," *A Book of Old Testament Illustrations of the Middle of the 13th Century*. Cambridge, 1927, pp. 1-55.

Jerchel, H., "Das Hasenburgsche Missale von 1409, die Wenzels-Werkstatt und die Mettener Malereien von 1414," *Zeitschrift für Kunstwissenschaft* (1937), pp. 22f.

Kempis, Thomas à, *The Imitation of Christ*. Translated and introduced by George F. Maine. Forward by L. M. J. Delaissé. London, 1957.

Kessler, H. L., "'Hic Homo Formatur:' The Genesis Frontispieces of the Carolingian Bibles", *Art Bulletin* 53 (1971), pp. 143-160.

Klaveren, G. van, "Utrechtsche schrijvers en verlichters van miniaturen," *Maandblad van "Oud-Utrecht"* 10 (1935), pp. 35-37.

Knierim, P. J. H., *Dirc van Herxen*. Leiden, 1926.

Krasa, Josef, "Astrolgické Rukopisy Václava IV," *Uměni* 12 (1964), pp. 466-486.

Krasa, Josef, *Die Handschriften Wenzels IV*, Vienna, 1971.

Krasa, Josef, "Humanistische und Reformatorische Gedanken in der höfischen Kunst Wenzels IV," *Acta Historiae Artium Academiae Scientiarum Hungaricae* 8, nos. 1-3 (1967), pp. 197-203.

Lampe, G. W. H. (ed.), *The Cambridge History of the Bible*. Vol. 2: *The West from the Fathers to the Reformation*. Cambridge, 1969.

Leendertz, P., "De prozabijbel aan Jacob van Maerlant toegeschreven," *De Navorscher* 11 (1861), pp. 337-346.

Le Long, Isaac, *Boekzaal der Nederduytsche Bybels*. Amsterdam, 1732.

Lieftinck, G. I., *Codices Manuscripti Bibliotheca Universitatis Leidensis*. Leiden, 1948.

Longnon, Jean; Cazelles, R., and Meiss, M., *The "Très Riches Heures" of Jean, Duke of Berry*. New York, 1969.

Lyna, F., "Les miniatures d'un manuscrit du 'Ci nous dit' et le réalisme préeyckien." *Scriptorium* 1 (1947), p. 106-118.

Madan, F., Craster, H. and Denholm-Young, N., *A Summary Catalogue of Western Manuscripts in the Bodleian Library at Oxford*. Oxford, 1937.

Marrow, James, "Dutch Manuscript Illumination before the Master of Catherine of Cleves," *Nederlands Kunsthistorisch Jaarboek* 19 (1968), pp. 51-114.

Marrow, J., "Dutch Illumination and the 'Devotio Moderna'," *Medium Aevum*, 42 (1973), pp. 251-258.

✓ Marrow, J., *From Sacred Allegory to Descriptive Narrative. Transformations of Passion Icono-graphy in the Late Middle Ages*. Columbia University, 1974 (unpublished doctoral dissertation).

McDonnell, Ernest W., *The Beguines and Beghards in Medieval Culture with special emphasis on the Belgian scene*. New Brunswick (New Jersey), 1954.

Meinsma, K. O., *Middeleeuwsche Bibliotheken*. Amsterdam, 1902.

Miner, Dorothy, "Dutch Illuminated Manuscripts in the Walters Art Gallery." *The Connoisseur Yearbook* (1955), pp. 66-77.

Nieuw Nederlandsch Biographisch Woordenbook, Leiden, 1911-1934.

Panofsky, E., "The de Buz Book of Hours. A New Manuscript from the Workshop of the Grandes Heures de Rohan," *Harvard Library Bulletin* 3 (1949), pp. 163-182.

Panofsky, E., *Early Netherlandish Painting*. Cambridge (Mass.), 1953.

Pickering, F., *Literature and Art in the Middle Ages*. London, 1970.

Plummer, John, *The Hours of Catherine of Cleves*. New York, n.d.

Pohl, M. I. (ed.), *Thomae Hemerken a Kempis Opera Omnia*. 7 volumes. Fribourg, 1922.

Porcher, Jean, *French Miniatures from Illuminated Manuscripts*. London, 1960.

Post, R. R., *The Modern Devotion. Confrontation with Reformation and Humanism*. Leiden, 1968.

Post, R. R., *Scholen en onderwijs in Nederland gedurende de Middeleeuwen*. Utrecht, 1954.

Priebsch, R., *Deutsche Handschriften in England*, II. *Das British Museum mit einem Anhang über die Guildhall-Bibliothek*. Erlangen, 1901.

Proost, K. F., *De Bijbel in de Nederlandsche Letterkunde als Spiegel der Cultuur*. Vol. 1: *De Middeleeuwen*. Assen, 1932.

Rickert, M., "The Illuminated Manuscripts of Meester Dirc van Delft's 'Tafel van den Kersten Ghelove'," *Journal of the Walters Art Gallery* 12 (1949), pp. 79-108.

Rickert, M., *The Reconstructed Carmelite Missal*. Chicago, 1952.

Rickert, M., "Review of F. Gorissen 'Jan Maelwael und die Brüder Limburg'," *Art Bulletin* 39 (1957), pp. 73-77.

Ringbom, Sixton, *Icon to Narrative. The rise of the dramatic close-up in fifteenth century devo-tional painting*. Abo, 1965. (Acta Academiae Aboensis, Ser. A, Vol. 31, nr. 2).

Rooy, J. van, *Gerald Zerbolt van Zutphen*. Vol. I: *Leven en geschriften*. Nijmegen, 1936.

Ross, D. J. A., *Illustrated Medieval Alexander Books in Germany and the Netherlands. A Study in comparative iconography*. Cambridge, 1971.

Rotermund, H.-M., "Rembrandts Bibel," *Nederlands Kunsthistorisch Jaarboek* 8 (1957), pp. 123-150.

Saint-Genois, Jules de, *Catalogue méthodique et raisonné des manuscrits de la Bibliothèque de la ville et de l'Université de Gand*. Ghent, 1849-1852.

Schlosser, Julius von, "Die Bilderhandschriften König Wenzels I," *Jahrbuch der Kunst-historischen Sammlungen des Allerhochsten Kaiserhauses* 14 (1893), pp. 214ff.

Schneider, Karin and Zirnbauer, Heinz, *Die Handschriften der Stadtbibliothek Nürnberg*. Vol. I: *Die Deutschen Mittelalterlichen Handschriften*, Wiesbaden, 1965.

Schoengen, M., *Jacobus Traiecti alias de Voecht narratio de inchoatione domus clericorum in Zwollis*. Amsterdam, 1908.

Schoengen, M., *Die Schule von Zwolle von ihren Anfängen bis zu dem Auftreten des Humanismus*. Freiburg, 1898.

Sharon, Hermon, "Illuminated Manuscripts of the Court of King Wenceslas IV of Bohemia," *Scriptorium* 9 (1955), pp. 115-124.

Smalley, Beryl, *The Study of the Bible in the Middle Ages*. Oxford, 1952.

Someren, J. F. van, *De Utrechtsche Universiteits Bibliotheek*. Utrecht, 1909.

Tabulae Codicum Manuscriptorum praeter Graecos et Orientales in Bibliotheca Palatina Vindo-bonensi Asservatorum, Vienna, 1868.

Thompson, E. Maunde, "Bibliographica on a manuscript of the Biblia Pauperum," *Bibliographica*, III, pp. 385-406.

Tümpel, Christian, "Studien zur Iconographie der Historien Rembrandts Deutung und Interpretation der Bildinhalte," *Nederlands Kunsthistorisch Jaarboek* 20 (1969), pp. 107-198.

Vermeeren, P. J. H., "De Nederlandse Historiebijbel der Oostenrijkse Nationale Bibliotheek, Cod. 2771 en 2772," *Het Boek* 32 (1955), pp. 101-139.

Vermeeren, P. J. H., "Op zoek naar de Librije van Rooklooster," *Het Boek* 35 (1962), pp. 142-55.

Vermeeren, P. J. H. and Dekker, A. F., *Koninklijke Bibliotheek. Inventaris van de handschriften van het Museum Meermanno-Westreenianum.* The Hague, 1960.

Vermeiren, Marie-Louise, "La Bible de Wenceslas du Musée Plantin-Moretus à Anvers," *De Gulden Passer* 31, nos. 3 and 4 (1953), pp. 191-229.

Vogelsang, Willem, *Holländische Miniaturen des späteren Mittelalters.* Strassburg, 1899. (Studien zur Deutschen Kunstgeschichte, 18.)

Vooys, C. G. N. de, "De Dietse tekst van het traktaat: 'De libris teutonicalibus'," *Nederlandsch Archief voor Kerkgeschiedenis* 4 (1907), pp. 117-134.

Vreese, W. de (ed.), *De simonia ad beguttas; de Middelnederlandse tekst.* The Hague, 1950.

Vries, Thomas de, *Duutsche sermoenen door magister Joan Cele Rektor der Zwolse school gehouden tot zijn clerken 1380-1415.* Zwolle, 1947.

Warner, G. F. and Gilson, J. P., *British Museum Catalogue of Western Manuscripts in the Old Rotal and Kings Collections.* London, 1921.

Wijk, N. van (ed.), *Het Getijdenboek van Geert Groote naar het Haagse handschrift, 133 E 21,* Leiden, 1940.

Winkel, J. te, *Maerlant's werken beschouwd als spiegel van de dertiende eeuw.* Leiden, 1877.

Wit, C. de, "Het Atelier der Utrechtsche Miniaturen en een Kapittel uit de Geschiedenis van het Karthuizerklooster Nieuw-Licht" *Oudheidkundig Jaarboek* 7 (1929), pp. 264-271.

Zijl, Th. van, *Gerard Groote, Ascetic and Reformer (1340-1384).* Washington, 1963. (The Catholic University of America Studies in Medieval History, New Series, 18).

INDEX OF PERSONS AND MANUSCRIPTS

1. *Elijah's Burnt Offering*, fol. 182v, British Library, Add. Ms. 10043.

2. *Shame of Noah*, fol. 15v, Munich, Staatsbibliothek, Cod. germ. 1102.

3. *Elijah's Burnt Offering*, fol. 27, British Library, Kings Ms. 5

4.   *Shame of Noah*, fol. 5v, British Library, Kings Ms. 5.

5. *Moses Crosses the Red Sea*, fol. 204, Cambridge, Fitzwilliam Museum, Ms. 289.

6. *Moses Crosses the Red Sea*, fol. 190v, the Hague, Museum Meermanno-Westreenianum, Ms. 10 A 18

7. *Song of Moses*, fol. 90r, British Library, Add. Ms. 38122.

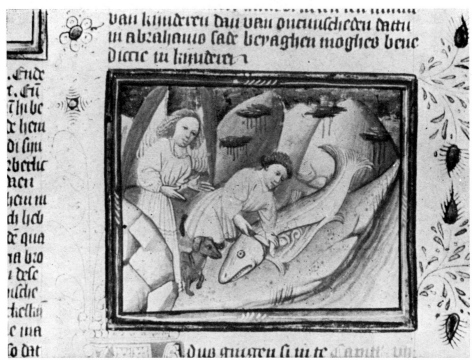

8. *Tobias Removes the Fishes Innards*, fol. 207r, British Library, Add. Ms. 10043.

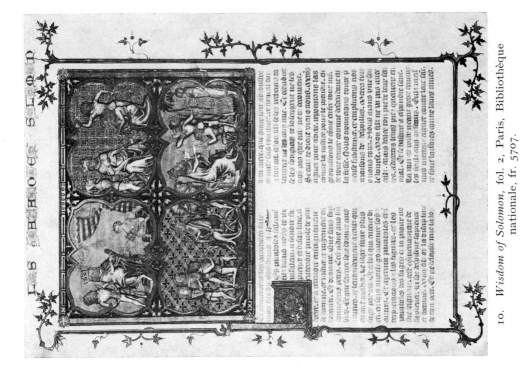

10. *Wisdom of Solomon*, fol. 2, Paris, Bibliothèque nationale, fr. 5707.

9. *Tobit and the Angel*, fol. 207, Cambridge, Fitzwilliam Museum, Ms. 289.

11.   *Abraham before Abimelech*, fol. 34v, Paris, Bibliothèque Nationale, fr. 15397.

12.   *Isaiah before Hezekiah*, fol. 99v, Nuremberg, Stadtbibliothek, Ms. Solger 8°

vij dage gebeit had so liet hi echter die duue vt
der arken vliegen En si quamen tsauonts te hem
en bracht in haren mont een rijs van eenre olyue
mit groiende blade rē Dair om ŏstont noe dat die

waters ōp gehouden waren bouen der eerden En
echter ontbeide hi vij dage en seinde die duue en
si en keerde vout meer niet weder te hem Dus
worden die wateren gemindert bouen der eerden

13.   *Raven and the Dove*, fol. 12v, British Library, Add. Ms. 10043.

14.   *David and Bathsheba*, fol. 158r, British Library, Add. Ms. 10043.

15. *Encircling of Jericho*, fol. 115r, British Library, Add. Ms. 10043.

16. *Lamech Kills Cain*, fol. 10r, British Library, Add. Ms. 10043.

17. *Lamech Kills Cain*, fol. 11v, Munich, Staatsbibliothek, Cod. germ. 1102.

18. *Barak Battles Sisera*, fol. 125r, British Library, Add. Ms. 10043.

19. *David Plays the Harp to Saul*, fol. 39r, Nuremberg, Stadtbibliothek, Ms. Solger 8°.

20. *David Slays Goliath*, fol. 146r, British Library, Add. Ms. 10043.

21. *Flight into Egypt*, fol. 145r, The Hague, Koninklijke Bibliotheek, Ms. 78 D 38 (II).

22. *Feast of Joseph*, fol. 64v, British Library, Add. Ms. 38122.

23. *Slaying of Absalom*, fol. 6or, Nuremberg, Stadtbibliothek, Ms. Solger 8°.

24. *David at the Pear Tree*, fol. 156r, British Library, Add. Ms. 10043.

25. *Moses and the Burning Coal*, fol. 41r, British Library, Add. Ms. 10043.

26. *Moses and the Burning Coal*, fol. 75r, British Library,
Add. Ms. 38122.

27. *Attempted Suicide of Herod*, fol. 146r, The Hague, Koninklijke Bibliotheek, Ms. 78 D
38 (II).

28. *Solomon's Temple*, fol. 169v, British Library, Add. Ms. 10043.

29. *Bezaleel and Aholiab*, fol. 117v, British Library,
Add. Ms. 38122.

30. *Making of Bricks from Straw*, fol. 78v, British Library,
Add. Ms. 38122.

31. *Birth of Samson*, fol. 238r, British Library, Add.
Ms. 38122.

32. *Fruit of Gilgal*, fol. 114v, British Library, Add. Ms. 10043.

33. *Anointment of David*, fol. 145r, British Library, Add. Ms. 10043.

34. *Moses Punishes the Israelites*, fol. 112v, British Library,
Add. Ms. 38122.

35. *Consumption of Blood before Saul's Altar*, fol. 143v, British Library, Add. Ms. 10043.

36. *David Feigns Mad*, fol. 148r, British Library, Add. Ms. 10043.

37. *Choice of Gideon's Army*, fol. 126v, British Library, Add. Ms. 10043.

38. *Torture of the Concubine*, fol. 25v, Nuremberg, Stadtbibliothek, Ms. Solger, 8°

39. *Kings Sons, Heads before Jehu*, fol. 191r, London, British Library, Add. Ms. 10043.

40. *Slaying of Jezebel*, fol. 218v, Vienna, Oesterreichische Nationalbibliothek, Ms. 2771.

41. *Slaying of Jezebel*, fol. 190v, British Library, Add. Ms. 10043.

42. *David Slays Goliath*, fol. 166v, Vienna, Oesterreichische Nationalbibliothek, Ms. 2771.

43. *Samuel Kills Agag*, fol. 165r, Vienna, Oesterreichische Nationalbibliothek, Ms. 2771.

44. *Abisag before David*, fol. 207r, British Library, Add. Ms. 15410

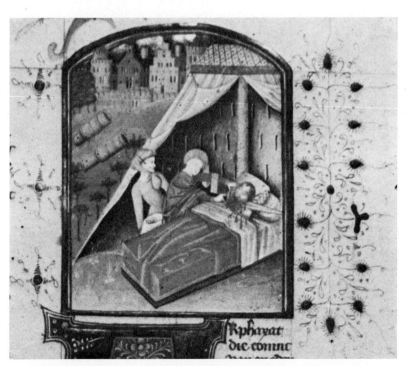

45. *Judith Slays Holofernes*, British Library, Add. Ms. 15410.

46. *Making of Bricks from Straw*, fol. 49v, Vienna, Oesterreichische Nationalbibliothek, Ms. 2771.

47. *Solomon and the Queen of Sheba*, fol. 202r, Vienna, Oesterreichische Nationalbibliothek.

48. *Stoning of the Blasphemer*, fol. 75v, British Library, Add. Ms. 10043.

49. *Terence des Ducs*, fol. 75v, Paris, Bibliothèque de l'Arsenal, Ms. 664.

50. *Plague of Locusts*, fol. 73r, Antwerp, Museum Plantin-Moretus, Ms. 15.1.

51. *Plague of Locusts*, fol. 84r, British Library, Add. Ms. 38122.

53. *Christ Learning to Walk*, fol. 155r, Cambridge, Harvard University Library, Ms. 42.

52. *Virgin at the Loom*, fol. 20r, Cambridge, Harvard University Library, Ms. 42.

54. *Annunciation,* fol. 20r, Cambridge, Harvard University, Library Ms. 42.

55. *Pietà Madonna*, fol. 155r, Cambridge, Harvard University Library, Ms. 42

56. *Adoration of the Magi*, fol. 57r, Cambridge, Harvard University Library, Ms. 42